THE ROUGH GUIDE to

Weddings

by

Nadine Kavanaugh and Ruth Tidball

Peter Buckley and Sean Mahoney

ROUGH GUIDES

www.roughguides.com

Credits

The Rough Guide to Weddings

Additional contributions: Keith Drew
Editing, layout, picture research: Kate Berens
Cover design: Peter Buckley, Diana Jarvis
Proofreading: Richard Lim
Production: Rebecca Short

Rough Guides Reference

Director: Andrew Lockett
Editors: Kate Berens, Peter Buckley, Tracy Hopkins, Matthew Milton, Joe Staines, Ruth Tidball

Publishing information

This first edition published February 2010 by
Rough Guides Ltd, 80 Strand, London WC2R 0RL
375 Hudson St, New York 10014, USA
Email: mail@roughguides.com

Distributed by the Penguin Group:
Penguin Books Ltd, 80 Strand, London WC2R 0RL
Penguin Putnam, Inc., 375 Hudson Street, New York 10014, USA
Penguin Group (Australia), 250 Camberwell Road, Camberwell, Victoria 3124, Australia
Penguin Books Canada Ltd, 90 Eglinton Avenue East, Suite 700, Toronto, Ontario, Canada M4P 2Y3
Penguin Group (New Zealand), Cnr Rosedale and Airborne Roads, Albany, Auckland, New Zealand

Printed in Singapore by Toppan Security Printing Pte. Ltd.

252 pages; includes index

A catalogue record for this book is available from the British Library

ISBN: 978-1-84836-260-4

1 3 5 7 9 8 6 4 2

Contents

Introduction

When it comes to planning a wedding, the thoroughly modern couple are up against a formidable set of unhelpful myths, stereotypes and external pressures. For starters, the wedding industry energetically promotes a **keeping-up-with-the-Joneses mentality**, instilling every bride with the idea that her wedding must be the wedding to end all weddings. But a wedding is just one day, and soon forgotten by everyone but you as the next year's set of invitations roll in. Aiming for **perfection** is not only cripplingly expensive, it's a sure route to exhaustion, disappointment and general insanity.

Without wishing to pop your blissful bubble of pre-wedding excitement, this book aims to keep your feet safely on the ground – because once you let go of those fantasies of perfection, you can set about the business of making your day as fun and fabulous as you care to make it. Your wedding day may indeed be the best day of your life, but it needn't be the sole object of your next eighteen months. This book assumes you've **already got a life** and shows you how you can fit wedding planning into your already busy schedule – as a fun shared project, not an all-encompassing obsession.

Another unhelpful myth is that this is *your* special day, and therefore you must have everything your own way. Sure, you're probably more excited about your wedding than anyone else, but ultimately it's not all about you, or even the two of you. A marriage brings together two families and two groups of friends: it's a **community occasion**, a chance for everyone to welcome this new person into their lives. Whatever the wording on your invites, you're the hosts of what's ultimately just a large and rather elaborate party – and as hosts you're responsible for everyone's enjoyment and comfort, not just your own. Of course you should put yourselves first a little more than usual, but avoiding the slippery slope into **bridezilladom** means you won't risk feelings of shame and regret when the red fog lifts.

When it comes to stereotypes, bridezilla's male consort is the **barely-there groom**, keeping steadily aloof from all the fuss as if the whole thing was someone else's idea. Again, you'll be doing yourself a disservice if you take this attitude: see p.4 for some reasons why you should get involved.

When you start planning your wedding, you're likely to encounter a long list of **shoulds** and **shouldn'ts**, in books, on websites, from friends or family: the bride and groom mustn't see each other on the morning of the wedding, you must have real champagne for toasting, you must dance the first dance in front of everyone. And there's certainly the odd do and don't in these pages: brides, don't be fashionably late for a UK civil ceremony, or you're likely to miss your slot and go home a spinster; yes, you really ought to send thank you notes for all your wedding gifts – even the truly hideous ones. But if this book has one thing to say about weddings, it's that once the legal bit is in the bag, you're pretty much at liberty to pick and choose, mix and match, to make a wedding that fits you.

For instance, **etiquette** is simply a fossilized version of a previous era's idea of good manners. Treat everyone as a human being and you won't go far wrong. The same goes for **formality**. While a degree of formality can help reflect the fact that this is a serious, significant business, treat your guests as what they are – the people you're closest to in all the world, not a bunch of strangers.

As for **tradition**, it's helpful to remember what a short pedigree and dubious origin many wedding traditions can lay claim to. The most notorious example is the diamond engagement ring, on which, we're told, the groom should spend three months' salary: an extraordinarily successful series of adverts by De Beers conjured this "tradition" into existence in a matter of years. Of much more ancient but no less questionable origin is the "giving away" of the bride by her father: along with carrying the bride over the threshold of the marital home, it's a throwback to a patriarchal society in which women were quite literally bought and sold. If a tradition has its roots in outmoded ways of thinking, let alone the mind of a marketing executive, don't be afraid to reject it. That said, it can be nice to join in traditions of long standing, to connect with the millions of others who've gone before. Such is the backlash against tradition and convention in some quarters that the pressure *not* to comply can be just as severe. Just remember: things don't have to be "alternative" to be meaningful.

About the book

Planning a wedding means keeping many balls in the air at once. Chapter 1, **Getting Started**, will set you off in the right direction, and the **timeline** on the inside front cover will keep you on track, reminding you what you should be thinking about when. Chapters 2 to 16 focus on **specific topics**: when each decision rears its head – whether it's choosing a best man, a photographer or a colour scheme – you'll find a chapter here with all the information and advice you need to tackle it confidently. You'll probably need to return to each of these chapters a number of times as your wedding takes shape. But before you know it, you'll be all set for the day itself; in the week preceding it, turn to Chapter 17, **The Big Day**, for some last-minute advice that'll prime you to sail through the inevitable hiccups and minor (or even major) crises.

The final four chapters are your armoury for keeping the whole shebang on course from proposal to honeymoon and beyond: chapters 18 and 19 will keep you sane and on the right side of the law, while chapter 20 provides a crash course in vendor-taming. The final chapter offers further sources of inspiration and information, including specific resources for particular priorities or circumstances. Having said that, we've catered for many concerns throughout the book, including budget, DIY and ethical issues, as well as giving specific advice about **civil partnerships** where relevant – though the vast bulk of the book is just as applicable to two brides or two grooms as it is to one of each.

Using your Rough Guides wedding timeline

The **wedding timeline** on the inside front cover isn't a checklist. Checklists are no good unless they're comprehensive and personalized, which – since every wedding is different – is impossible for a book like this. The timeline could form the basis of a more detailed and continually updated schedule of your own. But its main purpose is to help you see the big picture and avoid becoming overwhelmed by the sheer number of decisions that lie ahead. It'll make sure nothing slips through the cracks and help you to prioritize. Some things need doing first because they'll affect other decisions, some because the best suppliers get booked up months in advance. Either way, doing things in a logical order will make your life a lot simpler. These timings are not absolute latest deadlines, nor extra-early heads-ups: they're an indication of when's a good time to get stuck into that particular task, but depending on your circumstances or inclination, it may make sense to deal with it earlier or later.

The timeline works on the basis that you've at least **twelve months** to plan your wedding. If you've less time, don't just scale everything down: you need to catch up quick! So if you only have six months, mark everything before that "asap", and get cracking: that way, by the time you get to those last few weeks you'll be as relaxed as if you'd taken eighteen months over the process. So, not very, then…

Acknowledgements

The authors would like to thank Kate Berens for her committed and thoughtful editing. In addition:

Nadine would like to thank Sean Mahoney for his invaluable friendship and Nick Gilewicz for everything.

Ruth would like to thank everyone who's shared their experiences for this book, especially Libby, Matt, Charlotte, Mum, Dad, Graham, Haryun, Nicky, Helen and Emma; Andrew, for letting me write it; and Adam, for all sorts of things.

Peter would like to thank Caroline and Rosalie for all their love, help and support. Also everyone at Rough Guides who helped pull this book into shape.

Sean would like to thank his wife, June, for her patience and support, and his friends and family for their advice along the way.

Rough Guides would like to thank Keith Drew for his contributions on honeymoons, weddings abroad and international couples; Richard Lim for sharp-eyed, sensitive proofreading; and all the wedding participants and guests who generously provided advice and anecdotes for this book.

Picture credits

1 Getting Started

These days a simple change to your relationship status on Facebook can be enough to set the gossip wheels spinning. But however you choose to let people know, take a deep breath first and prepare for the onslaught. Aside from congratulations and demands to see the rock and hear the "popping the question" story (on which, see below), you'll soon be hit by a wave of questions about when, where and how you'll be sealing the deal. It pays to keep quiet about your plans until you've had a chance to mull things over: you'll be glad you did when it comes to paring down the guest list.

You're engaged

Throw a party if you like (see Chapter 15). But be sure to also **take time out alone** with your other half, just to get used to the fact this is really happening. There's no need to rush headlong into the planning, putting down deposits on dresses and venues like there's no tomorrow. You'll only have a brief period of being engaged, whereas you'll be married for ever: **enjoy this special status**, and the glamour of making constant reference to "my fian-say". (However much you've longed to use it, "my wife/husband" sounds hopelessly humdrum in comparison.) When you're ready, the following section will help you get the wedding-planning juggernaut on the road.

I secretly booked us on a flight to the Caribbean instead of returning to London from a holiday in New York – I proposed on a secret beach I had been researching for months! I made a few basic errors (not packing any beachwear for Charlotte) but I still managed to surprise her by going down on one knee as the sun set over St Kitts – and I think I got top marks for romance from all our friends and family!
MATT

Big-picture decisions you need to make

It's likely you'll arrive at this point with at least some idea of what your wedding will be like. But the truth is, right now, you really do have a **blank slate.** You still have the option of a quick dash to the register office. Equally, you could decide to get married abroad, or in a hot-air balloon. Now's the time to **consider all your options,** because once you start the wedding snowball rolling in a particular direction, it's difficult to significantly alter its course.

With so many elements involved, it can be hard to know **where to start.** Everything seems to depend on something else: the table linen needs to coordinate with those bridesmaids' dresses – so you'd better pick those first, right? Or at least figure out who the girls in question will be. But – dauntingly for the novice events organizer – in this case you need to start with the **big stuff.** Before you consider the colour schemes and confetti options, there are a few big-picture decisions you need to nail down.

❤ **Number of guests** Want to share this event only with your closest friends and family, or throw the mother of all parties and invite the whole town? You don't need to work out a definitive guest list yet, but a ballpark figure will help you decide whether venues and budgets are big enough.

❤ **Your budget** How much can you afford to spend? Perhaps more to the point, how much do you want to spend – how does your wedding rank among other spending priorities, such as a house? Are parents able and willing to help? See Chapter 2 for more things to consider.

♥ **Type of ceremony and party** Religious or civil? Formal or informal? Lavish or low-key? Offbeat or traditional? Figuring out the broad brush-strokes of your day will help you narrow down what kind of venue you're looking for. See Chapters 5 and 11 to help you decide.

♥ **Your attendants** Who will you ask to be in your wedding party? See Chapter 3 for advice.

All these choices feed into one another, so even at this early stage you need to think hard about your priorities. If you're dead set on marrying abroad, you can't expect to have lots of guests there with you. If the most important thing is sharing your day with everyone you care about, then you're going to need a substantial budget. Likewise, a flotilla of attendants can be expensive to dress and accessorize, whoever's footing the bill.

> ❝ *I was so happy those first few days, I wanted to share the love with everyone: before I knew it, I'd told four of my closest friends they'd be bridesmaids. It was horrible, two weeks later, to have to tell all but one that I'd spoken out of turn and we just couldn't afford so many.* ❞
> *ABBY*

Any way the wind blows doesn't really matter on the big day.

Hey, groom... get involved!

So, you are a groom-to-be, and already feel overwhelmed by all the talk of bridesmaid dresses, favours and blow-dried Shetland pony ring-bearers. Well, take a deep breath and realize that this is your day just as much as it is your fiancée's. Even though you might instinctively feel alienated from the whole "planning" business, the more you actually do get involved, the more likely it is that you will have a fantastic day; and it's a great way to get to know your in-laws a bit better too. Just think about all the aspects of the proceedings you might actually be able to influence and get right for you. For example, if you don't stick your oar in now, you might well end up with a buttonhole the size of a botanical garden, when you actually would have preferred a single stem; or wearing some hideous rented morning suit, when this was the perfect opportunity to go out and get something tailor-made. You have absolutely nothing to lose and everything to gain, so stop rolling your eyes and have your say.

Setting a date and booking the venue(s)

Once you've worked through the big-picture decisions, it's time to **set the date.** The first thing to consider is how far in the future you want your wedding to be. Do you need **time to save up?** If you can bear to wait, it's preferable not to start married life with a huge wedding debt (see p.19). As for the planning itself, beware of underestimating how much there is to be done. Even if you're determined yours will be a simple affair, there are still many different elements to pull together, and if you want the process to be enjoyable (which it should be), then it's best done at leisure, not in a frantic rush.

There is also something of a **vendor-booking arms race** among engaged couples, so that the best venues and photographers are being booked up further and further in advance. Fly in the face of this particular trend at your peril: no one wants to be picking up the scraps passed over by other couples. If you have a very popular venue in mind, and want to be married in midsummer, then you may need to book eighteen months or more ahead. Whatever your venue, if you want the full works then with anything less than nine months you're going to be hard at it. On a shorter timescale you may have more limited options – buying your gown off the peg rather than made-to-measure, for example – but it is possible to pull things together very quickly if you have to. You'll be amazed at what vendors can manage when the alternative is losing your custom.

Consider the likely **weather**, and how important this is to you. In all but the sunniest climates you'd be wise not to bank on fine weather (so make sure there's enough indoor space). But if you'd like a significant part of the day to be outdoors, or there's going to be a good deal of moving about between locations, then you'll want to give yourself the best chance of a sunny day. Many couples gravitate towards the summer months for this reason, but a **winter wedding** can be really special: you'll be walking the path less trodden, immediately giving you more scope for originality in your decorations and outfits, and you'll have less competition for vendors.

Here are a few other things to bear in mind:

♥ Avoid clashing with **major sporting events** (Wimbledon, the Super Bowl…), unless you're willing for the speeches and toasts to compete with the TV in the next room, and the radio under the table.

Wedding planners: who needs 'em?

Using a **wedding planner** needn't mean handing over control of your wedding: most are willing to be kept on as tight or loose a rein as you want, whipping the whole thing up fairy-godmother-style, or deferring every decision to you. They needn't do the whole thing, either, if there are certain bits you know you want to sort out yourselves.

Wedding planners can save you a lot of **time**. They should have a long list of **contacts** whose arms they can twist. They'll also, of course, be familiar with the tasks that need doing, and the various options available. They can do all the legwork and paperwork, leaving you the fun part of the process: choosing your favourite from among the options they've assembled. They'll also be there on the day itself to deal with any crises.

As for the downsides, there's the **cost**, of course. Planners may charge an hourly rate or a percentage of your budget – say, 10% to 15% – plus expenses. They may pay for themselves to a certain extent by negotiating better deals than you'd be able to, but inevitably they'll increase rather than decrease your total bill. And there's always the risk they won't put your interests first – they may be busy with other projects or favour certain vendors you don't like. Finally, no matter how much they keep you in the loop, you'll inevitably be **less involved**: you may feel less ownership of your big day, and you may come to regret missing out on all the wedding planning craziness.

If you do decide to hire a planner, make sure you pick someone you can trust: don't go with a complete rookie, follow personal recommendation if possible, and talk in detail with them before signing up – you'll need to feel some rapport. Give them a firm **budget** and make it clear overspending is not an option.

❤ **Holiday weekends** allow guests more time to travel home afterwards, but tend to be busy. Pick a holiday and you may get a high number of declined invites from guests attending other weddings or events.

❤ Check with your key players for any **prior engagements**. Don't spread the net too wide for this – stick to immediate family, groomsmen and brides-maids – or you'll end up with far too many conflicting priorities and may find no date that suits everyone. It's your wedding, so you can expect close friends and family to plan around it so long as you give them plenty of warning. But there's no point deliberately picking a date that's someone's fortieth birthday or graduation day.

Fortunately, of course, people don't tend to make a great number of plans a year or more in advance, so the personnel side of the equation is less tricky than it might sound. Those venues are a different matter, though, and the best advice is not to set your heart on any one place

Your wed-site

Tempting as it may be to populate your site with cutesy photos and heartwarming stories, look at your website first as a **reference tool** for your guests. You'll want to provide them with the location, time and date of the ceremony, reception, and any other events you want everyone to attend. (You may want to personally distribute information regarding private events like the rehearsal dinner to spare the feelings of the unin-vited.) Be sure to also include information about accommodation, direc-tions and parking for out-of-town visitors, and links to the places where you've registered for gifts. Most importantly, you'll want to prominently display your contact info on the very first page.

If you're already web-design savvy, you can buy a **domain name** for a year or two and build and host your own site. Otherwise there are a num-ber of easy and helpful **wedding website builders** available. The follow-ing list includes both free and paid options.

❤ momentville.com

❤ ewedding.com

❤ weddingchannel.com

❤ theknot.com

❤ weddingtracker.com

until you've found a date on which both it and your key players are available – and then secure it with a deposit and contract right away.

These decisions need to be made early, but they're also among the most important of all. Your choice of venue will colour your whole event. So before you dive in, read Chapter 6. And don't slap down a deposit on the first place you see, no matter how special it seems. Rush in and you risk wasting a deposit or, worse, getting stuck with a venue that just isn't right.

Once you've set a date and booked ceremony and reception venues, you can relax for a while. Unless you're on a very tight schedule you've probably a few weeks or months before you need to do anything else. But if you're raring to go, your best bet is probably the **photographer** (see Chapter 13). And after that, maybe it's time to start hunting for that perfect **gown** (see Chapter 8). For a detailed list of what you'll need done by when, see the inside front cover of this book – the box on p.vii advises on how best to adapt it to your circumstances.

Who's the boss?

If you've read this far, you may already be beginning to grasp the true dimensions of the task that lies ahead. But it's still easy to underestimate what's involved. Especially if you're reluctant to make an undignified big deal about your big day, it can be tempting to adopt a "We (or even I) can handle it" attitude. But the truth is that this is not just a party: it's probably the biggest party you'll ever throw and – unless you're in the events management business – it's likely you'll be breaking new ground in terms of both skills and experience. A successful wedding requires **teamwork**, and that means not only sharing tasks out between yourselves, but also getting help from others.

As for the **division of labour** between you and your other half, make sure you're both enthusiastic by allocating tasks according to your respective strengths and interests. Weddings involve lots that's stereotypically women's territory (flowers, big puffy dresses…), but there's plenty for even the most die-hard unreconstructed guys to get excited about: sharp suits, big cars, and enough alcohol to sink a battleship. Then, within reason, **stay off each other's turf**: you need to trust one another, respecting their opinion and right to make decisions. As for

> **Tip**
>
> Don't feel obliged to have strong feelings about every part of your wedding. It's okay not to care about the exact design of your invites or the frosting on your cake – it doesn't mean you're lacking suitable enthusiasm. And it'll make your life a lot easier if you can let some things go.

managing your **army of helpers** – whether that includes your mother or best friend – no matter how clearly you demarcate responsibilities at the outset, the likelihood is someone's toes will get stepped on at some point; see Chapter 18 for advice on weathering the inevitable storms.

A final word to the wise: though arming yourself with **ring binders** and **spreadsheets** might seem dangerously close to obsessive behaviour, the truth is they're more likely to save you from descending into insanity than the reverse. Get set up now and you'll be grateful for it further down the line.

2 Money

Love may be free, but weddings cost money – and lots of it. One of your first tasks will be to decide on a realistic budget. Realistic in two ways: it actually covers the amount you're going to spend on the wedding with minimal surprise additions at a later date, and it's a sum that you might conceivably be able to get your hands on. You can dream of throwing a huge bash at a palace with fountains of champagne and orchids dripping from the chandeliers, but your wallet may say no. Happily, with planning and creativity you can have a lovely wedding on any budget.

Where does it all go?

While the "New Gilded Age" and the "New Austerity" may duke it out depending on the stock market's latest performance, the cost of a wedding continues to creep up inexorably, albeit with some fluctuations depending on the state of the economy. In the US, the **average cost** of a wedding in 2007 was $27,490. By 2008 that figure had dropped to $21,814, but nevertheless, that's still an awful lot of money for one day. UK trends are much the same, with the 2008 average hitting £20,273, up from £14,643 five years before.

Of course, these **amounts vary** dramatically by region. And just because they're "average", it doesn't mean everyone spends that much or needs to. In fact, it's possible to have a memorable wedding for almost nothing at all – but you'll have to scale back from your original plan of 300 guests and a designer gown. Putting on a fabulous wedding is certainly easier if you've got endless pots of money, but for most of us, it's a case of making informed choices and prioritizing where to spend your cash. Just remember: it's about the love, not about the engraved invitations.

Breaking the costs down

Whatever your total wedding budget, the breakdown of costs is likely to look something like this:

- Food and drink: 40%
- Reception venue: 8%
- Clothes: 10%
- Flowers: 8%
- Photos/video: 12%
- Music: 8%
- Stationery: 3%
- Gifts: 3%
- Rings: 3%
- Ceremony: 3%
- Transport and parking: 2%

Obviously, these percentages will vary according to your circumstances and priorities. But as you set about constructing your wedding budget, it's a good place to start.

Based on the percentages above, this is how an "average" UK wedding (totalling £18,000) and US wedding ($25,000) would pan out. Note that the prices aren't convertible.

- Food and drink: £7200 / $10,000
- Reception venue: £1440 / $2000
- Clothes: £1800 / $2500
- Flowers: £1440 / $2000
- Photos/video: £2160 / $3000
- Music: £1440 / $2000
- Stationery: £540 / $750
- Gifts: £540 / $750
- Rings: £540 / $750
- Ceremony: £540 / $750
- Transport and parking: £360 / $500

It's suddenly easy to see — especially once you get some real quotes in from vendors — how these enormous sums are reached. For instance, £7200 or $10,000 may look like a princely sum to spend on a single meal, but if you invite 100 guests, this means that you have £72 ($100) to spend on each of them — a figure that has to include any taxes and gratuities (perhaps 25%), the drink, hire of linens, glassware and staff wages — as well as the food itself. If you want to throw a really nice party, then it's easy to rack up this amount.

Every couple's idea of a perfect wedding is different and you can **adjust these proportions** to match your own priorities, whether it's an extravagant bridal gown, a live band or a three-course, sit-down dinner. In some areas there's a lot more room for manoeuvre than in others. For example, a lot of the ceremony costs will be the same, no matter what your overall budget, whereas with music, you could spend literally nothing and just have an iPod playlist going, or spend a fortune on a series of live musicians. Similarly, flowers and decorations is an area where spending can vary dramatically, whereas unless you go for a really shoestring affair you're going to need to spend a fair amount on food

It's only money

Anyone about to commit to an even remotely traditional wedding is sure to ask themselves the question, "Why am I about to spend so much money on this one event?" After all, it's not as if you'll be able to live in your wedding once all your guests leave. Nor can you drive it away and use it tomorrow to run errands around town.

Don't go eloping just yet. While a wedding can seem at first like a huge waste of money, you are in fact making a significant and worthwhile **investment in your future**. Your wedding represents the start of your new life with your spouse, and all the time, effort and money you put into it will come back to you in love and support from your friends and family for years to come.

Yes, along the way you will feel gouged by vendors. You will most certainly end up spending more than you had planned. By the end there's a good chance you'll blindly hand your charge card to whomever promises to take care of the details threatening your sanity. But the community you've helped build on this one special day, between families and friends who are all there to celebrate you, is well worth the outlay.

We absolutely had to have...

"Emmanuel is from France but we live in Philadelphia and got married there. One thing that some people pass on but we absolutely had to have was a wedding video, because there are a lot of folks overseas who weren't able to make it in person." – OLIVIA

"One of the most important things for us was free booze. No one wants to go to a dry wedding (including me) and I think we spent almost as much on alcohol as we did for the reception hall. But people danced!" – JACKIE

"Finding a location with a panoramic view of the San Francisco Bay Area that was affordable was very difficult. This was the most important aspect for me because I wanted our wedding guests to be able to take in the beauty of where we live." – MICHAEL

"All my friends! It was awful trying to cut the guest list so we compromised in other areas. It really wouldn't have been the same without having all my friends there with me on the big day." – HELEN

and drink, and for this, like most of the discretionary costs, the sky's the limit if that's what you want.

For any priority on which you want to **splurge**, don't forget the effect on the rest of your budget. For instance, Vera Wang's bridal gowns start at around £1700 ($2500) – and go up to three times that, and more. If a designer gown is one of your essentials, then you've got

Organizing a wedding is perhaps easier if you've pots of money, but it's by no means a requirement for a fantastic day.

to plan around it. Even with a wedding budget of £18,000 or $25,000, the clothing allocation has to cover more than just the dress, and you'll have to up the percentage to cover shoes, undergarments, jewellery and more – not to mention the groom's wedding clothes. Which means other percentages must go down.

What dictates the cost?

- **Formality** The more formal the wedding, the more expensive it will be. Every element of the wedding (clothes, food, site, music) will have to be up to snuff. When the invitation requests "formal evening attire" or "black tie", guests will expect swank to match their tuxedos and evening gowns.

- **Date and time** Overall, summer weddings are more expensive than winter ones, and many venues have peak and off-peak pricing. Holiday weddings, no matter the season, are pricey. Weddings held on Saturdays cost more than those in the rest of the week, Fridays a little less than Saturdays, and evening weddings more than those held during the day.

- **Food** A sit-down dinner costs the most, mainly because of staffing. A buffet dinner is a bit less, and hors d'oeuvres plus cake is the cheapest evening option – though it runs the risk of underfed and cranky guests. Breakfast or lunch cost less than dinner and afternoon tea is the least pricey of all.

- **Reception venue** Rental fees vary dramatically, but keep in mind that a very plain site may cost you in decorations and flowers. While local parks or beaches are virtually free, there may be restrictions on alcohol consumption in public venues. If you go with an outdoor site, remember to factor in the cost of a tent or marquee in case of rain – not as cheap an option as it sounds.

- **Location** Big cities and tourist destinations tend to be pricey, although the potentially high cost of getting to and from a small town or out-of-the way locale should also be taken into consideration.

> *We saved some money by having our wedding on a Friday, which is cheaper than Saturday or Sunday. As a result, fewer people were able to attend, which further cut back our costs. Not that we didn't want everyone to come; it was just a side effect.*
> **KATRINA**

Keeping track: spreadsheets

By far the best way to plan a wedding budget and to track expenses – and what you've paid to whom – is to use a **spreadsheet**. If you've never used one before, dig up an online tutorial – there are plenty available on the Internet for free (check out tinyurl.com/MStrain or try spreadsheets.about.com). If you don't have access to Excel or similar software, there are web-based applications such as Google Docs or Zoho Office

Suite, which also allow you to check your figures from any computer connected to the Internet.

You can probably make a good **first guess** at how much money you'll be able to scrape together. Using the percentage breakdown on p.10, or your own tweaked version, create or use a spreadsheet that divvies up your total among the categories. Then it's time to make phone calls – to local vendors, to friends who recently got married in the area – in order to get some **real numbers.**

Enter these bids or estimates into columns next to the amounts you've budgeted, look at the sum at the bottom of each column, compare it to the total you wanted to spend, then pour yourself a stiff drink and take the rest of the day off from wedding planning. Until you've done it, it's hard to believe how expensive weddings really are.

Happily, there's no need to reinvent the wheel when it comes to wedding spreadsheets, as there are plenty of **templates** available online, like those from Microsoft (tinyurl.com/excelplan), The Knot (tinyurl.com/knotsheet), or Google Docs (tinyurl.com/googlesheet). You can customize these for your own wedding, and use them to compare various vendor bids as well.

Taxes and tips

When calculating the cost of any aspect of the wedding, from the flowers to the champagne to the roast beast to the reception hall, you must check if **tax is included** in the quoted price. It usually isn't. What gets taxed and at what rate varies from place to place. In order to prepare an accurate budget – and avoid a very nasty surprise when you open the bill – find out the total, tax-inclusive cost to you of any item or service.

When people are involved, **gratuities** are a factor as well. The catering company may add a percentage of the total onto the bill as a presumed tip, just as a restaurant might for a large party. You need to budget for the tip whether or not it's included on the invoice, and you'll want to know if it's already factored in – otherwise you might end up tipping twice. There are a ton of people you can tip if you want to: hair stylist, manicurist, make-up person, musicians or DJ, waiting staff, bartenders, cloakroom and parking attendants, drivers, delivery people from the florist, the baker, and more.

Footing the bill

Who pays – traditional

There's a long, detailed tradition dictating who's responsible for paying for which element of a wedding. In the past, the **bride's family** paid for the bride's and bridesmaids' clothes, the church fee and the reception, while the **groom and his family** ponied up for the marriage licence, the officiant's fee and the honeymoon. And he was supposed to provide her with a home to live in after the wedding, which she'd later earn by working on the farm or in the kitchen. Then there were **dowries** and elaborate family alliances that maintained the hierarchical ruling classes, none of which made much sense once women began to earn their own money.

Suffice it to say that times have changed. For the vast majority of people, weddings are no longer thought of as economic transactions, but are instead what were once quaintly known as "**love matches**". Of course, if the bride's dad is loaded and wants to pay, that's cool, too. However, it's worth noting that the people who pay generally get the most input into what they're paying for. If you want to make decisions about your wedding independently of your parents, then you're probably going to have to pay for it. Or some of it, at least. See Chapter 18 for more on dealing with "ownership" issues.

Who pays – contemporary

The good news is that wives are no longer bought and sold. The bad news is that you're on your own when it comes to figuring out who is going to pay for what. But here are the options.

You pay for the lot

If you both have good jobs and no debt, you might be able to **pay for your own wedding**. Once you've set a date and entered some vendor estimates into your spreadsheet, take the total budget and divide it by the number of months between today and your wedding day.

Wedding insurance

Your wedding probably accounts for one of the largest expenses of your life to date, and as such, insurance is a good idea. What you are actually covered for can vary dramatically, but you can generally expect a payout if you are forced to reschedule because of: bad weather; injury and illness; caterers, photographers or florists failing to materialize; or problems with the venue.

You will not, however, be covered for either the bride or groom getting cold feet and doing a runner! You might also find that you can be covered against stolen wedding presents, damage to the venue (though be aware that you may already be charged directly by the venue within their hire costs for this kind of cover), lost wedding rings, dressmakers going out of business, cancelled honeymoons, and the like.

You are obviously not expecting any of these things to happen… and more than likely they won't. But for a relatively small initial outlay (perhaps £100/$70 for a basic package), you could make the unthinkable a lot more palatable.

As for **where to buy cover**, there are many independent insurers specializing in this area, while most big-name insurers also offer policies. You may even find that the best deal to be had is with a company you already hold some other policy with (especially if you threaten to jump ship if they don't offer you a good deal). Whoever you go with, always make sure you read the small print.

That's how much you need to **set aside** each month in order to pay for the wedding. If it's going to be tough, see p.18 for tips on saving.

There's a thriving business in **wedding loans**, too (see box on p.19), but taking out a loan to cover your wedding isn't advisable. Educational or student loans and mortgages are worthwhile debt, but digging yourself into a hole for the sake of one day – albeit the most important day in your life – isn't.

Take the opportunity of planning your wedding to learn how you each **handle money**, to make compromises and become comfortable talking about this sensitive subject. It's great practice for married life, and while it may not seem romantic, it's far more so than worrying about how to make payments on a loan every month for years on end.

Parents pitch in

If the two of you can't save enough for the wedding by yourself, consider whether either or both sets of parents can contribute. Do the same basic calculation as above, but in reverse. Take a hard look at your monthly salary and expenses, and figure out how much money you can save each month, then multiply that by the number of months until "I do". Subtract that amount from the total you need: that's how much you'll need to ask for. But make sure that if your parents do offer to help they can actually afford it and are not themselves going to be racking up a hideous credit bill.

Everybody contributes

If you can't save the necessary sum and parents can't help, you may simply have to scale back. Or you can get creative about **funding sources.** Is there a wealthy, childless uncle in the picture? A godparent with a love of flowers who'd be thrilled to pay for the bride's bouquet? Could siblings pitch in? Consider asking a good friend if she'll buy you a wedding cake or case of champagne instead of a fancy blender. Small quantities from several sources might add up to enough to plug the gap between fantasy and reality.

> *My mother-in-law, who has only boys, was all too happy to hide behind the tradition of the bride's parents coughing up for the whole affair. She and my father-in-law didn't offer a penny, not even a round of drinks at the rehearsal dinner. But I was glad in a way: it meant there was no reason to let her interfere in our plans for the day.*
> **JULIA**

How to ask your parents for money

- ❤ **Don't wait** for them to offer. Ask directly and ask nicely.
- ❤ Ask for an **amount** of money that they can afford.
- ❤ Tell them about your **specific plans** and how much they will cost. Show them your budget so they can see you're being practical and careful with your/their money.
- ❤ Listen to their **suggestions** for the wedding. You don't have to take their recommendations, but do be polite, and remember that if they're controlling the purse strings, they have the ultimate power of veto.
- ❤ If possible, get the money **up front**, so you can pay for things as and when necessary, and you're not waiting for their okay on each decision.
- ❤ Show your **appreciation**. Offer thanks sincerely and often. Keep them informed about the wedding planning and where their money's going.

Depending on how modern you and your guests are, you could even suggest that people might like to make a **contribution** to the cost of the celebrations instead of buying you a present. Be warned, though, that people want to feel they're at your wedding because you want them there, not because they're paying their way. Another option might be to set up a website that allows guests to contribute to **honeymoon** expenses: see pp.179 and 198 for more information on setting up a honeymoon gift list.

Saving up and keeping costs down

Saving strategies

Whether you're paying for an entire wedding, or only a third or half, saving a large chunk of cash can be difficult. You need to start as soon as you become engaged. The longer you spend engaged, the more money you can save: you might even consider pushing back the wedding date to give you more time.

♥ Set a **savings schedule**. Figure out how much you need to save each month and do what you have to do to make it happen.

♥ Put money for the wedding into a **separate account**. This way, the money can't accidentally be spent on anything else. Also, sticking to your budget is easier when all expenditure comes out of one account.

♥ If you have time, look into **interest-bearing accounts**. While you may not be able to get much return on your investment, every little bit helps. Plus it'll make your savings harder to get at if you feel like spending them on other things.

♥ Take a long, hard look at your **day-to-day expenses** and identify areas where you could cut back; for example, reading a newspaper online rather than buying a paper copy each day would soon add up to significant savings, as would making coffee at home rather than treating yourself to a venti latte every morning.

> ❝ We planned the entire wedding in about six months, which saved us a ton, because everyone was trying to fill their empty slots. We also saved money by not going out as much as we would otherwise. We ate more tuna melts and scrambled eggs for dinner in those six months than either of us care to remember.
> *LUCIA* ❞

Wedding loans

There's no doubt that wedding loans are a bad idea. Lenders encourage couples to splurge on their big day, preying on your hopes and dreams for the perfect wedding, and then charge exorbitant interest, often up to 28%. If you are going to borrow money for your wedding, there are cheaper types of loan to go for. But any type of loan is to be avoided if possible. Of course you want your wedding to be a wonderful, memorable day – and it will be, no matter how much, or how little, you spend on it. But the day after the wedding, you return to normality and start your new life together as a married couple. Don't begin it with unnecessary debt dragging you down. Remember that the point of a wedding is to end up married to one another, not to hold the fanciest event your town has ever seen.

How to keep costs down

While you're thinking in terms of money, here are a few suggestions for how to keep the cost down but still have a great wedding. The relevant chapters contain more and more in-depth discussions of each facet of a wedding and its accompanying price tag. For shoestring weddings, see the box on p.24.

Guest list and invites

The easiest way to reduce costs is to **invite fewer people**. You can hold a very nice wedding for not much money if you invite only twenty guests – but choosing who those favoured twenty will be (especially if you have large families or a wide social circle) – can cause mayhem and potentially decades-long grudges. For more on putting together a guest list, see Chapter 4.

A reasonably computer-literate and design-conscious person can easily **knock up invitations**, wedding programmes, place cards and any other printed material. Many applications even offer templates to assist the artistically insecure. However, it's worth noting that most home printers can't handle the heavy cardstock usually used for formal invitations; professional printers will, however, be able to print your content for you. See p.42 for more tips.

Everything you can spend money on

There's no set formula for putting together a wedding budget, any more than there's a single template for getting married. In service of making your budget as complete, and therefore surprise-proof, as possible, here's a list of the many items that may (or may not) end up as line items on your spreadsheet.

Wedding planner
Wedding insurance
Loan interest

Guest list and invites
Save-the-date cards and postage
Invitation stationery
Calligraphy
Printing
Envelopes and postage
Reply cards, return envelopes and postage

Ceremony
Officiant's fee
Marriage licence
Organist
Choir
Singers
Programmes
Ring pillows
Aisle runner
Yarmulkes
Mass books
Chairs
Candles
Bellringers

Venue
Space rental
Special lighting
Table numbers
Tent/marquee
AC/heating
Floor
Lighting
Portable toilets
Cloakroom

Transport
Bride and groom
Wedding party
Parents
Guests

Weddings abroad
Hotel
Flights

Clothes
Bride:
   Dress or suit
   Ring
   Gloves
   Hair
   Tiara

   Veil
   Jewellery
   Makeup
   Nails
   Shoes
   Lingerie
Groom:
   Tuxedo, morning suit or suit
   Dress shirt
   Ring
   Tie or ascot/cravat
   Top hat
   Waistcoat
   Cummerbund
   Handkerchief
   Cuff links
   Manicure
   Shoes
Bridesmaids:
   Dresses or suits
   Gloves
   Hats
   Hair
   Jewellery
   Make-up
   Shoes

Groomsmen/ushers:
    Tuxedos, morning suits or suits
    Ties or ascots/cravats
    Waistcoats
    Cummerbunds
    Handkerchiefs
    Shoes
    Cuff links
Flower girl's outfit
Ring bearer's outfit
Alterations

Food
Wedding cake
Groom's cake
Cake-cutting fee
Hors d'oeuvres
Canapés
Main course
Dessert
Petits fours
Place settings
Linens
Place cards
Waiting staff
Meals for musicians, photographer, etc.

Drink
Bartenders
Bar setup
Glassware
Ice

Mixers
Garnishes
Wine
Beer
Spirits

Speeches
Microphone

Party
Band
Band platform
MP3 player
DJ
Sound system
Piano rental
Dance floor

Flowers
Altar flowers
Chuppah
Bouquet
Boutonnières/buttonholes
Pew bows or flowers
Flower baskets
Table centrepieces

Photos and video
Albums
Negatives
Film
Processing
Enlargements
Copies

Photographer's fee
Website
Videographer's fee
Copies

Gifts
Bridesmaids
Groomsmen/best man and ushers
Parents
Party favours
Welcome baskets for hotel rooms
Thank-you notes

Other parties
Engagement party
Bridal shower
Brunch
Rehearsal dinner
Bachelor/stag party
Bachelorette/hen party

Wedding night and honeymoon
First night's accommodation
Flights
Hotel
Meals

Red tape
Marriage licence
Wills
Pre-nup
New passport

Wedding party

US and UK traditions differ when it comes to financial responsibility in this area. In the US, the bride's and groom's attendants pay for their own clothes; in the UK, the couple often pays, so fewer attendants means an obvious saving. In either case, if you or your favourite people are strapped for cash, there are ways to get around buying matching dresses for bridesmaids, for instance choosing the **little black dress** as an outfit. See Chapters 3 and 8 for more ideas.

Venue and transport

A **shorter reception** will cost less – fewer hours of hall rental and staff wages to pay for – but make sure you allow time to meet and greet all the people who have trekked into town to see you wed. Consider other ways to keep costs down, like hiring fewer staff, offering buffet snacks rather than a sit-down meal, or making your own table centrepieces (see Chapters 9 and 12). If you can't afford to rent the space for more than a couple of hours, plan an **after party** at a nearby location. The formality level will go down, the fun will continue, and it's acceptable to ask guests to pay for their own drinks.

When limousine companies hear the word "wedding", dollar signs appear in their eyes. Most offer extravagant packages including flourishes like a red carpet, a bottle of champagne, or even a pair of doves or a trumpeter. All this costs big bucks – when all you really need is a taxi to get from point A to point B. Or better still, you can get a friend to tie a ribbon around their car and you're done. For more ideas, see p.81.

Clothing, hair and make-up

There are a million ways to cut corners on wedding clothes, from altering **your mother's dress** to going vintage to bidding on eBay. There are many gorgeous dresses in the world, and they don't all come from famous designers: perhaps your local boutique's up-and-coming seamstress would be interested in a commission. The groom can wear his best suit instead of renting. And when it comes to accessories, you could easily make a veil instead of buying one. See Chapter 8 for tips on saving money on jewellery, clothes and more.

If the bride is used to **doing her own hair and make-up** on a daily basis, then run with that: you don't need to pay a hair stylist to assemble some complicated updo that might not be the loose chignon you requested. If you're looking for ways to save money, have the bridesmaids and the bride all do each others' hair and nails. See p.105 for more on budget bridal beauty.

Food and drink

It's not worth trying to save money by making your own **wedding cake** when decent cake can be bought fairly cheaply at supermarket bakeries or local shops: tastings are usually free and a decoration of real flowers is both beautiful and inexpensive. Beyond cake, wedding guests generally expect drinks with which to toast your happiness and a bite of food to prevent the booze from going straight to their heads. Brunch, lunch or tea will all be **less expensive than dinner**. For drinks, an open bar with only wine and beer or a single signature cocktail will also keep costs down, or simply make it a **cash bar** after a certain hour.

Music

Do you really need a band? Or even a DJ? In the digital age, you can eliminate any danger of the reception being dominated by bad 80s rock or of being called upon to dance the Macarena. Make your own **playlist**, plug in your MP3 player and away you go. Better yet, make a few different playlists: for cocktail hour, for dinner, for dancing. Put one of your attendants in charge of slipping away to make last-minute changes should the mood demand it. There's more on DIY DJ-ing on p.151.

On the other hand, there's nothing like live music. You could ask at local colleges or music schools for a string quartet to play at the ceremony or a pianist to tickle the ivories during cocktails.

Decorations

Choose your venue wisely and no decorations may be necessary. A gorgeous old building or a botanical garden needs no further embellishment. A generic room may be vastly improved by low lighting and lots of **candles**. Candles, in fact, are a staple for the impoverished wedding planner. Use them instead of flowers as table centrepieces and save a

We were more concerned with what the ceremony stood for than what other people thought of it: the wedding truly is just one day, whereas the marriage is supposed to be forever, and thirty years from now, who is going to remember the centrepieces? So why spend a fortune on flowers that will die in a few days and that no one's going to remember?
MARIE

bundle. Scatter **flower petals** – boxes of those come cheap or, even better, you can dry them yourself (see p.163) – and the look is complete. Large **ribbons**, carefully draped and bowed, can also be bought inexpensively and used to decorate pews in church, chairs, or plain windows or walls at the reception venue. Crafty friends with time on their hands may be willing to help you make things that would cost a lot to buy. See Chapter 12 for more on flowers and other decorations.

Weddings on a shoestring

You may be broke graduate students or just unwilling to plunk down a fortune for a single day, but that doesn't mean you can't have a wonderful wedding. Try out these radical ideas for keeping costs really low.

♥ Forget bridal boutiques – hit the thrift or charity stores. Some wedding gowns end up there, and so do tons of evening dresses.

♥ Pay a tailor or dressmaker to fit a second-hand gown to your figure, or pull a *Pretty In Pink* and combine a couple of out-of-date models to make your own unique gown.

♥ Go in with other couples getting married at the same venue on the same day and split the cost of decorations.

♥ Get married in a friend's beautiful back yard when the roses are in bloom and don't buy any flowers at all.

♥ Make dinner a collaborative effort by asking guests to bring a dish – or a bottle – to share. Spread out blankets and throw a picnic.

♥ Cut the guest list all the way down and invite only immediate family or your ten best friends.

3 The Wedding Party

The "wedding party", in this sense, doesn't mean the dancing, drinking and cake-eating that follows the ceremony, but your entourage, the nearest and dearest who have a part to play in your big day. Other than the two of you, it's likely to include the maid (or matron, if married) of honour, best man, and as many bridesmaids and groomsmen or ushers as you like. These roles should be given to the individuals you feel closest to in the world, which can be absolutely anyone: best friends, siblings, children, cousins. Your parents, too, are an important part of your wedding party, though it's not usually considered necessary to dress them in matching outfits.

How many and who are they?

Particularly in the US, it's customary for the bride's side and the groom's side to have **equal numbers**. If there's a maid of honour and three bridesmaids, then the groom would have a best man and three groomsmen. While symmetry is great, this is also where so many brides and grooms run into trouble, as you may not have the same number of close friends. It's up to you as a couple to decide how important this is.

Of course, if you like you can have two or more best men or maids of honour, or none, depending on your circle of friends and your faith in their abilities. And there's no need to go along with **traditional gender expectations** either: should the bride's best friend be her brother, he can be her "man of honour" or "honour attendant". Ditto for a groom with close women friends: you can have a "best woman", "grooms-

Tip

If your closest friends are already spending a load of cash to travel or meet your sartorial demands, politely let them know they don't need to shell out for a present as well.

women" or "groom's attendants". The point is, these are the people you love, however many or few of them there may be. Choose the ones you want at your side when you say your vows.

There are practical considerations as well. All the wedding party, but especially the maid of honour and the best man, have **responsibilities** both before the wedding and on the day itself. When you ask a person to take part in your wedding, it's an honour, but you're also asking them to make significant investments of both **time** and **money**. These people will help you plan the wedding, make sure you don't lose your mind on the day, and, in the US especially, spend a fair chunk of change on clothes they many never wear again. Pick your wedding party with care and remember to thank them often.

Who's paying? Wedding party finances

In the US, the tradition is that members of the wedding party pay their own way. When you figure in clothes – dress, suit or tux – transport and accommodation, the price tag can be high, something worth keeping in mind when you put together the short list. If you and your friends are all loaded, then there's no problem. Otherwise, you'll need to consider how to defray costs for people you really want to be members of the wedding party but who might not be able to cover a swathe of sudden expenses.

One option is to **pay for some things yourself**. When asking your buddy to stand up with you on your wedding day, assure him that you'll pay for the tux rental if he'll agree to wear it. If one bridesmaid is flying in long-distance, tell her you want her at your wedding so much that you'd like to buy her plane ticket.

Careful **choice of clothing** can make a big difference as well. Have bridesmaids wear little black dresses (see p.107), ask guys to wear a dark suit with a white shirt, and they'll still look good standing together.

If you think a potential member of the wedding party **can't afford to come** to the wedding and it's not in your budget to make the trip happen, call and ask her carefully. Maybe she can pull off the flight after all – in which case, you should plan so that she doesn't accrue many other expenses – or if she can't, make sure she knows that you really are okay with her declining the offer.

UK brides and grooms often pay for the wedding party attire but not always. You'll want to consider your relative financial positions and relationship before deciding whether to ask your attendants to pay their own way.

Maid/Matron of honour

This is the big one. Being a maid or matron of honour – also known as the **chief bridesmaid** – demands time, money, patience, and a willingness to be immersed in the minutiae of a wedding that's not her own. Her job begins long before the wedding day. She helps shop for clothes for the bride and female attendants, and often pays for her own dress. She organizes the hen/bachelorette party and, in the US, the bridal shower. She keeps the bridesmaids in line and makes sure that they all get their dresses bought and fitted. It's her job to gracefully spread the word on where the couple is registered for gifts (assuming you haven't sent out that information already – see p.46). She may help out in myriad other ways – addressing invitations, scouting possible reception locations, dealing with cranky bridesmaids who think they don't look good in lavender.

On the day itself, she is the bride's Girl Friday. She makes sure that the bride is corseted, buttoned, blow-dried, lipsticked, veiled, and facing the correct direction when *Lohengrin* begins to play. She handles freak-outs and cold feet, hands out Valium if necessary, and holds the bride's bouquet during the vows. She probably signs the wedding certificate as a witness. At the reception, she makes sure that the bride gets something to eat and might give a toast. She charms disgruntled guests. She is the buffer who keeps the bride sane and happy on a wonderful but busy and potentially stressful day.

This is not a job for a flake, or for a friend who has just married off three other couples and is sick of the whole thing. Pick your most supportive, giving, sensible friend for this job. And once in a while, during the endless conversations about stemware and tiaras, remember to ask her what's going on in her life.

Best man

Back in the day, the "best man" was so called because he was the best with his sword. Whether the situation called for kidnapping a bride from the neighbouring village because your own ran out of marriageable maidens, or stealing the lady from disapproving parents, the best man was at the groom's side and ready for swordplay. He stood close

> **❝** My best friend from high school, now living 2000 miles away, asked me to be a bridesmaid, but not her maid of honour. I was a little sad that I'd been passed over. Once I saw her maid of honour in action, however – organizing a shower and a bachelorette party and keeping track of thank-you notes and helping her choose a dress and a million other tiny duties I'd never considered – I realized that the job actually involved quite a lot of responsibilities that I would not have been able to do justice to from far away. And I was ultimately glad she'd chosen somebody in the practical position to handle them.
> *KATHERINE* **❞**

during the ceremony in case of attack – or to prevent a feisty bride making a bid for freedom.

The contemporary duties of the best man are less likely to result in bloodshed. He is the groom's best friend – and again, he can certainly be a she. Like the maid/matron of honour, the best man should, ideally, be a fairly responsible, level-headed individual, since he has some **important duties**, and he's the one the groom's most likely to turn to when wedding-day butterflies hit.

The best man organizes the **bachelor/stag party** (see Chapter 15). In the US, he pays for his own tux and makes sure the **groomsmen** get their act together with regards to clothing. He makes sure the groomsmen and ushers know their roles, that they arrive on time, properly dressed and not too hung over – and that the groom does, too.

The best man stands next to the groom during the ceremony, holds **the rings**, and is often one of the witnesses to sign the marriage certificate. He may be delegated to hand over the officiant's fee after the ceremony. Traditionally, the best man makes one of the key speeches, with an affectionate and humorous tribute to the couple (see Chapter 10). Most of all, he offers care and support to the groom through the process of planning a wedding and then actually getting married. If you feel it's too much to ask of any one of your friends or siblings, you can always split the job between two or more best men/women.

Choosing your best man

Okay chaps, whatever popular culture might have led you to believe, the primary skills required by a best man are not the ability to publicly inflate a sex doll in under a minute or consume stupid amounts of alcohol. In short, it isn't all about your bachelor bash. When choosing a best man it's important to keep in mind the fact that he is going to play a **significant role** on the big day (see box opposite) and, with any luck, be available to help with a good deal of the preparations too – it's not uncommon to include his contact details on the invite so that questions about parking, dress code, etc, can be directed at him rather than you.

Discuss your short list with your wife-to-be, remembering that it would be infinitely better to choose **someone you both know well**. This character needs to be organized, resourceful, personable and reliable... not to mention funny and a good speaker. Perhaps you both already have the perfect man in mind, but do try and make sure you have the same perfect man in mind. Or consider ditching the idea of a single best man, and **dividing up the duties** among a number of close friends, both male and female; this can take an enormous amount of stress off a single individual and also make sure that each allotted task gets the attention it deserves.

Best man: duties on the day

Whether he thinks he needs one or not, give the best man a detailed running order of the day along with a list of tasks and cues. Looked at chronologically, the best man's day will likely go something like this:

- Make sure **the groom** is fed, watered, dressed and at the venue well ahead of the ceremony.
- Generally **usher the ushers** and hand out tasks to the willing and helpful.
- Take the lead with the **meeting-and-greeting** and, if necessary, make sure that everyone who needs a buttonhole gets one.
- Give the nod when everyone is seated and the **ceremony is ready to begin** (the groom will be about as much use as a chocolate teapot by this moment).
- During the ceremony, traditionally **the rings** are in his pocket, so make sure there are no holes in the lining the night before (no, really).
- For the rest of the day, generally **keeping an eye on the clock** and making sure that people are where they need to be for eating, cake-cutting, etc.
- **The speech**. Traditionally his big moment – for more on this momentous task, turn to p.140.

Depending on how the speeches go, your best man will either disappear all together at this point in a state of embarrassment, or triumphantly start knocking back the champagne before pouncing on the nearest eligible bridesmaid. Either way, don't expect too much more help out of him after that – with any luck he will have earned his stripes and the ushers or groomsmen can do the remaining shepherding of guests.

> *Being asked to be a best man can be a double-edged sword if you're not comfortable with public speaking. So I was doubly gratified when my oldest friend asked me to be one of two best men at his wedding. I had the more responsible role: organizing ushers, making sure he got up in time, looking after the rings. But the minute the ceremony was over I could relax, without fretting about the toasts to come. The speech was to be made by the other best man, an actor and sometime comedian – but not someone you'd want to trust your wedding rings to. His speech, written only that morning, went down a storm, and it even included a couple of anecdotes from my own history with the groom.*
> **RICHARD**

Bridesmaids

The rest of the wedding party have fewer specific duties than the big two; it's therefore even more important that you make clear what you expect of them. Otherwise if you assumed they were going to help out with the million little tasks that precede a wedding and they assumed not, bruised feelings will follow. In the case of the bridesmaids, their main job is to look pretty and, if possible, not cause trouble. By choosing them as bridesmaids, the bride is letting her dearest friends know

Bridesmaids wear the dresses given them without complaint – at least in the bride's earshot.

how much she values them and that she wants them to stand up with her at her wedding.

In return, bridesmaids buy the dress the bride picks out for them (according the US tradition, at least; see pp.26 and 107), which ideally should be attractive and flattering to all, and then wear it without complaining, at least where she can hear. They often **assist with general wedding planning tasks** like tying bows around invitations or making favours. They help plan the bachelorette/hen party. They attend the rehearsal and pay attention to their choreography.

On the big day they **march down the aisle** with the bride and stand at the front during the ceremony. They wear waterproof mascara so that when they cry their faces don't streak. At the reception they act as catalysts for getting shy guests out on the dance floor. Plus, if there are surly parental ex-spouses in the mix, or anyone else that might cause concern, a bridesmaid may be asked to keep an eye on the situation. She's an **auxiliary hostess**, helping to make the party go while the bride and groom table-hop.

The tradition of surrounding the bride with identically dressed women began as protection for the bride from evil spirits, who couldn't tell them apart and therefore didn't know whom to curse. Compared to this sort of selfless duty, the wearing of sea-green taffeta just doesn't seem that bad.

Groomsmen and ushers

The groom's attendants were originally the rest of the posse who went with the groom and best man to carry off the bride. Today, the **grooms-men** are the row of guys standing next to the groom in matching suits – a role specific to the US – whereas the **ushers** can be seen scurrying about directing traffic at the ceremony.

Their planning duties are fairly light, although they may assist the best man with putting together the perfect bachelor/stag party, whatever that may entail. Otherwise, they mainly have to take care of themselves: make sure they have an appropriate suit or rent the requested tux and shoes and have any necessary alterations done. Also get a haircut, take a shower, put on their clothes and show up on time.

On the day itself, if there are no ushers, then groomsmen may be roped into **usher duty**. Ushers will seat guests before the ceremony, handing out programmes or orders of service, for which they're expected to maintain a cheerful yet dignified demeanour. In the US, they may escort bridesmaids up the aisle, and will definitely stand at the altar with the groom during the ceremony.

The groomsmen/ushers decorate the **going-away car** – the tradition of tying shoes to the back bumper came from a desire to ward off evil spirits with leather, of all things – and generally provide a spirit of fun. At the reception, they have a good time, all the while making sure that others are enjoying themselves as well.

> *Being a bridesmaid in several weddings has been great... though once I was in weddings two weekends in a row, and had to buy two different shades of purple bridesmaid dresses! But there's something about being asked to be a bridesmaid, someone who they wanted to stand up there next to them, that makes you feel deeply honoured to be involved. And so I did whatever they wanted me to do, gladly.*
> *LUCILLE*

Tip

Springing usher duties on a groomsman who thought all he had to do was stand upright during the vows is asking for trouble. Be sure to let your attendants know what their role involves from the outset.

Parents

Longtime tradition has the **father of the bride** walking his daughter down the aisle to "give her away" to her new husband. While some brides kick at the obvious symbolism of male ownership, to others it's not a wedding without that tearful daddy's-girl moment. Even the most progressive of brides might want to consider her father's feelings in this matter – some dads have been waiting for this moment since the first pair of pink booties.

If you want dad to do the aisle walk, ask him, and let him know how much it means to you to have him there by your side. If you're not having him accompany you down the aisle, break the news early and gently so that he's not taken by surprise during the rehearsal. Some brides

Bonus families

Divorce, remarriage and the step-families that come along with the package are a part of modern life. While some ex-spouses get along delightfully, others would never consent to be in the same room together – except, of course, for your wedding. Every family is different, certainly, and will have its own issues to deal with. But a few points apply across the board.

❤ **Mothers and stepmothers** may both feel insecure and worry that the other has replaced her; this is best confronted head-on. A tactful chat with each one, during which you assure her that you love and value her and want her to be part of the wedding, may go a long way to smoothing ruffled feathers. Then offer each a small supporting role. Even if you feel closer to one than the other, a publicly even hand is best to avoid hurt feelings. Ditto for **fathers and stepfathers**.

❤ **Step-siblings**, however distant, get an invitation to the wedding at worst, and a request to participate in some way (read a poem, perhaps) at best. If they're your best friends, then they're a part of the wedding party, naturally.

❤ As for the **ex-spouses-who-hate-each-other**, this is where a diplomatic member of the wedding party comes in handy, keeping an eye on things during the reception – when the booze is flowing and tempers might flare – to ensure that everybody stays calm. Keep them on opposite sides of the room and well supplied with food and drink and everybody goes home happy.

"My parents are mortal enemies"

My wedding was in early fall, at a venue just outside the city. It was on the smaller side, just me and my husband with no groomsmen or bridesmaids. We wanted the whole thing to feel like a big dinner party instead of a big religious event, and we held the ceremony outside followed by a reception indoors for about 65 people. It was a great day, and hopefully you wouldn't have known that I'd spent so much time worrying.

My parents were divorced about 28 years ago, and they've both remarried and divorced other people since. I do have a very good relationship with both of my parents and my stepmother. But you could say that my parents are mortal enemies, so I had to take that into account in my preparations.

When I made my toast during the rehearsal dinner, I was careful to thank my whole family. That way I didn't have to say my mother's and stepmother's names, plus we only invited our fathers to speak to avoid any mother-controversy. For the reception, we were in a small room and I had to be very careful with the seating arrangement.

When the day came I was so overstimulated and there was just so much going on, I didn't have any time to worry. I leaned on friends to run interference in case they saw any drama unfolding. Everything went pretty smoothly, though halfway through my mother asked, "Why is your father staring at me?" But really, parents do have enough sense to behave themselves. The day isn't about them and their history, it's about their child.

Much of my sense of relief after the wedding was the psychological shift of not having to worry about separate families any more, but just one, the one my husband and I created together.

IRIS

give the tradition a twist by having both mother and father walk them down the aisle, or some choose mum alone. But if you want a male family member to do it, it can just as easily be a brother or uncle as a father. As with every other tradition, it's up to you. Regardless of the giving-away part, parents are usually given seats of honour in the front row for the ceremony.

During the reception, the father of the bride traditionally gives a **speech**, but this doesn't have to be the case – see Chapter 10. If you're not sticking to the UK tradition of particular speeches, then consider asking them both or all parents to make a toast – they may welcome the opportunity to express themselves.

Kids

> When I was two and a
> half years old, I was a
> bridesmaid at the wedding of
> my half-sister Judith. There's
> no doubt I looked adorable
> in pink broderie anglaise,
> carrying a dainty little flower
> basket. But apparently, half-
> way up the aisle, I announced
> loudly that I wanted a wee-
> wee and had to be rushed out
> before the ceremony began.
> I'm not sure my sister has
> quite forgiven me yet.
> **KATE**

Children are adorable, especially if they're yours or the offspring of someone you love. This doesn't necessarily mean they should have a place in your wedding party. As a general rule, avoid giving children under the age of four any duties and bear in mind that even older children, whatever their nature, bring an element of **unpredictability**: younger kids may wander off the aisle or burst into tears, older ones easily get the giggles. That said, many people choose to include special children in the wedding, usually in the roles outlined below, and if you have **children of your own**, you'll need to make them a part of it so they don't feel left out. Make sure you seat some family members at the front so any young children have someone to go to when their part's over.

- ♥ The **flower girl** precedes the bride, scattering flower petals out of a basket or, if indoors, carrying a flower or a small bouquet. A pair of children, of either gender, can fill this role as easily as a single child, and this may give both courage – kids are easily intimidated in front of a big crowd of strangers.

- ♥ The **ring bearer**, usually a boy, also walks the aisle, holding a fancy little pillow with two rings tied to it. These rings are often not the actual wedding rings, for obvious reasons. If you insist on having a small child carry the real rings, be sure to have a responsible adult tie the rings securely to the pillow just before he begins his walk. And have a tiny pair of scissors handy in case the knots are too good. A small boy does not have to carry a ring pillow in order to be included in the ceremony. He can carry a flower instead, and he'll be just as cute – though maybe not as happy doing it!

- ♥ If the bride's dress comes with a long train, kids can also be employed as **train bearers**, though it means walking at the same speed as the bride; you may want a more senior attendant to supervise and prevent any stepping on it or tripping over it.

The rest of the party

If you have more siblings than can fit into the wedding party or other people who are important in your lives but who, for whatever reason, aren't going to be bride's or groom's attendants, there are plenty more roles in the wedding.

One possibility is to ask some friends, male or female, to assist with **seating the guests**. This may seem like an odd honour to confer, but the fact that you've asked them to be a part of the wedding means a lot. Plus you can list these auxiliary members of the wedding party in the programme. They may dress similarly to the rest of the wedding party – tuxes or suits for men, dresses of a similar colour or cut to that of the bridesmaids for women – or they may simply have boutonnières (buttonholes) or corsages to identify them.

Another way to give a special person a role in the wedding is to ask him or her to **read a poem** or a religious passage. Or you could have someone **sing a song** or **play an instrument**, perhaps during the processional or recessional. An eloquent individual can be invited to **make a speech** or toast at the reception, especially if the best man gets tongue-tied in front of crowds.

4 Guest List and Invites

Deciding which of your friends and relatives makes it onto your guest list can be one of your first wedding-planning headaches. But if you think this is difficult, just wait till it comes to deciding who's sitting where for dinner. A more enjoyable task is designing your invites: it's your opportunity to set the tone for your wedding as a whole, giving guests a sneak preview of what's in store for the day itself.

The guest list

The number of guests you can invite will be limited by two things: the capacity of your ceremony and reception venues, and how much you can afford to spend on food and drink. Bearing these things in mind, set yourself an **upper limit**. Some people won't be able to come – ten percent is a reasonable estimate – so you could invite a few more than you're strictly able to accommodate or – safer – have a **reserve list** of people you'll invite once you've had a few "no"s. If you opt for the latter, it's best to send out the first round of invites early, and try to make sure people on your reserve list won't hear that invites have already gone to your first choices.

A good way to kick things off is by listing everyone you'd ideally like to invite (not forgetting to include yourselves, and members of the wedding party in the numbers). You'll almost certainly be ridiculously oversubscribed and so your task becomes the difficult one of reducing your list to the agreed size.

Paring down the guest list

To get a handle on the situation, you might start by highlighting the names of those who absolutely, definitely must be there. To decide on the fate of the remainder, it's often advised that you **divide the list into three** – bride's family, groom's family, couple's friends – and then strike out names until you have three reasonably even groups. This might not be feasible or fair if one partner's family is much larger than the other's, but bear in mind that if numbers are wildly unmatched, some guests – even the other half of the bridal couple – may end up feeling left out as the speeches become a string of family in-jokes.

This could easily be your first taste of wedding-planning conflict, so see it as a chance to practise your negotiation skills. Here are a couple of common sources of conflict.

💙 **Dad's golfing buddies** Especially if they're paying for the reception, your parents may want to invite some of their close friends: just remind them that this is a celebration of your marriage, and you may feel weird having it witnessed by people you don't even know.

💙 **Dealbreaker guests** Too-gorgeous ex-partners, perennially drunken and outrageous "friends", dad's new girlfriend – there's often a name or two that arouses such conflicting feelings that you can see no way out. Take a deep breath, and ask yourselves (as well as your parents and anyone else whose business it is) whether their presence really will be unbearable, or whether it can be managed through, say, a crafty seating plan and some ground rules. For more on dealing with step- and ex-families, see p.32.

Once you've got beyond the really awkward decisions, there are several more issues to consider.

💙 **Reception-only and evening-only invites** If your ceremony venue has a small capacity, or you'd like it to be a very intimate affair, you can invite some

Sorry, you're not on the list

As soon as you're engaged, friends and family will begin referring excitedly to the big day, what they're planning to wear and how much fun it'll all be. So it's likely you'll soon be faced with the painful task of letting someone know their invite won't ever be coming. It's not a comfortable conversation, but whatever you do, don't let it fester – vagueness is in danger of being blithely misread, and before you know it people will feel they've been messed about. In the very early days, before you've drawn up your guest list, you can honestly say you don't yet know how big a wedding you're going to have. But once you do know who's in and who's out – and the sooner the better – don't keep fudging the issue. And whatever you do, don't be tempted to add anyone on the spur of the moment because you feel sorry for them.

guests to join you only for the reception. Equally, if the food budget is tight and you can't afford to give all your guests a sit-down meal, you can invite some to come along for the evening only. Note: it's not an option to invite people only to the ceremony.

💜 **Children** For many, a marriage is all about family, and kids crawling around people's ankles are a cheerful reminder of the little'uns the couple may soon have of their own. For others, having their vows drowned out by wailing babies is the stuff of nightmares. If the latter's the case, you may want to make your wedding an adults-only affair. In which case, it's best to include a brief conciliatory note in the invites of parents rather than simply printing "NO KIDS!". Be aware, though, that this may still put some people's noses out of joint – or they may simply not be able to come. As with your guest list as a whole, consistency is the key to diplomacy: decide on a cut-off age and stick to it. The only exceptions should be children who are members of the wedding party (see p.34 for more on this).

💜 **Plus ones** These can put a major dent in your guest capacity. You should definitely allow guests to bring serious partners, even if you don't know them, but unattached guests needn't get a plus one if you haven't space. It would be considerate to offer a plus one to guests who'll know hardly anyone else, but there's no need to do it for cousins or single friends who'll have all their mates or family there.

> *Our biggest sticking point in compiling our guest list was couples whose weddings we'd attended in recent years. Is there a strict rule of reciprocity in such cases, even if the friendship's since faded? In the end we brazened it out and only invited those people to whom we were genuinely still close, but sadly it was the final kiss of death to our relationship with some of the others.*
> *DAVID*

Copying out addresses soon loses its appeal. Best get extra hands (with nice handwriting) to help out.

Invitations

Whether you make your own invitations, send e-invites or buy cards from a stationery supplier, think **substance** first, then **style**: figure out what you want to say and how you'll say it, then decide on a design that suits you and your big day. There's a formidable amount of **etiquette** baggage associated with wedding invitations: as always, it provides a helpful starting point, but don't let it hustle you into predictable options if you'd prefer something more original.

If you're on a long schedule you may want to send out **save-the-date cards** to ensure everyone knows not to make other plans. Six months before the wedding should beat all but the most ardent holiday-booker. All that's needed at this stage is the date: there's no need to mention venues or timings, particularly if you think they might change. An email or even a targeted Facebook message will do the job. Just remember this is your point of no return – you can't not invite someone you've asked to save the date – so if you're not 100 percent sure, hold off. The invites themselves can follow around three months to six weeks before the wedding day.

Wording

The **traditional wording** (see box below) is a helpful starting point – it includes all the information needed in a concise form. And it's easy to tweak it to fit your circumstances and personal style.

> ### Tip
>
> If you're getting married in spring or summer, save on postage by popping save-the-date cards in with the relevant Christmas cards.

Mr and Mrs John Smith
request the pleasure of your company
at the marriage of their daughter
Laura
to
Mr Adam Jones
at St Mary's Church, Tavistock
on Saturday 14 June 2009
at 2.30 p.m.
and afterwards at
The Bedford Arms, Tavistock

RSVP by 14 May
24 East Street
Tavistock

❤ The **opening line** indicates who's "hosting" the reception – in this example, it's the bride's parents. If the groom's parents are also making a significant contribution, you should probably change the first line to include their names. If you're hosting the wedding yourselves, you can put your own names here: "Miss Laura Smith and Mr Adam Jones request the pleasure of your company at their marriage…". Of course there are many potential name combinations if your parents are no longer married to each other – see tinyurl.com/gwmj4 for an exhaustive list of permutations.

❤ You can **vary the formality** by replacing words or phrases pick-and-mix style: "request the pleasure of your company" could become "would be delighted if you would join them to celebrate". And with the names of both hosts and guests you can be as formal or informal as you please, from Mr and Mrs John Smith or Peter Jones Esq. to John, Lucy and Pete.

❤ There's no real way round using the **third person** in a printed invite. If you really can't bear writing about yourselves in the third person, you might prefer to send a handwritten notecard or short letter signed by you both, with the venues and timings printed on a separate sheet to avoid having to copy them out each time.

Invitations: design it yourself

Given that most computers and domestic off-the-shelf printers can produce pretty impressive results these days, it's becoming increasingly difficult to justify splurging on designers and printers for either wedding invitations or save-the-date cards. Of course, there is the issue of whether you have the time and enthusiasm (and not to mention an eye for design) to do it yourself.

The very least you need is a word-processing package (such as Microsoft Word or OpenOffice), and if you take a look online it is pretty easy to stumble upon some templates to either use as inspiration or copy wholesale. Here are a few more dos and don'ts to get you started:

❤ Avoid using Microsoft **Clip Art**, or it'll end up looking like a jumble or yard sale poster.

❤ **Centre** your text on the page; maybe try italic text.

❤ Use a **spellchecker** and triple check all the details before you hit "Print". Print a test copy first.

❤ Experiment with putting high-quality heavyweight paper through your printer and maybe try some off-white tones. If your printer can't cope, you can still use your own original design but have it printed professionally.

❤ As for **ink colour**, you could consider brown or a very dark green or blue rather than the more formal black.

❤ If you go for a script-style font, make sure it's actually **legible**, or you run the risk that nobody will even realize it's a wedding invitation!

Design

The traditional invitation is a very simple "less is more" affair – embossed script on white or cream card, no borders, no bows, and certainly no pink fluffy hearts. But there's no reason to stick to that style if you don't want to. There are many independent designers out there offering far more creative ideas, or you could go hybrid: print traditional-style cards, and then jazz them up yourselves (see box on p.45).

If you've got a theme or colour scheme in mind for your wedding, you may want to tie your invites in with it, but don't worry if you haven't. More important is that your invites send guests the **right message** about what to expect on the day. A very traditional invite will give guests a heads-up that your wedding will be a formal affair (and that they should dress accordingly), while a more unusual/informal one will signal the same on the day.

Here's a few things to bear in mind when choosing your design:

- ❤ **The thicker the card, the better** – there's nothing worse than a card that flops waggishly on the mantelpiece. Go for a weight of 260gsm (70 pound) and upwards if you can afford it.

- ❤ Choosing a **postcard-style design** rather than a folded one will save on paper and may allow you to stretch to a thicker card.

- ❤ **Engraving** is the gold standard for your text. **Thermography** aims to provide the same effect more cheaply – ask for a sample so you can judge whether it does so convincingly enough for you.

- ❤ Don't be seduced into style over substance: pick a **typeface** that's legible.

- ❤ Remember that a large card might require extra postage.

Choosing your supplier

These days, it's perfectly possible to make and print your own invites (see the box opposite). But if you'd rather leave it to the professionals, there are plenty of options available.

- ❤ **Stationery** and **wedding stores** will have glossy catalogues and samples and can help you choose both design and wording. But you'll pay a premium for all that hand-holding. In both the UK and the US, the majority of invites are produced by just a handful of companies – so there's no point traipsing round in the hope of finding anything different. But once you've found one you like, you may want to see if anyone else can supply it more cheaply.

> ❝ My mother-in-law fancies herself as something of a 1930s society hostess: one must, she believes, follow correct form in invitations – wording, font and even paper weight. Fortunately, my fiancé alerted me to this fact, so the first she saw of our invite design – featuring a cute but most definitely unacceptable line drawing of two lovebirds – was when her own invite landed on the doormat.
> **ROSALIND** ❞

How many?

You don't need one invite per person – probably most of your guests will be part of a couple or family and can share. But don't order the bare minimum, as you're likely to need some to accommodate mistakes or to send to extras, and you might like to have a couple left over for keepsakes. As setup costs make up a substantial portion of the print price, it's much more economical to print a few extra now than to reorder later. Depending how mistake-prone you are, 10 –20 percent extra might be a good idea for both invites and envelopes.

Defining your dress code

From your perspective, the **dress code** is there to make sure that people turn up at your wedding dressed in a way that isn't going to make your photos look ridiculous – the last thing you want is a group shot that looks like a quarter-final line-up of *America's Got Talent*. There are all manner of tantalizing codes you could opt for (everything from "Beach Formal" to "Boating Elegant"), but if they are remotely spurious or open to interpretation, you more than likely won't end up with the result you want on the big day. Instead, it's far safer (and less stressful for your guests) to go with one of the following.

❤ **Formal** This tends to indicate that the wedding party are going to be in morning suits (or tuxes) and guests should be at their most dressed up, with ladies wearing the biggest hat they can find and men their best suits. If you want people to wear "Black Tie" and "Evening Gowns" for the party, make sure that this is spelled out.

❤ **Semi-Formal** Here we're really talking dark suits and cocktail dresses for both the day and the evening. But be warned, those with a traditional outlook can sometimes misinterpret "Semi-Formal" as meaning "Black Tie" in the evening.

❤ **Smart Casual** (aka **Informal**) You'd hope that this would be interpreted to mean nothing less smart than sports jackets or blazers for chaps and, again, dresses for ladies. But be warned that it's likely to be a green light for some men to wear jeans; if this is not going to be OK, say so.

The bottom line is that you need to have something written on the invite, but you will also have to follow up, having discreet conversations with specific guests who you feel might need a little more guidance.

❤ **Online/mail-order companies** are able to charge less because they don't offer such a personal service. Once more, you'll see the same designs on different sites, but again it is worth shopping around, because different sites are targeted at different audiences and priced accordingly. There's no denying it's a slog trawling through badly designed sites and making sense of differing pricing structures, but if you do some careful research, and ask to see printed samples before ordering, you could save a packet compared to buying in-store. Don't expect to have the whole thing sorted in an hour or two, however, or the end result could be a big disappointment.

❤ **Independent designers** vary widely in cost: some are surprisingly good value compared to the big brands, while others are expensive but provide a unique work of art in return. Look for adverts in bridal magazines, search the web, or browse indie art galleries for handcrafted greetings cards and ask whether the designer will take on a commission.

Evening/reception-only invites

Ideally, if you're inviting some guests to the reception or evening only, you should get a **separate batch of invites** printed for them. As opposed to an email or verbal invite, this shows that you'd really value their presence, even though you can't invite them for the whole day. Make it absolutely clear what time you'd like them to arrive, and what if any food and drink there'll be (if it's a paying bar by that time, best say so – though it'd be nice to welcome them with a glass of bubbly, if you can).

You may want to ask these guests to RSVP to give you a rough idea of who's coming, but since numbers probably aren't so critical for this part of the day, you needn't chase late replies if you don't want to.

Tip

No matter how easy you make it for them, there'll be some – perhaps many – guests who don't RSVP. It's perfectly reasonable to phone them two or three weeks before the wedding to confirm – just say the caterers are hounding you for numbers.

All that glitters... jazzing up invites

It'd be easy to get carried away here and end up with something reminiscent of those mother's day cards you made back in junior school – but with some thought, a few trial runs and just a little restraint you can easily give your invites that special something. Unleash your inner artist using the ideas below – just make sure your finished creation will fit in its envelope and survive the journey.

- ♥ Punch **holes** on the edge or corner of your card and feed through **ribbon**.
- ♥ Wrap the card in coloured **tissue paper**, sealing it with a **sticker**.
- ♥ Buy or cut out shapes in coloured card and glue to the front of your invite.
- ♥ Use ribbon or paper to create a "**belly band**" in a complementary colour: fix it into a loop with double-sided tape and wrap around the invitation.
- ♥ If you're feeling mischievous, pop a pinch of **confetti** into the envelope to surprise the unwary.

What else to include

While the invitation itself will outline the basic details of the day, it's a good idea to enclose a sheet or two of further information, as detailed below. Out-of-towners in particular will appreciate help with planning their trip.

- ❤ **Hotels** Provide a list for a range of different budgets, as close to the reception venue as you can find. If accommodation is scarce, you may want to block-book some rooms on behalf of your guests.

- ❤ **Maps and directions** You'll need to cover various modes of transport plus phone numbers of local taxi firms and information about car parking. If your wedding involves multiple venues, don't forget to tell guests how to get from one to the next.

- ❤ **Gift registry** Some feel you shouldn't give out details of your gift registry unless asked, but if you don't, the assumption may well be that you haven't got one. In the US, however, it's simply not done to mention gifts in the invite.

- ❤ **Dress code** Defining a dress code at this stage gives guests plenty of warning (see box on p.44 for more info).

- ❤ **Reply cards** Including a reply card (perhaps a pre-stamped and addressed postcard) will encourage guests to get around to replying sooner rather than later. You might include on it a space for guests to specify any dietary requirements.

Assembling and sending

As with pretty much any wedding-related task, expect this to be a time-sink, and for the "fun" to quickly wear off. If you can summon up any help, try to form a production line of people doing different tasks to avoid confusion. It is possible to hire a **calligrapher** to address your invites for you, but otherwise get the person with the best handwriting to do the job. Take an invite to the post office or weigh it yourself to check what postage is needed.

5 The Ceremony

Although you may find that much of your energy – and budget – is consumed by the reception venue and catering, the ceremony is of course the heart of your wedding. Whatever your circumstances, you'll have a number of options, allowing you to choose a ceremony that is true to you and your beliefs. The first section of this chapter outlines the various possibilities, while the second provides a rundown of what to expect from the different types of ceremony. The final section goes into detail about various ceremony specifics – from music, readings and vows to confetti.

Your options

Religious ceremonies

If you're practising **members of a religion**, you'll probably want to be married in your local church, synagogue or temple. Unless either of you is divorced (see box overleaf), this should be quite straightforward. If only **one of you is religious**, you may well still be able to marry within your faith – check with your minister for your religion's position but, for example, a Catholic priest will usually be happy to marry a Catholic to a non-Catholic, provided you can convince him that the marriage will not endanger the faith of the Catholic partner, and that any children will be raised within the faith. If you're of **different faiths**,

See Chapter 19 for details of the **legal process** required for any of the ceremony options covered in this chapter. Your officiant will, of course, be able to help you with this.

things are a little more complicated, but there are still various options (see opposite).

If you're **not regular churchgoers** – even if you're not religious at all – you may still be able to marry in church. All British citizens have the right to marry in a **Church of England** or **Church of Wales** ceremony, so long as neither partner has a previous spouse still living. However, your choice of church is limited: one of you must live in the parish, be on the church's electoral roll, or have one of seven other qualifying connections (see tinyurl.com/ChurchChoice). In the US and Scotland, on the other hand, there is no such restriction on which church you can marry in, leaving you free to **shop around** (fees vary in the US and Scotland, while they're set nationally in England and Wales). However, by the same token, there's no legal obligation on any minister to marry you, so if you are not religious you may find it difficult to find a priest who is willing to perform the ceremony. If you're struggling, try the **Unitarian Church**, a non-denominational church willing to conduct a religious ceremony for those of any faith or no faith.

Religious ceremonies after divorce

The **Unitarian Church** will conduct a religious ceremony for divorcees, and the **Church of Scotland** is usually happy to do so. However, priests of most **other Protestant denominations** will only do so in certain circumstances (they will want to understand the reason for the divorce, so you need to be prepared to talk frankly about it). They will, though, probably offer to conduct a blessing ceremony – a brief church service in which you to ask for God's blessing on your new union.

Divorced **Catholics** will need to be married in a civil ceremony unless, in exceptional circumstances, they are granted an annulment by the Church. Again, your priest will probably be happy to conduct a brief service of blessing after your civil ceremony.

Judaism permits remarriage after divorce, although you will need to seek a Jewish divorce: a civil divorce is not sufficient to dissolve a Jewish marriage. **Islam**, too, permits remarriage after divorce in certain circumstances. **Hinduism**, however, does not recognize divorce.

Options for couples of different faiths

Depending on your faiths, some of the following options may not be available to you, as some religions are unwilling to give their blessing to interfaith marriages. Talk to your respective ministers to find out.

♥ You may be able to have an **interfaith ceremony** conducted jointly by ministers from your two faiths. For example, a Catholic and a Protestant priest may be willing to do a joint ceremony. Alternatively, you could have a ceremony presided over by an interfaith minister – someone who, whatever their faith background, will conduct a ceremony which respects both your faiths.

♥ You may be able to have a religious ceremony conducted by a minister of **one of your faiths** that includes prayers or rituals from the other faith.

♥ You could have a religious ceremony conducted in one faith followed by a **blessing ceremony** in the other faith, which celebrates the new union even though it doesn't formally "marry" you.

♥ If neither of your faiths is willing to marry you, or you want to marry on "neutral ground", you might prefer a **non-denominational religious ceremony**, such as those conducted by the Unitarian Church.

♥ You could simply have a **civil ceremony**.

Check out **interfaithmarriage.org.uk** for a wealth of information. It's a UK site, but most of the advice is applicable wherever you're based, and it also offers links to websites with US-specific information. **Interfaithfoundation.org** trains and ordains interfaith ministers in the UK; its website includes a directory of ministers.

Non-religious ceremonies

In the UK, civil weddings are conducted by the local **registrar**, either in the **register office** or at an **approved venue** (in England and Wales these need to be permanently moored, have a roof, and be accessible to the public, among other requirements, while in Scotland the rules are more relaxed). A UK civil wedding cannot contain any religious elements. At a register office you're usually restricted to a simple and brief ceremony. The ceremony at an approved venue may be more elaborate, but it can still feel a little brisk. For this reason, you may want to consider following your civil ceremony with a **Humanist** wedding or **DIY** ceremony (see p.60): these are often not legally recognized, but allow you pretty much

> See tinyurl.com/civilvenues to search for approved venues in England and Wales, and tinyurl.com/civilscotland for a list of approved premises in Scotland.

infinite scope to craft a ceremony that is meaningful to you.

In the **US**, regulations vary from state to state but are generally more flexible. Judges and various other **civic officials** are licensed to perform civil wedding ceremonies and can do so anywhere you like, including outdoors. In some states it's relatively easy to obtain a one-off licence to conduct a marriage, so a friend could marry you if you chose.

Many civil ceremony venues offer the possibility of holding your reception at the same site, saving on transport costs (see p.73 for more on the pros and cons of the single-venue option). When choosing your venue, be sure also to consider the **seating capacity**: will it accommodate all your guests, or necessitate a restricted guest list for this part of the day? If you intend to marry **outdoors**, what are your options in case of bad weather, and is the location sufficiently private?

Same-sex partnerships

Since 2005, same-sex couples in the UK have had the right to enter into a **civil partnership**, which confers the same rights as marriage (see tinyurl.com/civilpart). Although the registration of a civil partnership doesn't automatically involve a ceremony, many authorities will offer some form of ceremony on request. This may be a basic affair in which you simply get to say vows to one another before you sign your names. Or it might be a full-on commitment ceremony, similar to a civil wedding ceremony (see p.58).

If your local register office doesn't offer the ceremony you want, try a different one, or an approved venue. As with civil weddings, civil partnership ceremonies cannot include any religious elements but you could have a religious blessing ceremony (see p.49) afterwards. Some Church of England priests conduct blessings for same-sex couples, though the Unitarian Church is a more likely option. For a small fee, the Lesbian and Gay Christian Movement (lgcm.org.uk) can put you in touch with a willing priest. The Catholic Church is opposed to any recognition of gay partnerships, as is Islam, but liberal rabbis will conduct a Jewish blessing ceremony.

If you're not religious, you could follow your trip to the register office with a **Humanist ceremony** (see p.60).

The US federal government doesn't recognize marriages or civil unions of same-sex couples. A number of states, however, have passed laws that give most or all of the legal benefits of marriage to same-sex couples. Massachusetts, Connecticut, Iowa, Vermont, Maine and New Hampshire are the only states that allow **same-sex marriage**. California briefly offered same-sex marriages from May to November 2008, and the approximately 18,000 marriages that squeezed into that window remain valid. However, California does offer Domestic Partnerships, as do Oregon, the District of Columbia, Washington, Nevada, Maine, Maryland, New Jersey and Wisconsin. Civil Unions are performed in Vermont, Connecticut, New Jersey and New Hampshire, while in Hawaii you can legalize your Reciprocal Beneficiary Relationship or, in Colorado, your Designated Beneficiary Agreement. Rhode Island recognizes marriages performed in Massachusetts, though it doesn't perform any itself.

Best advice is to check with your home state and keep watching the news for changes in the law.

What to expect

Protestant ceremonies

Whether your ceremony is **Church of England**, **Episcopalian**, **Baptist**, **Presbyterian**, **Methodist** or **Lutheran**, the basic elements of the Protestant marriage service are roughly the same, although wording varies between denominations.

As guests arrive, your ushers should show them to their seats. The front few rows are generally reserved for close family. The rest of the guests are traditionally seated with the bride's friends and family on the **left** facing the altar, and the groom's on the **right**. However, if your families are significantly different in size or your friendship groups are so merged that many of your friends are likely to be stumped by the question "bride or groom?", you can simply let guests sit where they like. The groom and his best man wait at the front of the church.

When the bride and her attendants arrive, the guests stand for their **procession** to the front of the church. Customarily, the bride processes on the arm of her father, but you may prefer to be accompanied by both your parents, or by someone else significant to you; equally, you can walk up the aisle on your own.

After **welcoming** the congregation, the minister asks them, and then the couple themselves, whether they know of any reason why the couple may not be lawfully married. The minister will then ask the couple to confirm their intention to be married. Then may follow the "**giving away**" of the bride by her father. Many brides object to the patriarchal connotations of such a ritual and so many denominations omit it, perhaps instead asking both sets of parents or the whole congregation to declare their support for the marriage.

Next follows the **exchange of vows and rings**. In the US, many denominations now allow you to write your own vows (see p.63), as long as they don't undermine the Church's view of marriage. If you're marrying in the Church of England, you can't write your own vows, but you do get to choose between old and new wordings (essentially the choice is whether the bride wants to "obey").

> Go to **tinyurl.com/Church-Services** for links to orders of service for a Church of England ceremony. Other denominations will be similar.

Quaker weddings

Quaker weddings reflect the simplicity of the Quaker worship tradition. There's no procession, no music, no minister. Instead, the couple simply sit at the front of the meeting house facing the congregation. Anyone present may stand and speak if they wish, or remain silent. When they feel the time is right, the couple stand and **make their vows** to one another. (The vows will have been agreed with the Elders in advance.) After a further period of reflection, the Elders will signal the end of the meeting, and the **marriage certificate and register** will be signed. **Rings** may be exchanged at any time, perhaps after the vows or the signing of the register.

After rings have been exchanged, the minister will pronounce you "**husband and wife**". And they may invite the groom to "**kiss the bride**"; if you'd rather not perform for the crowd, you can certainly agree with your minister in advance to leave this out.

Now that you're officially married, the rest of the ceremony constitutes a celebration of that fact. In the US, a popular way of doing this is through the lighting of the **unity candle**: the couple each hold a lighted candle, and together use them to light a third. There will be **prayers**, and probably a brief **sermon**. In some churches, **Communion** (the Lord's Supper) is celebrated – something which will add significantly to the overall length of the service. In addition, the ceremony will likely be punctuated by one or more **readings** (see p.61), and perhaps two or three **hymns** (see p.66).

One final requirement to seal the deal is the **signing of the register** (in the UK) or the **license** (in the US). The bridal party disappear into the vestry for this brisk piece of paperwork; once they emerge, it's generally to head straight down the aisle and out of the church.

Catholic ceremonies

Guests are seated and the bride processes to the front of the church in the same way as for a Protestant ceremony (see p.51). The priest introduces the service, and then a **hymn** is sung (see p.66). Next comes the "liturgy of the word": **readings** from the Old Testament, New

Go to **tinyurl.com/ CatholicService** for the order of service for a US Catholic wedding; a UK Catholic ceremony will be largely the same.

Striking the balance between a traditional and very personal ceremony.

Testament and Gospel, a responsorial **psalm** and a **homily** (a brief sermon, practical rather than theological in nature, delivered by the priest).

Then the priest will ask the couple to **state their intentions**. They must confirm that they are marrying of their own free will, and that they are committed to the Catholic Church's vision of married life – namely that they intend to be faithful to one another for the rest of their lives, and to try for at least one child. This is followed by the **exchange of vows and rings**. Some churches may allow you to write your own vows or at least add a few lines of your own, but many will insist you stick to the set wording.

The **lighting of the unity candle** (see p.52) may follow at this point. Some Catholic priests object to this ritual, though, in which case you can always incorporate it into your reception. Next come **prayers** and a **blessing**. At this point, **Mass** may be celebrated, if both of you are Catholic. Including Mass will more than double the length of your ceremony, meaning it lasts about an hour in total, so you may prefer not to include it.

After a **final blessing** and **dismissal** – and, in the UK, a detour into the sacristy to make your **civil declaration** and **sign the register** – it's time to process out of the church together as husband and wife.

Marriage preparation

Many ministers will offer some form of marriage preparation to engaged couples. They might invite you to take a **compatibility test** intended to winkle out differences of opinion worth talking over. They might also offer **advice** about dealing with conflict and communicating better with one another. They'll also be able to help you explore any **specific challenges** you'll be facing, such as chronic illness, ageing parents or family objections to your relationship. Although you may feel your relationship is in pretty good nick – you've decided to get married, after all – you may still enjoy the chance to reflect on what all this wedding planning is ultimately in aid of: the rest of your life together.

The **Catholic Church** is particularly hot on marriage prep: in the US, there is an extensive, compulsory course known as **Pre-Cana**. This might be spread over a number of weeks or take place during a single, intensive weekend. It's likely to be made up of small groups of engaged couples and led not by the priest but by long-married couples who've of course more personal experience of marriage than a Catholic priest can have. In the UK too, your priest may require you attend such a course; at the least, he will want to meet with you both and speak at length about the Church's attitude to marriage, to ensure you understand the commitment you're entering into.

If your minister doesn't offer anything much in this line, or what's on offer doesn't appeal (and if you're having a civil ceremony there most probably won't be any course available), you can always do it yourself with the help of a good book. Try Elizabeth Martyn's *Before You Say "I Do"* or Monica Mendez Leahy's *1001 Questions to Ask Before You Get Married*. Both will get you thinking – and more importantly talking – about your hopes and expectations of marriage.

Greek Orthodox

The couple enter a Greek Orthodox wedding ceremony together, followed by their guests. Unlike in other Christian ceremonies, **rings are exchanged** at the beginning of the service. Notably, the couple do not speak any vows to one another; in fact once they've confirmed to the priest that they are **willing and free to marry**, they remain silent for the rest of the ceremony. **Prayers** follow, and then the priest joins the couple's hands; they stay joined until the end of the service. Next, the priest places **crowns or wreaths** on the couple's heads. After a couple of readings, the bride and groom drink three times each from a **common cup**. They then **walk around the altar** three times. (In the Orthodox tradition, many ceremonies are repeated three times, to represent the Holy Trinity.) At the end of the ceremony the priest removes the crowns and separates the couple's hands, reminding them that only God can break the union into which they've entered. Russian Orthodox traditions are largely the same.

Unitarian ceremonies

The Unitarian Church has its roots in Christianity but is the ultimate nonconformist sect: it is committed to individual choice in matters of faith and so will offer a **personalized wedding ceremony** to all comers, no matter if you're divorced or a member of another religion.

There's no set format to a Unitarian wedding ceremony – the minister will be ready to work with you to craft a service that is meaningful to you. They will probably have various **templates** from which you can pick and choose, but they won't want to include rituals or words that mean nothing to you, let alone anything that makes you feel uncomfortable, so they'll be open to the idea of building your ceremony entirely from scratch, so long as you include the **minimum wording** that ensures your marriage will be legally recognized. That said, there's no assumption that your ceremony needs to be non-traditional in order to be meaningful: if you want to use the words and vows familiar from mainstream Christian ceremonies that's fine. Equally, you'll be able to include **rituals from other faiths and traditions** too, meaning your ceremony can reflect your heritage. There need not be any explicit references to a god or gods: Unitarians would still consider the ceremony to be religious, because it's based on your personal beliefs and convictions.

Jewish ceremonies

Jewish ceremonies vary depending on whether they're Orthodox, Conservative or Reform. Although a **rabbi** must be in charge, with his permission it's possible for another person to officiate; there's no law saying the ceremony has to take place in a synagogue either. More important are the ancient laws and traditions that date in some cases from biblical times. Before the ceremony proper the couple sign the **ketubah**, essentially a marriage contract, which harks back to the days of dowries though now represents a more balanced acknowledgement of spousal duties; it's often followed by the **bedeken**, or formal veiling of the bride by the groom, representing his intention to clothe and protect her.

The bride may be escorted by her father or both parents to the **chuppah**, a canopy under which the ceremony proper takes place, symbolizing the home the couple will have together and a reminder of when Jewish weddings were mainly held outdoors. Once there, depending on the religiousness of the service, she may **walk round the groom** up to seven times.

During the service **vows and rings are exchanged**, **blessings** may be read by close friends and family, and there may be **singing** by a cantor and other **prayers**. But regardless of how strictly or not ancient traditions are followed, the event will undoubtedly conclude with the **smashing of a glass**. This is thought to be in remembrance of the destruction of the temples in Jerusalem and forms a poignant reminder of loss even in the midst of celebration.

The newly married couple then get a chance to catch their collective breath before the reception – when they will be raised high in chairs and paraded around during the Hava Nagila. They spend some time in a secluded **private room** where they can absorb the events of the day before moving on to the party that awaits.

Muslim ceremonies

Beyond the straightforward requirements of Islam, Muslim wedding customs are mostly defined by the **culture** in which they take place. In Asia, for instance, a week or so before the day, there are parties with singing and dancing, and just prior to the wedding the bride and key women in the family might have their hands and feet painted with henna.

Called the **nikah**, the wedding itself is more contractual than religious, leading to many interpretations of the ceremony. There is a payment made (called **mahr**) to the wife, which is hers to keep even if she has nothing of her own. Orthodox customs dictate that men and women be separated, including the bride and groom. Once the mahr is paid (even if only a token amount – the wedding ring will sometimes suffice), the officiant meets with the man and woman separately to ask for their **agreement to the union**. Afterwards the couple may be brought together to sign the **marriage contract**, and then, again depending on local customs, an elaborate meal may be consumed in combination with a reception.

Hindu ceremonies

The traditions surrounding Hindu weddings are as varied as the communities across the Subcontinent. In the West, where there's a greater chance that a couple's families come from different regions with different traditions, they must agree to a balance, though they sometimes simply choose to perform as many rituals as time allows.

Custom dictates that the most appropriate **wedding day** is chosen by means of astrology, and family from both sides come together days before the ceremony to perform displays of respect and to exchange gifts. When the wedding day arrives, brides usually wear a red sari, grooms sometimes ride in on a horse (this is more common for families of northern Indian descent, and if the wedding can be staged outdoors, continues to be practised in the West), and the couple always meet in front of a fire under a flower-decorated canopy called a **mandap**.

The ceremony can last many hours, with a Hindu priest or Brahmin leading the assembled in **songs** and **prayers**, many of them in Sanskrit. Family members and the couple perform a number of rites, again dependent on regional traditions. The most important of these rites is the **sapta padi**, where the couple circles the fire seven times while the priest reads aloud the seven vows, petitioning the gods for a future abundant with food, strength and prosperity, happiness and family, harmony and friendship. After the ceremony, the once separate families solidify their new community by sharing in a giant feast.

Sikh ceremonies

A Sikh wedding is a **sacred ceremony** seen as the joining of two souls into one, and as such there's no paper contract to sign. Known as **Anand Karaj**, it creates a partnership of equals, without any consideration to caste, race or family history, just so long as both the bride and the groom are Sikhs. The event, officiated by a guru, nearly always takes place in the gurdwara (temple), with families convening prior to the day to perform ceremonies of respect toward one another.

Brides dress in traditional clothing with a gold-embroidered shawl adorning the head, while grooms switch their everyday, modestly coloured turbans for red or dark pink models. There are a number of **rituals** to be performed before the couple meets, but once the ceremony is in full swing the highlight of the event is the **four nuptial rounds**. With the bride holding the end of a sash draped over the groom's shoulder, the couple walk around the book of sacred scripture, symbolizing its central role in their lives. Meanwhile, the guru leads the **singing of four prayers**, asking the couple to live together lovingly and full of god's spirit. A meal follows the ceremony and there may be a reception, though it is not expected.

Civil ceremonies

In the US, the civil ceremony can be carried out by a number of different public officials, including county clerks, justices of the peace and judges, while what actually happens on the day is very much up to the individual couple.

In contrast, **UK civil ceremonies** can seem a little brisk and prescriptive, especially when carried out in council chambers. This doesn't have to be the case, however, and even with a relatively short time set aside, there are loads of opportunities to make it special.

You will normally arrange to meet your registrar the day before the wedding to run through readings, vows and music. At this stage you don't want any surprises, so be fully prepared and don't be afraid to make full use of the staff at the registrar's office during the preceding months: they are there to answer your questions and clarify exactly what you can and can't do. The main thing to remember is that God doesn't get a look in: not in the music, not in the readings and not in the vows, so make sure you know the exact origin of any material you want to use.

It's only in England and Wales that civil ceremony venues need to have a roof.

As for the ceremony itself, the registrar normally kicks off with a few welcoming words, housekeeping statements and a comment or two about the binding nature of what is about to happen. From there things can happen pretty quickly. The father of the bride might pass his daughter's hand to the groom and then take a seat, or perhaps the registrar will dive straight in with the **general vows** before inviting the best man to step forward for the **exchange of rings**. A brief **reading** is probably best slotted in between the registrar's opening statement and the first set of vows.

Before you know it you'll be husband and wife and find yourselves at a table, along with your witnesses, signing the official **marriage records**. This can take a while and is also presented as an opportunity for friends and family to take photos. Finally, the registrar will introduce you to the assembled masses as Mr & Mrs X, before ushering you out of the room to the accompaniment of cheers and clapping.

Humanist and DIY ceremonies

If you and your partner are non-religious and feel constrained by the formality and prescriptive wording of civil ceremonies, you might want to consider a ceremony that reflects your own values and allows you the freedom to have the kind of wedding day that you want. In a handful of countries around the globe (including **Scotland**, **the US** and **Norway**) this kind of ceremony is recognized as official and lawful, as long as it is carried out by a registered "celebrant" from a recognized Humanist society.

The alternative approach (which is the route that must be taken in **England and Wales**) is to hold a register office civil ceremony to fulfil the legal requirements of marriage (perhaps with only a very small circle of family and witnesses present), and then have a second, larger wedding for the extended masses, with a completely personalized ceremony: your own script, vows, magicians, dancing ponies… whatever you like. One very good reason to do this is that in England and Wales it's the only way to **hold a ceremony outdoors.**

However you play it, the important thing is that you regard the Humanist ceremony as the symbolic beginning of your married life together, over and above the register office formality. Though Humanist

To find out more, visit humanism.org.uk, americanhumanist.org, humanism-scotland.org.uk and handfasting.info.

celebrants are a good choice when finding someone to conduct your ceremony, assuming you already have the legal angle covered, there really is no reason at all why it can't instead be a close friend or relative – this can make for an incredibly personal and emotionally charged experience, and will also mean that the key player of your big day is someone who will remain in your lives for years to come.

When planning the ceremony itself, it's worth doing a bit of **research into wedding traditions** from around the world, especially those with a **pagan** basis, as they often contain some very beautiful and symbolic rituals that can be incorporated into a modern script – a binding of hands with ribbon perhaps, the exchanging of small symbolic gifts, or the highly ceremonial and ancient "**handfasting**" ceremony.

Readings, vows, music and more

Readings

If yours is to be a church wedding, you will probably be required to include at least one **Bible reading**. Some ministers will insist that all your readings are from the Bible; others will allow you to include a non-religious text, so long as it doesn't undermine the Christian view of marriage. If you're having a **civil wedding in the UK**, the reverse is true: all readings must be secular, though the law has now been relaxed so that references to a god are allowed, as long as they are in an "essentially non-religious context". Your officiant will of course be able to let you know whether your proposed reading is permissible.

Readings are a great way of involving friends or family who didn't make the cut to be part of the wedding party. But think carefully before **choosing readers**, for your sake and theirs: reading with passion and meaning is harder than it looks. People may not want to disappoint you by saying no, but if their last experience of speaking to a crowd was in junior school, they may well struggle. Whomever you choose, **invite them to practise** at the wedding rehearsal (see p.69) so they can get used to the venue's acoustics.

Three sources of reading ideas

❤ **WeddingguideUK**'s readings pages (tinyurl.com/ wedguide) include most of the traditional favourites; before heading into uncharted waters, see if any of these move you as they have so many others.

❤ Browse the "ceremony readings" discussion topic on the **Indie Bride forum** (tinyurl.com/indie-readings) to pick up some truly original ideas.

❤ Unitarian minister Carl Seaburg's book **Great Occasions** is a good source of fresh ideas, compiling poetry and prose from literary greats and less familiar names alike.

Three alternative Bible readings

❤ **The Song of Solomon** "Rise up, my love, my fair one, and come away. For, lo, the winter is past, the rain is over and gone, the flowers appear on the earth…": In the Song of Solomon, the Bible harbours some of the most passionate, erotic, vivid love poetry ever written: dive in and pick a passage that resonates for you.

❤ **Ruth 1:16–17** "Whither thou goest, I will go": A simple promise to bind your life to that of your beloved.

❤ **Ecclesiastes 4:9–12** "Two are better than one": Practical words on the benefits of partnership.

Go to **biblegateway.com** to see the full text of each of the above, or any other passage you have in mind. It also allows you to compare the same passage in a huge range of translations, so you can pick the version you prefer – from the poetic language of the King James to the down-to-earth language of more modern renderings.

Five readings from around the world

❤ **Alsace-Lorraine**: Albert Schweitzer, "We are each a secret to the other…", from *Memories of Childhood and Youth*. Straight-talking advice on the fact that loving and believing in someone does not require knowing their every thought (tinyurl.com/ eachasecret).

❤ **Lebanon**: Khalil Gibran, "Fill each other's cup but drink not from one cup…". More words of wisdom about giving your partner space to be their own person (tinyurl.com/drinkcup)

❤ **India**: Rabindranath Tagore, "It is for the union of you and me". The subcontinent's greatest poet captures the sense that you were born for one another (tinyurl.com/tagoreunion).

❤ **China**: I Ching, "When two people are at one". The strength that comes from a deep understanding and commitment to one another (tinyurl.com/ wed-ching).

❤ **UK**: Head off-piste within Shakespeare's sonnets and choose no. 29, "When in disgrace with fortune and men's eyes", a funny, joyful take on how the love of a good woman (or man) makes bearable whatever life throws at you (shakespeare-online. com/sonnets/29).

When it comes to **choosing your readings**, there are several things to consider.

❤ It's worth remembering that marriage is about **way more than merely falling in love**: many great love poems look no further than those first heady moments, but if your readings are to do justice to the promises you're making, they should celebrate commitment, partnership, trust and the qualities needed for long-term love.

- Think about **length**. It's much harder to concentrate on something read aloud than it is to read from a page. If you don't want your guests' attention to flag, around 300 words should be your upper limit. On the other hand, there's no harm in going for something short and sweet: a reading of just a few lines, read clearly and leisurely, can lodge in listeners' minds in a way a longer piece won't.

- Does it work **out of context**? An extract from a longer work (perhaps a play or novel) can work really well, but be sure it'll make sense as a stand-alone piece, as more than a few words of introductory explanation are likely to detract from its impact.

- Consider **song lyrics** as an alternative to poetry. Bear in mind, though, that while some lyrics stand up well to being read aloud, others sound banal without the tune.

Your vows

Depending on your ceremony, you may be able to choose the way in which your affirm your vows. You might **recite them** from memory, **read them** from a book or card, **repeat them** line by line after your officiant, or **simply respond** "I do" at the end. Whether or not you've written your vows yourself, it's advisable not to go in entirely unsupported. If you want to recite your vows from memory, keep a crib card to hand in case your mind goes blank. The rehearsal is a good dry run: you'll need to get used to raising your voice so as to fill the space, and speaking more slowly and clearly than usual. Your officiant will be able to give you feedback on how you're doing.

Writing your own vows

In some cases you'll have the option to write your own vows, or at least add a line or two to the basic wording (see pp.51–61 for the likely policy in your case). You may prefer not to: there's a certain appeal to the idea of taking your turn to intone those familiar, weighted phrases, making the same promises as have so many others over the centuries. But using your own words does give you a unique opportunity to **define what marriage means to you**. Writing your vows, and talking about them with your partner, can be a great way of discovering exactly what you believe you're committing to, and how you feel about that.

> *I promise to keep you warm, hold your hair when you're sick and the rest of you when you're healthy! Oh, and to love you always. I pledge to do my share of the dusting, the hoovering, the washing up, making the bed, cleaning the bathroom, the ironing, mowing the lawn, washing the car, decorating the house and – if I am still physically able at the end of the day – to love you… I vow to understand you when I don't; to admit that I am in the wrong when I mistakenly think I am in the right; and to bring you flowers more than once a year …*
> **GLYN**

> *I promise to care for you in sickness and in health, unless it is self-inflicted and two o'clock in the morning; not to nudge you too hard when you are snoring… I pledge to cook for you sometimes, not to use you to warm my hands and feet every time they're cold and to accept your bad habits as being what makes you lovable… I vow to admit that you are right sometimes…*
> **NICKY**

> *You have my heart because you have earned it... I celebrate our life together and rejoice in the still-growing horizons of our love. I promise that I will always be by your side. I will be here when you feel like being quiet, and when you need to speak I will listen... I promise to give you the best of myself. I will respect you, have faith in you, and always think the best of you. I promise to keep letting you know the goodness I see in you. I will be kind to you, laugh with you, dream with you and help you bring your dreams to life. I promise to be always your true friend and wife and to love you forever.*
> SAMANTHA

I thank you for all that you have given me; your passion for life, love and friendship has enriched my world... I celebrate the life we share, and I'm excited at the thought of all that lies ahead. As we take this new leap together, I promise that whatever life may bring and however we may change, you will always fill my heart, and I will always hold and cherish you there. I will stand by you and I will share everything with you. I will trust you and I will be true to you. I will listen to you and I will love you forever.
GREG

Finding vows online

Rather than writing your own vows from scratch, it's far easier to do a bit of research and find something tried and tested. From that starting point you can add bits, take bits away, splice a few different sets of vows together... whatever you like. The Internet is the obvious place to start your search: try one of the following sites.

- ♥ weddingvowsden.com Some useful tips and a Celebrity Vows section with, among others, Kurt Cobain and Courtney Love's vows.
- ♥ elegantvows.com Take a look at the free selection on offer, and then if you still want more, cough up $8 for the full monty.
- ♥ weddings.about.com/cs/bridesandgrooms/a/vowwording.htm About.com is a fantastic resource for all aspects of wedding organization. Scroll down to the bottom for the link to a further article about the "exchanging of the rings" bit.
- ♥ myweddingvows.com A good selection here, including offerings for Buddhists, Quakers and various other groups; there's also a whole bunch of specifically appropriate verses from the Bible.

And finally, make what you will of this extraordinary outpouring of emotion: tinyurl.com/vowsvideo.

Before you start, check with your officiant whether there are any **restrictions** on what you can say, or any **legal minimum wording** you need to include. Your vows are a very public declaration of your love and commitment, so avoid allusions to any past difficulties and focus on your hopes and good intentions for the future. It's easy to embarrass your guests: if there are private things you want to say to one another on your big day, save them for when you're alone together. **Positive** statements – "I will always support you" – tend to work better than negative ones – "I will never let you down". As for your **choice of language**, remember the point of the exercise is to say how you feel in your own words. There's no need to contort your words into a more poetic-sounding order, or address one another as "thee": the result will feel fake. Depending on the formality of the ceremony, the odd hint of levity (see the quote on p.63) may leaven the mix, but a string of one-liners or gimmicks is likely to be as distancing as over-formality. Finally, think Oscars acceptance speeches: no matter how much you need to get off your chest, **less really is more**.

Don't leave writing your vows until the night before the wedding: it is likely to take **much longer than you think** to figure out what you want to say, let alone how best to express it, and inspiration will come more easily without the pressure of a looming deadline. Recent research has shown that people brainstorm far more effectively alone than in groups, so you may find you do better to work separately, at least at first, before conferring. But don't leave your vows as a surprise to your partner. Your vows can be matching, or quite different, reflecting the different things each of you brings to your relationship.

Music

Your first musical choice is between **live** and **recorded** music. Some venues may not allow live music, while others (particularly churches) may feel recorded music is inappropriate. Recorded music will, of course, be cheaper, and you'll be able to pick your favourite version of your chosen piece, rather than being vulnerable to the interpretation of hired musicians. But make sure there's suitable **amplification**: it takes a surprising amount of noise to sound impressive in a large space, let alone outdoors.

As for live music, the default option for a church ceremony is the **organ**: it's the most effective way to fill the space and accompany any hymn singing – after all, that's what it's designed for. But there are plenty of other possibilities, from a **string quartet** or **brass band** to **classical guitar** or **steel drums**. Again, though, it's important to think about the size of the building the music will need to fill, and the number of guests: while a lone trumpeter may provide a show-stopping accompaniment to the bride's entrance, you'll probably need at least a quartet to provide adequate support for any hymns. And save that solo voice or harpist for an interlude (see below), when your guests will be sitting quietly.

If you're marrying in a church, you may be able to call on the services of the regular **choir** to lead the hymns and perhaps sing an anthem. Be sure to hear them live before committing: some can be teeth-grindingly bad, in which case you might still ask them to sing the hymns, but forgo listening to them murder "Ave Maria" during your unity candle ceremony. There may also be the option of **bellringing** – though, as with choir and organist, don't assume the ringers will turn out just for the love of it: there'll probably be a fee.

> *We asked my little sister, an accomplished cellist, to play during the processional. We had her choose a favourite piece, and it was gorgeous. Also a great way to include a much-loved family member without adding yet another reading to the ceremony.*
> **PAUL**

Prelude, processional and recessional

If the church organist will be playing these, you need to take their **ability** into account. Your priest will be able to advise if certain ambitious pieces are beyond their capacity, or those of their instrument.

♥ The **prelude** is background music, played as guests arrive. If you don't have specific pieces in mind (and, brides, remember you won't be there to hear them anyway), you might still want to suggest an overall mood: perky and upbeat, or quiet and reflective.

♥ The **processional** accompanies the bride's entrance. It needs to last long enough for you to reach the front, but not go on long beyond that – so consider how far you've got to walk! It's best to pick a relatively slow piece, or you'll find yourself hurrying down the aisle in sympathy with its tempo.

♥ The **recessional** is played as bride and groom leave the ceremony together. A more upbeat choice tends to work best, to match your pace as you bowl down the aisle in your enthusiasm to start your new life together and, more immediately, get that party started.

Various **wedding CDs** include popular choices for each of the above: you may well be able to pick one up second-hand on eBay or elsewhere, or borrow one from the CD collection of your local library. Alternatively, listen on YouTube; see tinyurl.com/wed-music for the titles of pieces to search for.

Wagner's "Wedding March" has been the theme tune to so many bridal entrances that it may seem almost compulsory, but there's no reason why you can't break the mould. If you want something more unusual but don't have ideas of your own, **ask your organist** or band leader – they'll have had even more occasion than you to become tired of the clichéd favourite and may be happy to suggest alternatives.

Hymns

While civil ceremonies give little scope for audience participation in the music, Christian ceremonies usually include a couple of hymns. Make sure your choices are **well known**, without too many high notes, so that your guests feel comfortable about joining in and don't retreat into an embarrassed mumble. And keep the number of verses relatively short, to prevent flagging: it's fine to miss the odd verse out of a long hymn (just make sure the accompanying musicians know). Your priest may have a list of suggestions, or lend you a hymn book to choose from. Alternatively, visit tinyurl.com/wed-hymn and tinyurl.com/hymnplayer, which between them provide words and audio files for over fifty popular wedding hymns. Whichever hymn you choose, ensure the accompanist knows to play the **tune** you prefer: some popular choices have two or more variants.

Interludes

If you're having a **unity candle ceremony** or need to **sign the register**, a short piece of music can fill the silence. Equally, a musical interlude can be included just for its own sake, perhaps between readings or after the prayers.

If any **friends or family** have musical talents, this is the most obvious way to include them. Make sure, though, that any piece you have in mind is within their capability, and is something they feel suits their voice or playing style and that they can feel enthusiastic about. It may be best to ask them for suggestions. Remember to check your officiant

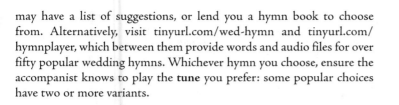

Civil ceremony playlist

Religious music isn't allowed during a civil ceremony in the UK, so you need to make sure that your choices are approved by the registrar before the big day. You can make them as personal as you like (though remember that your gran might not have quite the same fondness for Barry White that you do) or try to choose something that fits with more traditional expectations of wedding music. Here are a few traditional suggestions that fit with register office requirements.

❤ **"Sheep May Safely Graze" by Bach** Particularly nice when everyone is milling around beforehand.

❤ **"Trois Gymnopédies" by Satie** These are lovely pastoral piano pieces that might work well during the signing of the register.

❤ **"The Bridal March" by Wagner** The traditional choice for that gliding down the aisle moment.

❤ **"Hornpipe in D" from** *The Water Music* **by Handel** Not for everyone, as it is pretty grand, but another potential choice for the bride's entrance.

❤ **"Wedding Day at Troldhaugen" by Grieg** Sure to get feet tapping and help you keep in stride as you make your entrance.

is happy with your selection before confirming: in particular, religious ceremonies may not allow secular pieces, and vice versa.

If a piece is to accompany a particular bit of action, make sure it's long enough: you don't want everyone sitting in silence while you're posing for pictures in the vestry. On the other hand, beware of anything too long: these are wedding guests, not a concert audience, and their listening stamina may be limited, no matter how high the quality.

Orders of service/programmes

For some civil ceremonies, where there's little in the way of audience participation, there's no need for orders of service, as your officiant will be able to let people know what little they need to do. You may want them all the same, to act as a **keepsake.** For church weddings, it is possible to refer guests to the relevant pages of the service book, but the multiple options at some points can be confusing. An order of service ensures everyone knows what's going on and what's expected of them.

You officiant will be able to provide a **template.** To some extent, you can choose the level of detail you want to include.

- ♥ Any **responses** guests are expected to make should be printed, preferably in bold so they don't miss their cue.

- ♥ You may want to include the text of your **vows and readings,** so the order of service acts as a keepsake – but the downside is guests may not really listen to the speaker, or may listen too critically, picking up on any slips that might otherwise have passed unnoticed.

- ♥ You can simply include hymn numbers for reference to hymn books, but it is easier for guests if the words of **hymns and psalms** are included on the sheet.

- ♥ You might want to list the members of your **wedding party,** and include a **message of thanks** to guests for coming.

- ♥ A quotation or couple of lines from a song or poem too short to have been chosen as a reading could be included as an **epigraph.**

- ♥ If you're including traditional or **unusual rituals** in your ceremony, you might want to explain their meaning to guests.

Orders of service needn't be as fancy or on such heavy card as your invites, so are easily designed and **printed** yourselves. This means you can put off hitting "Print" until just a few days before the wedding, and

What time's kick-off?

The timing of your ceremony really depends on your plans for the rest of the day, as once your guests are through that door you'll need to keep them entertained until the party's over. A long **dead period** between ceremony and reception will leave guests in the lurch – literally all dressed up with no place to go. Are you intending to feed your guests an evening meal and have dancing into the small hours? If so, a late afternoon ceremony will avoid you and your guests flagging while the night is still young. But beware of too tight a schedule: you need to allow **time for transition** from ceremony to reception. See p.145 for more detail on blocking out your reception schedule.

so accommodate all but the most last-minute changes of plan. Make sure to show it to your officiant and proofread the entire thing before you do print, especially the hymns – guests are much more likely to spot a typo if they're singing the words themselves.

Rehearsal

Your officiant will usually arrange a rehearsal the night before the wedding at the ceremony venue. If that's not possible it could be any time in the preceding week (earlier than that and you'll forget what you've been told), or somewhere else if the venue's not available – though this is not ideal. Everyone who's got a **special role to play** in the ceremony should be at the rehearsal. That includes the whole wedding party, plus readers, candle lighters and so on. If friends are providing music during the ceremony they may prefer to have a quick practice in situ just before the guests arrive on the day itself. The aim of the rehearsal is to ensure that all the key players know where to stand, what to do and when. Your officiant will be able to prompt and hint on the day, but things will go more smoothly if their directions don't come as a total surprise.

Confetti and alternatives

These days, paper confetti is pretty much a no-go. Many venues ban you from throwing it in the grounds and you may even be landed with a fine for littering if you allow guests to throw it in the street. Of course, some

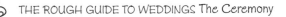

of your guests will probably arrive armed with packets of the stuff. Make sure they know it can't be used: your officiant may mention it in his or her welcoming address, or you can print a note in your order of service. And if you can stretch to it, get your ushers to hand out a more acceptable confetti alternative along with the orders of service as guests arrive.

- ❤ **Birdseed** An alternative to the traditional **rice** – but beware, it's painful if pelted and will sneak into the most well-guarded cleavage, making for an uncomfortable rest of the day. It's a boon for the local bird population, though; rice, on the other hand, can kill them.

- ❤ **Rose petals** See p.163 for a recipe for drying petals – fresh ones will go brown before you get the chance to use them.

- ❤ **Bubbles** One of the more helpful offerings of the wedding tat industry, mini pots of bubbles, perhaps in the shape of a champagne flute, are now widely available – and even the strictest venue would be hard-pressed to find a reason for banning these.

6 Venue and Transport

As we say throughout this book, your wedding is about you, and while there may be some restrictions on the type of legal ceremony you can have (see Chapter 5), with the reception you have the freedom to keep it as big or small, smart or casual, as you like. Wherever you choose to hold your wedding, you'll also need to consider how to get yourselves and your guests there.

Choosing your venue

Which country, which city?

Tradition says the wedding should take place in the **bride's hometown**. If that's where your roots are, then go for it. Otherwise, gather around a globe and give it a spin. You could get married absolutely anywhere at all. (If you're seriously considering getting married abroad, skip to Chapter 7.)

That said, you'll need to decide a long way in advance, since the great sites get booked up fast, especially during peak times. Aim to have both ceremony and reception venues booked six months before your preferred wedding day – see p.4 for more on picking a date.

Religious ceremony venues

If you're planning on a religious ceremony, don't book a thing until you've got an **officiant** on board and know his or her schedule. Different countries, states and religions all have their own rules for where a ceremony can be performed (see Chapter 5). Talk to the officiant you've chosen, or to the one attached to the particular location you're after, to find out what the requirements are. It won't do you any good to have a gorgeous reception site booked up if it turns out you can't actually get married anywhere nearby.

It's worth narrowing your wedding location down as far as you can before you begin serious venue-shopping. Choice is a great thing, but too many options may leave you frozen in indecision. Think about the kind of **style** that appeals: urban or rural? elegant or homey? Questions like these will help you focus your search. You'll also need to consider **travel time**. How far will your guests have to travel, and how expensive and inconvenient will that be for them? Also, check how far you will have to travel on the day of the ceremony. More than twenty minutes in the car and your gown may be wrinkling and your make-up sliding.

Hunting the perfect space

Once you know the approximate geography of where you want to get married, there are plenty of ways to find out about actual wedding venues. Searching online will also let you winnow out the unsuitable spots without having to trek all the way out to them. Don't expect to find prices quoted, but you should be able to look at pictures and get a sense of the place from its website.

❤ **Bridal/wedding shows** bring together tons of local wedding professionals under one roof, offering info on venues and providing tastings of their food. For more on navigating wedding shows, see Chapter 20.

❤ The **caterers**, **photographers** and **DJs** in an area will know all the usual locations and might also be able to suggest out-of-the-way sites that would work.

- Look at wedding announcements in the **local papers** to get a feel for where couples wed. Accompanying pictures may also help you get a sense of the style of a particular venue.

- **Tourist offices** exist to get people to spend money in their area, so they're a great resource for planning a wedding. They may also know whether museums, government buildings, parks, beaches and the like are available for weddings. And in the US, a chamber of commerce should be able to suggest hotels, banquet halls, country clubs and other suitable locations, as well as local vendors.

- For a touch of grandeur, contact the **local historical society**. They'll likely be able to tell you if any of the local castles, estates, stately homes or plantations can be rented out for events.

- **Recently married couples** will undoubtedly have passed on a couple of places for innocuous personal reasons. They'll also be able to tell you why they didn't choose certain places, which is worth finding out sooner rather than later.

> *I loved getting married in a rose garden. The site was beautiful, which was no surprise, as it's designed to be that way – and it was a great natural setting for photos as well. The garden was right next to our reception venue, which was convenient for our guests.*
> **Nick**

One venue or two?

If you're getting married in some sort of house of worship, then this one's easy, as chances are you're not going to stay there for the party, let alone dinner. Similarly, if you're marrying at a register office in the UK you'll be herded out the door pretty swiftly to make way for the next couple. In other cases, the ideal solution is to find a **single venue with two rooms or spaces** – one appropriate for the ceremony, the other, mere steps away, perfect for a party. But should this elude you, you'll need to decide whether you're going to use the same room for both your ceremony and reception or choose two separate venues for the day's events.

The pros of using a **single room** for both ceremony and reception are that you only need to choose one place, which cuts down on the aggravation of site-hunting, plus there's no need to think about how to get everyone from the ceremony site to the reception. Cons are that the room may require redecorating between the two events: someone will need to roll up the carpet, shift the flowers, move the chairs out of their orderly rows and put them around the tables that have just been whisked out of storage, covered and set, and they'll need paying to do

How much room do you need?

Aim for a location that's the right size for your guest list. Too crowded and it will quickly overheat, whereas a room with too few people in it can feel depressing. How many square feet you need depends not only on **how many people** you plan to invite, but also on how you're going to **use the space**. Here are some basic recommendations **per person** or, in the case of a band, **per instrument**:

Ceremony … 8 sq. ft/0.75 sq. m

Cocktails (no seating) … 6–8 sq. ft/0.5–0.75 sq. m

Cocktails and dancing (some seating)… 8 sq. ft/0.75 sq. m

Cocktails and hors d'oeuvre stations (some seating)… 12–13 sq. ft/1–1.2 sq. m

Sit-down dinner with round tables … 12 sq. ft/1 sq. m

Sit-down dinner with rectangular tables … 8 sq. ft/0.75 sq. m

Sit-down dinner and dancing …13–15 sq. ft/1.2–1.4 sq. m

Band… 20–25 sq. ft/1.8–2.3 sq. m

Dance floor … 3 sq. ft/0.25 sq. m

this. Of course the guests need to be elsewhere while all this happens, which necessitates a cocktail hour and a bar in the next room. And if this all takes too long, your guests may end up sloshed before the reception even begins.

Using **two separate venues** comes with its own benefits and drawbacks. There's no room transformation needed, and besides, you may simply want to be married in one place and hold the party in another. However, two sites means, at a minimum, two rental fees, and could involve double the amount of flowers and other decorations as well.

Most importantly, consider how you and your guests will get to the reception, and how long it will take to move everyone. Very little walking should be expected of those wearing formal clothes and high heels, no more than a block or so, especially if they're supposed to dance all night. You must arrange, or at least have a plan for, **transporting everyone** from point A to B (see p.80). Timing is crucial, as well. Make sure the reception site is all yours and completely set up by the time the speediest guest could arrive. This is especially important to consider if there is an expanded guest list for the reception – some couples like to keep the ceremony intimate and then throw a big party. Particularly in this situation, you don't want restless reception guests kept waiting if the ceremony starts late or runs late.

Catering options

Many places have **on-site catering**, meaning there's a chef who comes as part of the package and whose food you will be eating if you hold a reception there. These include hotels, restaurants, country clubs, banquet halls – anywhere you'd expect to find a kitchen. They generally insist that you use their staff and their food, so make sure you like what they serve. They probably won't allow you to bring in food from elsewhere, with the possible exception of a wedding cake, although in that case they may charge a cake-cutting fee. On the plus side, it's convenient to have chefs and servers who are used to working in the location, and venues with on-site catering are also likely to include essential items like glassware, plates, linens, tables, chairs, bar setup and staffing in their price, so you don't have to shop for all these separately.

Any other venue that doesn't generally hold banquets – your backyard, a museum or a local historical site – counts as **off-site**, which means you're free to hire whichever caterer tastes best to you. Be sure to find out exactly what the caterer supplies so that you can budget for all those important extras, like forks or ice, that may not be part of the package.

> ### Tip
>
> When getting estimates from caterers or hall managers, always check if taxes and tips or service charges are included in the price. See Chapter 20 for more on dealing with vendors.

> ### Alternative venues
>
> Sometimes, the best venues are those that don't normally do weddings, as the staff will tend to make a real effort for you and be open to interesting ideas. Why not ask a favourite bar, music venue or café if they might be interested in hosting your reception? Or perhaps there is some amazing building nearby that would be your dream venue – an abandoned lighthouse or old music hall perhaps? Find out who owns it and make the call. You have nothing to lose by asking and you might end up with something really special, and really cheap.

Visiting the venues

Once you've got a shortlist of places that meet your basic needs and look good online, it's time to **check them out** in person. For anywhere that's got staff included, you're not just evaluating the physical spaces themselves, but also the **professionalism and courtesy** of the people you interact with. After all, these people will be working at your wedding, and you want to be sure that they're willing to do as you ask and do it with a smile. You shouldn't have to feel anxious about calling up the caterer to discuss room arrangements.

When you make appointments, ask who will be showing you around. Ideally, it should be the same person with whom you'll make all further arrangements and who will be responsible for your event on the day. At the venue, **take lots of notes** and ask for brochures and references from people who have held events there. Find out how the space is usually set up and whether you can move furniture to suit your own needs or bring in items of your own. Don't forget to check out the toilets. Make sure you've got a way to keep the spaces straight in your own mind – it's easy to get them muddled after you've seen ten different banquet halls. Here's a list of the questions you'll want to ask:

- ❤ Is the **date** you want available?
- ❤ Is the **time** you want available?
- ❤ **Who** from the venue will be supervising on the day? Can you speak with that person?
- ❤ What is the space rental **fee**? What deposit is required? What is the payment plan?
- ❤ Will **other weddings/events** be booked for the same day? Will there be enough time to set up and take down decorations? Is there any chance of an overlap?
- ❤ **What time** will the florist, caterer, videographer, band, be able to set up?
- ❤ **How many hours** will you have the site? Is there an overtime fee for staying longer?
- ❤ Is there a **minimum** rental time?
- ❤ Is there a reception **package**? What, exactly, is included?
- ❤ Are **tables**, **chairs**, **plates**, **glasses**, **cutlery/silverware** and **linens** included?

Tip

Bring along a camera and, if the venue permits, snap a few pictures of the space to help jog your memory when discussing them later. Make sure to take pictures of the aspects you liked least as well as the things you loved about a space.

- Is staff included? What staff?
- Are tax and gratuity included in the prices?
- What spaces are available? Are there any places in the venue that are off limits?
- Where can you take photographs?
- If the event is supposed to take place outdoors, what is the rain plan?
- What is the square footage?
- How many people can be accommodated? For a sit-down dinner? For buffet stations? For cocktails and hors d'oeuvres? With dancing?
- Is there on-site catering? Can you bring in outside food?
- Is there a cake-cutting fee for an outside cake?
- Is there a list of recommended or required off-site caterers?
- Are there kitchen facilities? Refrigerator? Freezer? Ice machine?
- Is there a bar? If not, can you set one up? Does the venue have a licence? Does it supply wine/beer/spirits, or can you bring in your own? Are mixers and garnishes provided? A bartender?
- Is there a good sound system?
- Is there space for a band to setup?
- Is there a piano? Is there a fee for using the piano?
- Is there a dance floor?
- Where do the guests enter? Is the entrance clearly marked?
- Where is the parking? Is there enough?
- Where is the coat room?
- Are there adequate toilet facilities?
- Is the space accessible to any guests with disabilities?
- What decorations are permitted?
- What decorations are offered (potted plants, candles, chair covers, etc)?
- Does the venue have insurance? What does it cover?
- Will they provide a list of references for you to call?
- What is the cancellation policy?

Guests with disabilities

Give the guest list a hard look and consider whether anyone on it may have trouble **accessing** the ceremony or reception site. The few steps you bound up cheerfully may provide an insurmountable barrier to your grandmother. Look for wheelchair ramps or elevators/lifts and make sure that toilets, portable or stationary, are accessible to all. If your nearest and dearest include people who are elderly, disabled or ill, keep their needs in mind when picking your locations. A gorgeous outdoor spot that requires a long trek over uneven ground may not be the best choice.

Home weddings

Getting married at home can seem like the perfect answer to the venue question, especially if you or your parents have a big, beautiful house or a big, beautiful garden, and holding your wedding at the house you grew up in or the one where you live now ensures a deeply **personal event**. However, contrary to what you may imagine, a home wedding is not necessarily any cheaper or easier than one anywhere else.

The big question is **where to put everyone**. Where will they sit, eat, dance? If the guest list is longer than for a dinner party, you likely don't have enough plates for everyone to eat off or chairs for them to sit in. That means renting absolutely everything, from tables and chairs to glasses and forks. Your best bet is to find a caterer who will supply these items along with the food. If it rains, can everyone fit in the house? If not, you'll need a tent or marquee (see p.79). These aren't the only issues to consider, however.

❤ What about your **kitchen**? Is it suitable for caterers to prepare food in? Is the **refrigerator** big enough? Can the **freezer** hold all that ice?

❤ Will the house's **wiring** stand up to the strain of the day's electrical needs? An evening ceremony in the solemn stillness of twilight is gorgeous, but the guests will require **light** to dine and dance by. You may need to rent a generator.

❤ Few homes have enough **toilets** for a wedding. A good estimate is one per 35 guests. You do not want to have septic tank problems on your wedding day, or long lines of bursting guests. Fortunately, portable bathrooms have come a long way, and you can rent upscale ones complete with lights, running water, even air conditioning – though they're not cheap.

❤ **Parking** is a major issue that's easy to overlook. You may need a **permit** to park cars along the street by your home, and even then, the street may not be long enough. If there's a nearby car park then you can reserve spaces there and maybe provide a shuttle. Or in the US, you can hire staff to provide valet parking. Better yet, encourage carpooling.

❤ **Noise** levels may be an issue. Check with your local council or precinct for noise regulations. You may need a special permit, and, you will probably have to invite all your neighbours or risk their wrath when the party rages past early bedtimes.

❤ Who will **clean up** after the party, and when? Don't plan on doing it yourself, or on drunk guests sticking around to help tidy up – that is beyond the best man's purview. Hire a cleaning crew or a fleet of maids to take care of the mess outside and in. Alternatively, talk with friends and family and elicit promises from responsible parties that they'll help clean up – or better yet, organize a cleanup effort themselves – on the day after. In the afternoon.

❤ Finally, bring a critical eye to your house and garden. Are there **repairs** or **improvements** that you would feel bound to do before the wedding? These can be a significant hidden cost – or even worse, may fall behind schedule, so that tarps and sawdust provide the ceremony backdrop rather than fresh paint and rose bushes.

Outdoors: tents and marquees

Plan for **rain**. For an outdoor wedding, this means a tent, aka a marquee, and a good one, too. The sort of delicate canopy you can assemble yourselves will do very little to block a gusting downpour. Marquee rental agencies book up at least as far in advance as other desirable wedding vendors, so **reserve yours early** – though you should also discuss the cancellation policy. Many agencies charge a percentage of the fee if, three days before the wedding, you decide to trust a sunny weather report.

Get a tent or marquee with **sides** that can be left down if it rains but rolled up to let in the sunshine should the weather choose to cooperate. However nice it sounds, say no to a clear ceiling: the greenhouse effect will have you sweltering if the sun shines.

> ### Tip
> With family and friends running loose over your house, pick **one room that's off limits**, where the two of you can dress, freak out, breathe deeply, kiss, or simply take a moment.

Just as for any other space, the question arises of how many **rooms** you need. Do you want separate tents for the ceremony and reception? What about one for the portable toilets you'll probably require? And one for the caterers?

You'll need a **flat surface** for the tent. Also, consider how well the area drains: a rainstorm from the previous week could leave a swampy residue. A **floor** will add substantially to the price tag, but you may want one anyway for dancing. There are several different grades of flooring available, from basic matting to wooden boards – with a wide range of prices attached. Otherwise, you might want to suggest that all of your female guests wear wedge heels.

A marquee presents its own special set of problems for **decor**, being a vast expanse of smudged white, interrupted only by industrial poles. Factor in the expense of disguising these when you consider the cost.

All those lights coupled with that big stereo system may require a **generator**. If you're planning on heating or air conditioning a tent, the generator becomes a necessity. Make sure you set it up far enough away from the tent that the roar doesn't drown out the vows or speeches.

Transport

Once you've sorted out where the wedding is to be, you can plan for **how to get there**. This may seem like a detail easily sorted out at the last minute, but if your wedding happens to be on a Saturday in June or around the time of the local prom, it's best to book as early as possible. Unless your ceremony and reception are held in the same place, you'll have to plan for transporting guests as well as the wedding party.

Wedding party

UK tradition dictates that the bride and her father arrive in one car while the bride's mother and her attendants arrive in another. The groom is simply expected to get himself to the ceremony before the guests arrive, so he doesn't need a flashy car. **In the US** there are no such traditions to guide your choices, though feel free to adopt the British custom to avoid having to decide who rides with who.

For the less traditional couple, the ride to the wedding can provide time for an intimate moment during a very busy day. The bride and groom may enjoy a few minutes together before they take their vows. Or mum and dad may appreciate the chance to offer words of wisdom to their little boy or girl. However, if you're the traditional sort who believe that the groom shouldn't see the bride before the moment she walks down the aisle, then you've got to plan for at least two vehicles – and who's going to ride in each.

It's a nice touch to chauffeur the **wedding party** to the ceremony, too. Plus, that way you're assured they'll arrive on time. This is where, admittedly, a **limousine** comes in handy, since a stretch limo can carry ten to twelve passengers and even a regular limo will usually hold six. Peace of mind combined with ease and comfort may make the price seem a lot more reasonable.

Limo companies generally charge extra for weddings, though a black or silver limo will generally cost about ten percent less than white (which won't go with a cream dress anyhow). As with any other vendor, check out the goods in person and get all details, up to the plate number of a specific vehicle if you're particular, in writing. If limos aren't your style, a traditional car like a **Rolls Royce** or **Bentley** is a very classy option. Or maybe a **vintage car**, especially if you don't

> **Tip**
>
> When renting a car and driver, ask about the cost for them to wait; it may be the same as, or less than, two or three separate trips to ferry you to the ceremony, from there to the reception, and then away to your next stop, whether home, hotel or airport.

DIY bridal car

The bridal car can be a quite a major expense (especially if you have your heart set on a vintage Rolls Royce or a replica of the "General Lee" from *The Dukes of Hazzard*). And while the moment that the bride appears from said vehicle is a great thing for the photographer to catch, most of your guests will be seated inside waiting for the ceremony to begin. In short, if you want to save a small bundle of cash, this is a good place to do it. What's more, it doesn't mean compromising on style. Many taxi firms (and private taxi drivers) are more than happy to spruce up their cab and don a silly hat for a fraction of the cost of using a commercial "wedding car" company. You could also ask a friend if they might want to get involved – but preferably one with a good-looking motor. That way, you might be looking at the cost of a bit of ribbon for the front grille and perhaps a chauffeur's cap, found on eBay, for your friend to wear.

> *My dad had arranged for a fancy car to pick up me and my bridesmaids from the place we were having our make-up done before heading to the ceremony. We were all done up and waiting for it to arrive. We waited. And waited some more. We didn't have the number of the car company and couldn't get hold of my dad at that point, so one of the bridesmaids who lived nearby walked to get her own car, an old banger, and drove us all to the ceremony in that. Everyone was so relieved to see me – they were starting to think we weren't going to turn up.*
> **JESS**

Daisy, Daisy… what happened to a bicycle made for two?

need the space of a limo. You could even ask your parents or a member of the wedding party to give you a lift. See the box on p.81 for more DIY suggestions.

Friends of the couple, led by the best man, often sneak out and decorate the vehicle the couple plans to make their getaway in. If it's a vintage rental that absolutely must not be decorated, give your pals a hint in good time. Otherwise, expect anything from a restrained "Just Married" sign in the back window to dirty slogans painted on the windows and streamers, shoes, and cans trailing behind, depending on the best man's sense of humour.

Why can't the groom see the bride?

The superstition that it's bad luck for the groom to see the bride on the wedding day comes from the times when marriages were contractual affairs between families. Then, the bride and groom might never have laid eyes on one another until they said "I do". Hiding the bride from the groom on the day of the ceremony was insurance against a groom fleeing an unappealing bride. Ditto for the veil.

More recently, the superstition has attached itself more firmly to the dress as well as to the day – the groom isn't supposed to see the bride's gown. Many contemporary brides follow through on this, more in the hopes of knocking their sweeties out with how gorgeous they look as they walk down the aisle.

Absolutely **do not plan on driving yourselves** to or from the wedding. A jitters-driven fender bender on the way to the ceremony or, even worse, a drunk driving charge on the way home are too great a risk.

Of course you don't have to arrive by car. **Horse and carriage** is one traditional, if not always practical option, but depending on the venue this is another way you could make your wedding special: do it like Audrey Hepburn in *Roman Holiday* and arrive on a white Vespa, travel to a waterside reception by **boat**, or slide off into a winter wonderland by **bobsled**. If distances are small, you could even get to the ceremony on foot, surrounded by as many attendants and guests as you like.

Transporting your guests

Sometimes your ceremony site and reception venue are across town from one another. Envision a rainstorm: the guests pour forth from the church into the wet and each one tries to hail a cab. This is a worst-case scenario, yes, but even on a sunny day you don't want everyone to get blisters trekking from one venue to another. Consider **hiring a bus**. If that's not in the budget, you can easily make some calls and ensure that everyone has a ride, whether with a friend or relative or in the fleet of **taxis** you arranged to line up at the crucial moment.

> *I'm a keen horse-woman and wanted my horse Katy to be part of the wedding. Glyn, my husband-to-be, also grew up with horses and wanted to be in on the fun. So arriving at the ceremony on horseback was the perfect option. I rode side-saddle and he rode next to me on a white 'charger'! Getting on and off was a challenge in my pencil-thin dress, but Glyn was able to lift me down, which was very romantic.*
> **NICKY**

For those guests who are visiting from **out of town**, a map of the area with their hotel and the ceremony and reception sites prominently marked can be a life-saver. A simple home print job will suffice, and you can email it to them before the wedding.

Welcome, overnight guests!

In the US it's common practice to book a **block of rooms** at a single hotel for wedding guests to stay at. The guests have until a certain date to book these rooms, ensuring that conveniently located (and, hopefully, reasonably priced) accommodation is available to those who don't know the area. Hotels often offer discounts on these blocks, or give the bride and groom a break on the honeymoon suite. The couple often provide a **welcome bag** for these guests as well, containing items like local treats (such as Texas hot sauce or Boston Baked Beans candy), a couple of bottles of water, a granola or chocolate bar, and any other small item you think your guests might appreciate – ear plugs, mini lip balm, IKEA slippers, aspirin.

You should also include an **information packet** along with the treats, including the map provided to all out-of-town guests, a reminder of event times and details of travel distances and any shuttle services to and from the hotel. An info pack will save you the hassle of many a last-minute phone call. If you know the area well, you could also include a list of favourite nearby shops and restaurants, as well as any other places you think people might enjoy spending time when not at your wedding.

As a final touch, you might consider adding some **essential information**, including the number for a local cab service and the address of the hotel, on a business-card-sized piece of paper just big enough to fit in a wallet. This little cheat sheet will be especially appreciated if your reception has an open bar.

In the UK much of this information is sent out with the invitations rather than dropped off at the hotel. In any case, it's probably a good idea to supply the best man and ushers with the phone numbers of **local cab companies** for guests in need.

7 Weddings Abroad

Why not have your dream day in your dream destination? One in six British couples gets married overseas, lured by sunny skies and the chance to say "I do" on a tropical island far away from home; the number of US couples marrying abroad is far fewer. Many of the factors you'll need to consider when choosing your wedding destination – what time of the year you want to get married, how much you want to spend – also apply to planning your honeymoon (see Chapter 16), and a lot of couples marrying overseas start with the honeymoon and work backwards.

Do-It-Yourself?

Given the amount of organization required in planning a (successful) wedding abroad, and the often complex rules and regulations, the majority of couples book through a **specialist tour operator**: with most reputable agencies now offering an overseas wedding service, you'll have plenty of choice. You'll get your own dedicated wedding planner, who will be able to advise you on what each destination or resort offers, and will take responsibility for arranging the necessary paperwork.

However, if you're getting married in a country where services cost a lot less than they do at home, there's a great temptation to **organize the wedding yourself** – you can stay in control of the whole occasion (which

Tip

If you can't face the paper-work headache involved in making sure your destination wedding is legally recog-nized back home, consider having a **secret home wed-ding** before you head out – just you and a couple of witnesses. Your guests need never know your foreign cer-emony is just for show.

you can't always do with package weddings abroad), and you can save money by missing out the middle man. But you'll also be responsible for organizing the entire event, from researching legal requirements to arranging accommodation for your guests – and, in some cases, all from a couple of thousand miles away, and maybe in a foreign language. If you do want to be your own boss, make sure you've considered the following:

💗 What are the **legal requirements**? If you don't have the right paperwork (see p.90), you won't get married, and the necessary documentation can vary enormously from country to country and take months to prepare. Meeting any such requirements must be factored into your wedding schedule.

💗 Are there any **residency rules**? Most countries, reasonably enough, require that you live there before you can get married there, though this may not be too onerous: see p.90 for more.

💗 Who's going to be **the officiant**? Is your wedding going to be a civil cer-emony, in which case you'll need to recruit the services of a local judge, justice of the peace or government official, or are you planning a religious wedding that requires an appropriately qualified officiant? Many resorts and hotels have on-site wedding coordinators who can help with finding the right person for the job.

💗 What about **your guests**? Organizing a wedding abroad also means look-ing after all your guests' requirements. You'll need to make sure there's enough accommodation at or near the venue and, even if you're ultimately not paying for it, to reserve it well in advance – you don't want your guests staying in a different resort on the other side of the island. If they're travel-ling with you, are there enough activities to entertain them while you sort out any necessary on-location paperwork? Do you need to organize any-thing for them to do after the day itself?

The pros of getting married abroad...

Organization

If the thought of planning your own wedding makes you sick with dread, then getting married abroad can be the perfect antidote: you'll get everything you want without having to do much of the work, and a lot of the **big decisions** that would normally weigh you down – which flowers should you have? who's going to make the cake? how many

Tip

Wedding insurance is a good idea if you're getting married in your own country; it's a necessity if you're tying the knot abroad. A decent policy should cover you for every-thing from flight cancellations and lost luggage to accidents overseas.

Civil partnerships abroad

British couples in a same-sex relationship will need to get married in a country that also has a partnership or union that is recognized in Schedule 20 of the UK's Civil Partnership Act (see tinyurl.com/sched20 for more). Countries that currently appear in Schedule 20 include Australia, Canada, France, Germany, the Netherlands, New Zealand and the USA, though residency requirements can differ within each country – in Canada, for example, provinces that offer a "union civile" rather than a "marriage" come under French law and have a residency period of around thirty days.

Couples need to register their civil partnership thirty days in advance and submit documents proving they are sane, in good health and not already married.

guests should you invite? – are either someone else's responsibility or are made redundant by the situation. Destination weddings invariably come as a package, meaning that the day is mapped out for you, with each individual component, such as transport to the ceremony, food and music, part of the all-inclusive service.

The location

Weather at a UK wedding, even in the height of summer, can be unpredictable, and you should always cater for the chance of rain. You don't need a crystal ball, however, to know when it's going to be sunny in the Bahamas. And, of course, there's the exotic **backdrop** – white-sand beaches in the Indian Ocean, winding Parisian streets – to give your wedding photos that touch of originality.

The cost

It might sound odd, but heading to the other side of the world to get married can often work out cheaper – at least for the couple themselves – than doing it at home: for UK residents the average cost of a wedding abroad is just £6500, whilst US citizens opting to tie the knot overseas might save up to $20,000 over a traditional wedding.

> *The great thing about getting married in Italy – apart from the guaranteed good weather and the romantic setting – was that we didn't need to spend weeks agonizing over a 'theme' that would distinguish our wedding from all the others our friends were going to that year. The reception was in a beautiful old hilltop farmhouse; the flowers, fresh lavender picked from the field that morning; the wedding breakfast, a spread of rich Tuscan cuisine. So you could say it was handed to us on a plate.*
> **CECILLIA**

Tip

Remember that your flight tickets must match the names on your passport – see p.222 for more.

The honeymoon

Getting married abroad kills two birds with one stone: once you've decided on the destination, you've essentially decided on the honeymoon as well (or vice versa). You'll have much less in the way of planning to do and will certainly save money. What's more, your family will be there to enjoy it with you – which, of course, could easily be seen as a disadvantage too.

... and the cons

Lack of control...

Having everything planned for you may suit time-poor couples, but if you've got your heart set on a certain flower arrangement, have always wanted to arrive at the church in a vintage car, or have promised your brother's mate that he could do the DJ-ing, then you may find the **limited options** at an overseas wedding a little too restrictive.

... and lack of a personal touch

Few alternatives means that there will undoubtedly be a lot of **other couples** getting married in the same place as you who have made exactly the same choices. You might find it hard to stamp your identity on the event. At some of the more popular resorts and beaches, there can be an unsatisfactory conveyor-belt feeling to the occasion, with your Big Day just one of a number of (very similar) others.

Fewer guests...

It's easy at a traditional wedding to end up inviting distant relatives whose faces you can't even picture, but get married abroad and you could face an entirely different problem: a wedding attended by only the bride, the groom and the two other people who could afford the trip. It's fine to spend a fortune on your dream day – just don't expect everyone else to be quite so enthusiastic.

... but at higher costs

Those guests that do make it to your wedding will have to foot the bill for their own travel and accommodation expenses – normal etiquette

is for the couple to only pay for the ceremony and reception. Guests attending weddings abroad will spend, on average, £1250 more than they would at a wedding in the UK.

It can be hard to find time alone if your guests are effectively going on honeymoon with you.

Red tape

It's difficult to know which would be worse: travelling halfway around the globe only to realize you can't get married because you forgot to sign a slip of paper at your local town hall three months ago, or returning home to find that your "wedding" isn't legally recognized in your own country and you're not actually married after all.

Generally, as long as your marriage is legally performed in a country whose marriage law is recognized in your home country, it will be **legally valid**. Weddings carried out abroad cannot be **registered** in the

Tip

You can check what **visas** you'll need for your destination at fco.gov.uk/travel or state.gov/travel and which **vaccinations** are recommended, and other specific travel-health advice, at fitfortravel.scot.nhs.uk or cdc.gov/travel.

UK, but you can arrange for a record of your marriage to be kept at the General Register Office, which also makes it easier get copies in the future. You'll need to get your documents translated if they're not in English.

Meeting the **legal requirements of your destination** can be more complex: in France, for example, UK citizens might need a Certificate of Custom Law (*certificat de coutume*); in Italy, they'll need a Certificate of No Impediment; and in Sri Lanka a Single Status Statutory Declaration (see box below). In Mexico, all documents must be translated into Spanish, certified by a Spanish-speaking lawyer and, with UK documents, legalized by the Foreign & Commonwealth Office. For specific advice on whether your marriage will be recognized at home, and to find out which documents you'll need, contact the local **British embassy** or consulate (fco.gov.uk has a list), or, if from the US, the **Attorney General** of your home state. It can pay to check with a

> *We got married in my wife's home town in Mexico. I had my hippy hair cut, watched La Franja win against America, turned up right on time to our wedding in the oldest cathedral on the continent, and enjoyed the reception with wife, outlaws, home-made beer, tequila, mariachis, ex-pat rock band and karaoke.*
> **Peter**

Certificate of No Impediment and the Single Status what?

A **Certificate of No Impediment** (CNI) confirms that there are no objections to your proposed marriage, and is a requirement in several popular overseas wedding destinations, including Aruba, Greece, Italy and Turkey. In the UK, CNIs can be obtained from your local register office (go to tinyurl.com/find-register to find yours), unless you're marrying an Irish national, in which case they must be applied for through the Foreign & Commonwealth office in London; they usually take around a month to issue and are valid for six months. Some countries require your CNI to be **translated** or **legalized**. Note, too, that in Italy you'll need to exchange your CNI for a Nulla Osta at the nearest British consulate to where you're getting married.

Many countries, including Antigua, the Bahamas, the Dominican Republic, Kenya, the Seychelles and Sri Lanka, require a **Single Status Statutory Declaration**, proof that no impediment exists for you to be legally married. In the UK, you'll need yours stamped and certified by a solicitor no more than three months before the return date of travel. No such document exists in the US, so instead you'll need what's known as an **Affidavit of Eligibility to Marry**, which can be signed at the American embassy or consulate in the country in which you're getting married.

lawyer as well. No matter where you get married, every destination will require both the bride and groom to have original documents or certified copies of:

- ❤ A full ten-year valid **passport** with more than six months remaining before expiry
- ❤ Full **birth certificates**
- ❤ If under 18 (or 21 in some countries), **parental consent**
- ❤ If divorced, the **decree absolute**
- ❤ If widowed, the **marriage and death certificates** of the deceased spouse
- ❤ **Deed poll** proof of any name change
- ❤ **Adoption certificate** if relevant

In many countries, you'll need to show **proof of residency** before you can get married. This isn't as bad as it sounds, as it usually requires a stay of between just one and seven days, though exceptions include Mauritius (fifteen days required for a religious ceremony), England (foreign nationals need to reside in England for seven days before applying for a marriage licence but then have to wait fifteen days to get married) and France (forty days).

8 Clothes

That big white dress is a potent symbol of a wedding, but the bride's not the only one who needs special clothes – nor is she actually required to walk the aisle in a meringue of a gown. The groom, too, will likely be decked out in rather swankier attire than usual, and everyone else in the wedding party, from the bridesmaids to the groom's parents, needs to be suitably dressed.

Does it have to be a white wedding?

The most important thing to remember when choosing your wedding clothes is to please yourself. As with everything to do with weddings, there's no tradition too old to break, no rules that must be followed to the letter. Both the bride and groom should feel good as well as gorgeous on this important, exhausting and wonderful day.

In general, the type of clothes you pick out for both the bride and groom depend on what kind of wedding you're going for. This is especially true for the bride, who has a tremendous range of looks she can choose from. A suit can be just as chic as a dress though not as glamorous, and there's nothing that says the bride can't wear trousers. A skirt suit can feel either contemporary or sweetly vintage, depending on the cut and fabric. Your mother's dress can be updated or tailored. On the other hand, if you want to be princess for a day – tiara, train, puffy skirt and all – don't let anyone talk you out of it.

Your clothes may be influenced by your choice of **theme**, whether 1950s sock hop or black-tie elegance. The overall colour palette should probably also be taken into consideration. It's not necessary for the

> ❝ Virginal white didn't really fit with the statement Greg and I were making by getting married. We had been together for sixteen years and our wedding was a celebration of all we had already shared and a way of looking forward to our continuing future together. Though I did consider wearing ivory, I kept an open mind when looking around for my dress and when I saw it I immediately knew it was right. Scarlet felt bold, strong, dramatic – it suited my colouring and (I hope) my personality. What also counted, quite apart from the colour, was the shape. It was a gorgeous, flattering halter neck, which I felt sure I would wear again. That said, I haven't yet worn it again, four years later – it feels too imbued with the magic of that day.
>
> SAMANTHA ❞

bridesmaid dresses to actually match the pink cosmopolitans you plan on serving, but you should probably consider whether any colour choices at the ceremony or reception will clash.

White in its various shades is generally the colour of choice for Western brides, though plenty of brides add a splash of colour with a stripe or sash, or even wear a colourful dress. In China, however, brides wear red for luck – white is the colour of mourning there and in many other countries too. Look around the world and you can find a wealth of contradictory meanings associated with every colour. So if meringue isn't your style, wear a colour you like and that looks good on you.

Keep in mind that, ultimately, it's just clothes. You each have an opportunity to get a really great outfit that looks great on you, so try to enjoy it rather than stress over it.

Blame Queen Victoria

It's all **Queen Victoria**'s fault: she wore a **white dress** for her wedding to Prince Albert in 1840. In fact, her white satin gown and orange blossom headdress with lace veil were considered shockingly plain by royal standards, which typically included silver, jewels, velvet and fur. But when the next generation of British royalty married in white satin and orange blossoms, the style was set. Besides, only the very rich could afford to wear a colour that was so difficult to keep clean, so a white dress announced wealth.

During the Victorian era, less wealthy brides simply wore a **new best dress**, usually in a more practical colour than white. Wedding dress styles then, as now, followed the current fashion. Victorian propriety demanded high necklines, long sleeves and long skirts. When brides did wear white, it was usually ivory or cream, which had the benefit of being more flattering as well as not showing every little fleck of dust.

During the **twentieth century** wedding gowns mimicked the styles of the times, from the flapper dresses of the 1920s to the caftans of the 70s. It became more common for wedding gowns to be bought for the single occasion, and pure white became the colour of choice. Over time, with the invention of washing machines, white came to symbolize the purity of the woman in the gown rather than her affluence.

Where Victoria kicked off a royal trend, **Diana** ran with it. When Lady Di married Prince Charles in 1982, her gown was pure Victorian revival, and the image of those puffy sleeves and that huge skirt became the epitome of the traditional wedding dress.

Whatever the weather

The weather's a crucial consideration for wedding clothes. Brides won't enjoy the day if their arms are blue from cold at a **winter wedding**, nor if they're sweating under heavy brocade fabric in August. Men's suits can be stifling on a **hot afternoon**. Give the temperature some thought when setting the location and time of day for the big event, and then pick clothes that will be comfortable in that environment. If you're getting married abroad, check online for average temperatures during the month – and for the chance of precipitation.

In **colder months**, brides-to-be might want to go for an elegant long-sleeved dress, or else wear long gloves and have a shawl, shrug or stole handy. Plan ahead and make warm clothes part of the outfit rather than something thrown on at the last minute. Remember your bridesmaids, too – a pashmina shawl makes a great gift.

Don't forget the **shoes**. Strappy sandals are gorgeous for summer but adding tights is not a good look. Plus, wearing closed shoes in cold weather will prevent your toes becoming blocks of ice.

You can choose to let your choice of clothing dictate the season for your wedding.

The bride

Stalking the dress: where to look

Unless you're having the most casual of weddings, the bride's dress is going to be one of the most exciting and expensive articles of clothing she will ever wear. It's a good idea to take into account the sorts of styles you already know look good on you and to remember to flatter your personal body type. But this is also a moment to consider wearing something really spectacular. Flip through some **magazines** – bridal or simply high fashion – or look at **designers' websites** to get some inspiration. These can help you figure out what you're looking for.

However, unless you can commission a custom-made gown, it's best not to get too locked in on a single design, or you may find that nothing available quite matches the ideal in your head. Go out armed with lots of ideas but an open mind, and try on a lot of different styles. Also, remember that a dress on the hanger and a dress on you will look totally different. Your body provides the structure for those flips of fabric to hang from and cling to.

You should absolutely check out your favourite stores on the chance they will happen to have a gorgeous dress that you'd enjoy walking the aisle in, but if the old stand-bys fail, never fear. From gigantic bridal chains to tiny boutiques and vintage stores, there are hundreds of places that make every sort of dress, or you could have one made to order. And it doesn't have to be the biggest single cost of the entire wedding.

Bridal salons and stores

The home of the custom-made, designer gown. **Make an appointment** before you go (on a weekday if possible, to beat the crowds) and a "bridal consultant" (salesperson to you and me) will take you by the hand and lead you through the process of buying a wedding dress, plus, if you want, shoes, veil, headpiece and other fripperies. On the plus side, weddings are what these stores do, so they know their business, and will be able to suggest fits and colours that suit your figure and skin tone. The downside can be a high price, though it varies with the type of store.

> **Tip**
>
> It can be fun – and informative – to try out lots of different styles, but don't feel you have to search endlessly for the perfect dress. When you find a dress you love, buy it.

> **Tip**
>
> On dress shopping excursions, bring along a trusted companion or two who combine exquisite taste with complete honesty. Keep the guest list short, however. Too many cooks make the activity a chore and will likely end up giving you contradictory advice when you least need it. Don't bring along anyone with a tendency to give you faux compliments, however kindly meant.

Discount outlets and sample sales

If you can do without the pampering, check out a discount bridal outlet. These warehouses are stuffed with racks of dresses, often **last year's designer styles**, colours that didn't sell well, or off-brand knock-offs. Still, you may be able to find a designer gown for significantly less than you'd pay elsewhere – just remember the price may still be in the thousands.

Sample dresses are those other people try on in bridal salons. In theory, every size is represented, but in practice these are mostly useful to the size 2, 4, 6 or perhaps 8 bride in the US (in UK sizes, that's 4 to 12). Note that wedding dresses run small, so the samples may look bigger than they are.

Online

Use the Internet to find shops and look at their wares, to check out designers' latest looks, and to shop at untraditional venues – like eBay. Great **vintage dresses** (or vintage look, in some cases – be sure to read the fine print) can be found at vintagewedding.com or tinyurl.com/vintvix. For **used dresses** from any era, in the US check out preownedweddingdresses.com or wornitonce.com; in the UK, try sellmyweddingdress.co.uk or theweddingdressmarket.com. Better yet, do your good deed for the day, offering the proceeds from your gown sale to a charity like Oxfam – check out tinyurl.com/oxfambride for locations of their bridal departments – or bridesagainstbreastcancer.org.

Be prepared to do major **alterations** on a gown you buy online, since you can't know how it fits before it arrives – and buy a size up, especially in a vintage dress (sizes have become larger over time). It's much easier to take a dress in than to let it out.

> ### Tip
>
> A camera can be an invaluable tool for dress shopping. Have your companions take photos of you in the dresses you like best, and be sure to note down which dress was where and how much each cost. You can compare your favourites at home, away from high-pressure sales pitches, and solicit more opinions on the finalists if you're having trouble choosing.

> ### Renting a wedding gown
>
> It is possible to rent a wedding gown, just like your groom can rent his tux. This is a great option for the bride who can't see the point in spending big bucks on a dress that she'll wear only once – and then have to pay to preserve. Look for bridal rentals online or ask at an upscale costume shop.

Custom-made dresses

This is horrifically expensive if you're working with a famous designer, but at the tailor shop around the corner it can be quite affordable, especially if your tastes run to the **simple and elegant** – a look that can be prohibitively pricey at the salon. A local tailor or seamstress – or a struggling young designer – can make a wedding dress just for you. Really good fabric is costly and you'll have to pay for labour, but you could still end up with a unique wedding gown that fits you perfectly for a few hundred pounds or dollars, rather than thousands.

Second-hand

Vintage, or even plain old **thrift stores/charity shops** often receive wedding-gown donations. Selection is iffy – it's whatever happens to come through – but you may end up with a great and unusual dress for a minuscule price. Branches in expensive areas are the best bet – people give where they live, so a Salvation Army store on Manhattan or a charity shop in Chelsea will generally have higher-end stock than branches elsewhere.

Wearing your **mother's gown** can be charming and saves you the trouble of shopping. If she agrees and you adore her dress, go for it.

Dressing for two

There's no reason why you can't be **pregnant** and a glowing bride at the same time. Wedding gowns specifically designed for pregnant brides do at least exist these days, which they didn't a few years back, but you still won't get the same range of choice if your dress needs to elegantly drape a baby bump. Bridal salons may not keep maternity dresses in stock but can often order them from a catalogue. Or you could do it the other way around, and try a boutique that caters to the stylish mum-to-be. Don't let anyone tell you whether you can or cannot wear white: wear whatever colour you like.

Shop early, but make sure to buy close to your wedding day so that you can still fit into that great dress. A sympathetic shop attendant can likely help you find the most suitable gowns and will be able to advise on your changing shape over time. Needless to say, it's absolutely essential to schedule a final fitting as close to the wedding as possible.

Sew your own

Don't even think about it unless you or a close friend does this sort of thing regularly. As with the local tailor, your best bet is a **very simple** gown. Buy **extra fabric** in case you mess up – and get it all at the same time, from the same bolt, since there can be slight variations between batches. Give yourself plenty of **time**, and enlist a friend to help with the final fittings. It is impossible to both model a dress and pin the last darts into place.

Choosing your dress

Shapes and lengths

There's something out there to suit everyone, no matter what shape or size or colouring. If you can buy clothes then you can buy a wedding dress. If you've never really thought about what suits you, have a look through your wardrobe and decide which necklines and lengths you enjoy wearing. If you're big on top and look better in scoop or V-necks, then that's the neckline of the dress to go for. If you hate your arms, get a dress with sleeves. On the other hand, if you've got legs you like to show off, there's no reason you need to wear a floor-length gown. There are shapes for all shapes.

First of all you'll need to choose the **shape** of your dress, whether it's A-line, a ball gown, mermaid or Empire line. **Length** can range from touching the floor to as short as you dare. With **necklines**, there's a huge range of options, both revealing and demure. When it comes to **sleeves** you'll need to consider the weather and if you're happy wearing a shawl or shrug or not. Climate also comes into play when it comes to choosing the **fabric**. Colour aside, a wedding dress can come in various types of fabric, from heavy velvet or brocade to silk and chiffon.

The style of gown will usually fit in with your overall wedding theme. If the bride is wearing a taffeta princess dress, then the groom is likely up there next to her in a tux or morning suit. If you were planning a casual wedding and then fall in love with a ball gown, you may have some rethinking to do.

Tip

You probably already know what you look good in. Don't let the fact that this is a wedding dress fluster you. Unless you're actively seeking a radically different look (dressing up as a fairy princess), you'll feel most comfortable – and therefore look most beautiful – in a style you're familiar with.

Embellishments

On a wedding dress, the rich fabric is often a blank canvas. From appliqués or beads to seed pearls or silk flowers, just about **anything can be sewn onto a gown**. Whether it's crystals, bows, sequins or ribbons, try to use a restrained hand and don't add too many different elements. If you want a ton of decoration, choose a single item and have a lot of them, such as a lacy pattern sewn in seed pearls all over the skirt. An overly busy dress looks cheap, no matter how much you paid for it.

Fittings and alterations

When you buy a dress off the rack, it rarely fits perfectly. It's snug in the bust, gathers at the waist or feels a bit long. These are the perils of having our clothes made to fit mannequins rather than human beings. We learn over time to frequent shops that use models which approximate our measurements, but this isn't always possible when it comes to your wedding.

For your wedding gown, you may choose to go the extra mile and have **those little imperfections fixed**. If you're buying from a bridal salon, they'll likely do the fitting in-house. If not, find a tailor or dressmaker – perhaps test him or her first on a less important project – and have them

Before you buy...

… or before you walk out of the store with the finished product, do a quick quality assessment.

- ♥ Are any embellishments or buttons sewn securely on?
- ♥ Are there loose threads?
- ♥ Are the seams securely sewn?
- ♥ Are there any stains or marks?

If you've placed an order for a gown to be picked up later, you should have several things in writing:

- ♥ Price
- ♥ Delivery date
- ♥ Price for fittings/alterations
- ♥ Cancellation policy

pin and tuck and sew your dress until it fits as if it had been made for you. Have your last fitting a week or so before the wedding, so that your dress perfectly matches your current weight (many brides yo-yo up or down from nerves or dieting gone awry). Be warned, though: having a perfectly fitted piece of clothing can be a revelation and you may be spoiled for life.

Trains, veils and tiaras

On your wedding day, you have the chance to go around in stuff that would normally elicit a raised eyebrow, at the very least. While these embellishments are far from required, the contemporary world offers so

Of course you don't look silly, darling…

few chances for anyone aged over seven to wear a sparkly crown, it seems churlish not to.

A **tiara** is clearly de rigueur for the princess-style bride or anyone who "just love[s] new places to wear diamonds" (thank you, Marilyn Monroe). Sparkling or be-ribbonned **hair clips** are an extremely popular option, and can even hold recalcitrant strands of hair in place as well as looking lovely. A **headband** pulls hair back from the bride's face, plus it provides a docking space for the veil.

The wedding **veil** dates back to the days when a groom didn't set eyes on his bride until after the ceremony was over. Never mind the symbolism, many brides feel their look isn't complete without that floating bit of fabric. Lengths run from shoulder to the 75-inch chapel and the 108-inch cathedral, which is functionally a sheer train.

A **train** is an extension of your wedding dress that trails out behind you. If you're getting married outdoors, make sure you get a carpet for the bride to walk down, as grass stains will never come out. Trains start out just brushing the floor but can extend as far as 12 feet – or more – from the bride's waist in the case of the monarch train, a style that's probably best left to actual royalty.

Some trains are detachable, while others are designed to be looped up into a scallop near the hem or an elaborate bustle – essential if you're planning on dancing the night away. Make sure the maid of honour or other bride's attendants have instruction and practice at rearranging the train before the wedding day.

The rest of the outfit

What goes on underneath

In an ideal world, the lingerie you wear on your wedding day would be sexy, lacy and barely there. In real life, however, the more exciting the dress, the more draconian the undergarments required to hold you in place underneath.

For a strapless, spaghetti strap or halter dress, you will likely need a **strapless bra**. These do exist in sizes for the amply endowed – and they do work. For a really supportive strapless bra, you could go for a bustier, which includes a corset type of body section in order to more firmly

Old, new, borrowed, blue

The Victorians strike again, this time with dressing instructions for the bride: "Something old, something new, something borrowed, something blue and a silver sixpence in her shoe." The **old** connects the bride to her family and her past. The **new** represents her new life as a married woman, and is often a gift from the groom or his family. Something **borrowed** symbolizes the willingness of the bride's friends and family to help her out should she ever need them; ideally, borrow an item from a happily married woman, so that her wedded bliss can rub off. As for the **blue**, the colour means faithfulness, loyalty, and purity – before white became all the rage, wedding gowns were often blue. The last part about the **sixpence** has been dropped off contemporary recitation, but the bride was supposed to put a coin in her left shoe to attract wealth. A penny will suffice, if you want to do the whole thing, or wedding stores sell keepsake sixpence coins for just this purpose.

This tradition is rather nice, with its emphasis on continuity and community rather than having everything new from a shop. Wearing mum's earrings and your best friend's veil is sweet as well as practical.

hold you in place and up. A backless dress requires a **backless bra**, which ingeniously fastens at the bottom of your back. Go to a good department store or a bra specialist and explain your needs, then be prepared to pay amply for these wonders of engineering.

Be sure to **try on** all your planned undergarments under the dress to make sure they do what they're supposed to and don't show. Make sure you can move, as well – after all, you're going to hug tall guests and dance with your new husband. If you plan on control-top stockings or tights or smoothing knickers – anything from Lycra shorts to body stockings that go from just under your bust down over the stomach and through the thighs – then you need to have your **dress fitted over them**. Beforehand, practise wearing one around for a decent amount of time to make sure it doesn't cut off blood flow to any limbs.

The last thing you want on your wedding day is a **panty line** for all to admire – if you're wearing stockings or tights, you can forgo panties altogether. Otherwise, acquaint yourself with a G-string or thong, or shop for anything marketed as **invisible** – then give it a test run to check it lives up to the hype.

Once you have the serious matter of foundation undergarments settled, go out and get some sweet little nothings to change into for the wedding night.

Can you walk in those?

The shoes you wear with your wedding gown should be gorgeous, fun and, most crucially, **comfortable**. You're going to walk down the aisle, stand during the ceremony, table-hop during dinner, then dance all night. Even if you usually wear four-inch stilettos, this is the day for a low heel, or even none at all – a prudent maximum is two inches. If any part of the wedding's outdoors, go for a flat or a wedge heel – and warn any women in your wedding party to do the same.

Satin shoes can be **dyed** to exactly match the shade of your dress if you feel it's necessary. Otherwise, consider **gold** or **silver** shoes, or a basic **white** that doesn't clash. Professional dancer's shoes are designed for comfort and can be a great way to go. For a touch of the tomboy plus ultimate comfort, consider white pumps or tennis shoes.

As with your underwear, bring either the chosen shoes or ones with the same heel height to dress fittings to ensure that the skirt is hemmed to the proper length.

Jewellery

Your wedding can seem like a logical time to load up on gorgeous jewellery, but before you drape yourself in gems, consider your overall look. If your dress is already festooned with pearls and crystals, too much jewellery can easily take it from classy to overkill.

The neckline of your dress will determine if a **necklace** is appropriate, and how much of one, from a delicate chain to a chunky art piece. Don't get **earrings** that clash with your tiara, and consider your planned hairstyle when deciding betweens studs and dangly chandeliers.

Pearls are classic, and if your mother has a string, that will work nicely for "something old" as well. If you want pearls but there are none in the family, turn to the Internet for assistance. Jewellery of all kinds gets a huge markup at the store; buy pearls direct from China, diamonds from estate sales, and save a bundle.

> ### Tip
>
> Analogous to cultured pearls, created jewels are the exact same material as those mined out of the ground, except that the molecules line up in perfect rows. Only a jeweller with a special magnifying tool can tell the difference. They really are diamonds, or rubies, or sapphires or emeralds – except that they cost a great deal less than those nature squished out of coal.

Wedding rings: gold, silver, platinum, palladium...

Aside from the aesthetic decisions that need to be made about what style of wedding band you and your partner opt for, you'll also need to consider the **type of metal** your rings are made from. At the very least it's a good idea to know a little of the jargon before you visit a jeweller.

The obvious choice is **gold** (traditionally yellow gold). Bands do not tend to be pure gold (24-karat) however, as by itself gold is a very soft metal that's easily bent and misshapen. Thus, expect to buy rings that have a mix of gold and other metals that increase their strength. Most people choose something between 14 karats (a stronger blend) and 20 karats (a purer blend); 18-karat is a good bet and gives both strength and good colour.

If you prefer the look of **silver**, you could... er... go for silver. However, you might also consider **white gold**, which looks similar to silver but has a golden gleam and doesn't tarnish like silver (though it will need replating). There's also the more unusual **rose gold**, which has a pinkish, copper-like finish and is sometimes found in Russian three-hooped rings alongside a white and yellow hoop.

Other options include the very expensive, heavier **platinum** (which looks similar to white gold) and the increasingly popular **palladium** – a cheaper, whiter and stronger metal from the same family as platinum. Both of these will develop a slightly hazy and attractive patina over time.

Let go of the handbag

Your wedding day is not the time to be lugging around that huge bag that contains your life. At most, you'll want to carry a **delicate clutch** containing your ID, lipstick and a hankie for joyous tears, but even that doesn't come down the aisle with you. Leave it in the dressing room or give it to your mother or matron of honour to hold. Ditto for any other wedding-day necessities, from hairspray to a spare pair of stockings. For more on what to carry on the big day, see p.202.

Bridal party beauty

There are two ways to handle wedding hair and make-up for the bride and the women of the wedding party. One is to **hire a professional** to do you up, the other is to **do it yourself**. Unlike baking a three-tiered cake or fixing canapés for 100 hungry guests, you probably have some experience doing your own hair and make-up, so if you're looking for a place to pinch pennies, this is a promising spot.

Either way, be sure to do at least one **complete run-through** before the morning of the big day. You don't want to be fighting with a hair stylist or struggling with a curling iron while the clock ticks down to "I do".

Hair

If you're getting married near home, talk with your **regular stylist.** She knows your hair and she knows you, so she's a good bet. Otherwise, the process is the same as for any other vendor: ask around. Get advice from the salesperson at the bridal salon, talk with recently married friends, even stop a well-coiffed woman in the street to get the name of her salon and stylist – this will always be taken as a compliment. Be sure to bring along any hair pieces – headband, tiara, veil – to the run-through, so the stylist knows what she's got to incorporate. A picture of you in the dress isn't a bad idea, either, so she can see the look you're going for.

For **DIY hairdos**, get together with your bridesmaids and pool your accumulated styling tools at a "hair party". You'll be amazed at the amount of hot rollers, curling irons, straighteners, blow-dryers, pins, clips and gunk of every description you can assemble – enough to do any style in creation. For instructions for how to get a complicated updo or exactly the right flowing waves, the Internet is a great resource. In particular, check out YouTube and Videojug for how-to videos.

Make-up

A hair stylist will often be able to do your make-up as well or know someone who can, or the salon may have a make-up person on staff. A **trial run** is as important for make-up as for hair – get it all done, then take some photos in similar light to that of the ceremony and reception venues (time of day, indoor or outdoor, natural or electric) to see how you look. You'll likely be wearing a lot more make-up than you're used to, and it will look different in pictures than in life. You want to look good both on the day and in the photos.

Some **make-up counters** (Bobbi Brown, Shu Uemura) will do wedding make-up sessions for a cost that's often reimbursed if you buy the items recommended. Then you'll get some new stuff and a demo on how to do it, and you don't need to buy anything if you don't want. If you do usually do your own make-up you may want a different look, if you don't then you need to come up with a look from scratch. You could take your bridesmaids too and then get together and make sure you can replicate the look, and that it photographs well. As with hair, YouTube offers useful tutorials for looks from sex kitten to vamp. Some of the big cosmetics companies also have online resources: check out Bobbi Brown's bridal looks at tinyurl.com/bb-bride.

Even if you don't usually use a **foundation**, it's worth considering as it will look great in photos. Another clever product for a big make-up day is **primer**, which gives make-up something to grab onto and makes it last longer. Bigger brands often sell mini sample-size containers good for a few uses, if it's not something you're going to apply every day.

Bridesmaids – you can wear it again

Every bridesmaid throughout history has heard those fateful words, assuring her that whatever the bride has chosen for her to wear will inevitably become a wardrobe staple. This may even have been true once or twice. But for the most part, not. Everyone knows that bridesmaids' dresses, like wedding gowns, are pretty much for **one-time use**.

Who pays for the clothing of the wedding party depends on your finances and traditions. In the US, they pay for their own clothes; in the UK, it's more of a grey area as to whether the wedding party or the bride and groom cover their attendants' outfits. Of course, any of these rules can be broken, depending on who's got the cash. The important thing is to make sure everyone involved is clear about who's paying for what.

However strong your vision of how your bridesmaids will look, it's not fair to subject your attendants to outfits they're not going to feel happy wearing. Far better to come up with a few options and get their feedback before taking things further. And definitely let them have a say in accessories and shoes.

The dress...

Back in the day, bridesmaids **dressed identically** not only to each other but to the bride as well, thus fooling any evil spirits intent on harming the bride. These days, if you want every woman in the wedding party to wear a **matching** dress, be sure to choose a style that will flatter everyone's body type and a colour that suits their skin tone and hair.

Many bridesmaid dresses come in a range of styles. You may decide to choose the **colour**, then let each woman pick the style that suits her best, thus maintaining a cohesive look but allowing some freedom of expression. Or choose a single **style** of dress and let them pick the colour, from a range of jewel tones or autumn shades or blues.

You could even go **freestyle** and let your attendants wear what they please, or perhaps stipulate that they pick out something in, say, pink. Independent-minded bridesmaids (or broke ones who are paying their own way) will appreciate the freedom.

... and the rest

Like the bride, bridesmaids can wear satin **shoes** dyed to match their dresses. Alternatively, ask them to wear black strappy sandals, gold flats, or whatever, and let them pick shoes they like and that fit them comfortably.

Matching **jewellery** can be a great gift from the bride to her attendants. Otherwise, let each woman wear her own jewellery – a small spark of individuality that will help her feel more comfortable in an outfit she may not have chosen.

Settle well in advance whether you're getting a professional stylist or doing one another's **hair and make-up**, as well as who's paying for any services rendered. Identical hairstyles may be going a touch too far – better to let each person determine her own style for the day with perhaps some input from you, so the overall look works. Ditto for make-up. The same pink will not go with every skin tone.

The groom and attendants

Formalwear for guys is more straightforward than the oodles of options available to the female of the species, but there's still room to get lost. Also, while yes, you can wear any style of suit at any time of day, the **rules of formality** remain more firmly in place for menswear than for women's. If you decide to go by the book, the time of day and level of formality of your wedding will make some of your sartorial choices for you. Those of Scottish ancestry may choose to go with the kilt.

The rules of formality

❤ **Semiformal day** Wear a suit with a nice shirt and tie.

❤ **Semiformal evening** A good dark suit or a black tux/dinner jacket, worn with black bow tie and either a cummerbund or vest/waistcoat. See p.112 for instructions on tying a bow tie.

❤ **Formal day** A formal suit or a grey stroller coat (essentially a shorter version of a morning jacket).

❤ **Formal evening** This means black tie: black tux, black tie, cummerbund or vest/waistcoat. Alternatively, a white dinner jacket worn with tuxedo pants.

❤ **Really formal day** Cutaway or morning coat with charcoal striped trousers, grey waistcoat, wing-collared shirt, ascot/cravat or striped tie. Very old school, very classy. A top hat completes the look, if you want to go all the way.

❤ **Really formal evening** White tie and tails. This is Fred Astaire, baby. Go all out with a white waistcoat or vest, wing-collared shirt, and black patent leather shoes. Again, one of life's few chances to don a top hat.

Jackets, coats, cummerbunds and more

As you may have gathered from the delineations above, there's more to men's fashions than just suits versus tuxedos. As with every other set of rules, these are made to be broken as often as you like – the most important consideration is to feel both comfortable and handsome. It's not all about the bride. The groom gets to strut his stuff as well.

Consider your sartorial heroes: have you always wanted to be James Bond? Here's your chance. Alternatively, head out to a well-stocked men's department or menswear store and try on a lot of different styles of suit. See if you like how you look in tails, or a white dinner jacket, or with a brightly patterned vest/waistcoat peering out from behind your suit jacket. This is you, only spiffier.

Getting the right fit

Formalwear that doesn't fit right looks terrible and feels uncomfortable, too. With your arms at your sides, fingers extended, the hem of the jacket should be no longer than your middle finger. The jacket should fit comfortably at the neck and shoulders and fasten across your midsection without straining, and you should be able to move – stand, sit, dance. The shirt sleeve should touch the top of your hand and the cuff should peek out from the jacket sleeve by no more than half an inch. The shirt, too, should fit comfortably at your neck, shoulders and waist; ditto for the vest or waistcoat, the bottom of which should cover the trouser waistband. The waist of your trousers should fit comfortably whether standing or sitting and the hem should skim the heel of your shoes in back and just break over the shoe tops in front.

Tailored suits

The experience of having a suit tailor-made is something that every man should indulge in at some time in his life. Aside from the fact that you will end up with an outfit that fits you perfectly, it can really get you in the mood for the wedding, especially if you have been feeling a little neglected while your wife-to-be zips around town to have dresses fitted, eyeballs waxed and goodness knows what else. Yes, it might cost more than an off-the-peg suit, but you're worth it.

Choosing a tailor is a very personal thing, and you should visit several different boutiques before you commit. As well as the very traditional, slightly musty set-ups, expect to come across more modern establishments with a better understanding of current trends and fashions.

Think seriously about the weight of the **fabric** you choose: you're going to feel hot under the collar whatever the weather, so a lighter weight is always a good move. You also need to choose whether to go for a **three-piece** or a **two-piece**. The latter is generally cheaper, though waistcoats (vests) do look really special and give you a few more options on the day, especially when it comes to ditching the suit jacket when you get on the dance floor in the evening.

Many tailors have their own **signature details** that they always try to include in their suits (a certain number of cuff buttons, storm collars, etc), but it's your big day, so you shouldn't feel obliged to include anything that you don't want.

Expect to go for at least **three fittings**, the last only a couple of weeks before the wedding, and always take someone with you whose opinion you trust and whose style you respect. It's also nice to keep your better half out of the loop, so that they get the wow of seeing you dressed to the nines at the same moment that you get the wow of their dress. (However, if at the very least you can find out the colour of her gown, you could try and get the hue of your suit's silk lining to match.)

Finally, make sure you get the whole process started early as it can take **several months** for your suit to appear after the initial measurement session.

To rent or buy?

If you're going to be married in a full-on morning suit, the question doesn't arise, but if you're wearing a tuxedo, the question is murkier. Renting a tux will cost up to around thirty percent of the price of buying the same item. If you go to three or four formal events a year, then buying a tux begins to make financial sense, especially if you go for a conservative style that will remain in fashion for a good few years.

Those who do rent should check over their clothes with care to ensure that there are no holes, burns, stains or smells. Pick up rentals a few days before the wedding if at all possible so that the store doesn't run out – they shouldn't, if you've made your reservation, but mix-ups do happen, and imagine your distress on your wedding morning when one guy's coat isn't available.

Obviously if you're wearing a regular suit then it makes sense to buy it outright.

Completing the look

Men's formalwear offers what used to be the only opportunities for guys to sport some bling.

- **Cuff links** are worn in French cuffs, which don't have buttons at the wrist, and come in every conceivable shape and pattern, from art deco platinum studs to golf balls or Scrabble letters.

- A **tie tack or pin** will keep your tie in place and ranges in look from a sleek clip to an ostentatious jewel.

- No ascot (cravat) is complete without the **stick pin** that holds it in place.

- Dress up a breast pocket with a **pocket square handkerchief** – either in plain white or a colour and fabric that matches your necktie or vest/waistcoat.

- **Suspenders/braces** can be either plain or a surprise of colour, but aren't worn with a vest/waistcoat or cummerbund.

- Don't forget the **shoes**. As with the bride's, comfort is crucial as you'll be on your feet most of the day. Try to wear them in beforehand and make sure you've tried them on with your suit.

> *My father-in-law is short and stout, my husband on the rangy side, and his best man – well, put it this way, he usually gets his clothes from that shop called High and Mighty. The hire shop clearly didn't specialize in unusual sizes. My husband's morning coat fitted okay, thank god, but his best man couldn't bend his elbows, and his dad's tails were practically trailing along the ground.*
> Lucy

Tip

This is going to be the first day of the rest of your life – push the boat out and buy some new underwear.

1 A bowtie uses the same knot you use to tie your shoelaces. Start by adjusting the bowtie to your neck size, then wrap it around your collar and bring the ends even.

2 Now tie a simple knot tight against your top button. In this diagram, the lighter shade represents the back of the tie, while the darker shade represents the front.

3 Take the lower, hanging portion of the tie, and fold it up into the shape of a bow, with its middle in line with your top button. This will be the front of your tie.

4 Flip down the end you've been keeping pointed upward, bringing it directly over the centre of the bow you made in figure 3.

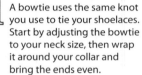

5 Pinch the bow together and pull it to the side, revealing a hole behind it.

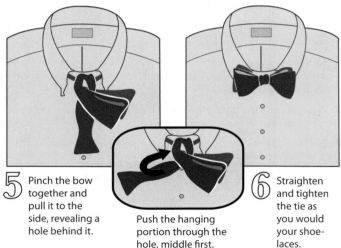

Push the hanging portion through the hole, middle first.

6 Straighten and tighten the tie as you would your shoe-laces.

Illustration by David Ardito, 2009

Male grooming tips

You may not want to think about this, or you may not care, but if nothing else there are the photos to consider – you want to appear worthy of your bride and for everyone to see how lovely you look together, not how big that zit on your face is.

Avoid using fancy new moisturizers or aftershaves that might irritate your skin just before the wedding. You don't want to get sunburnt either in an ill-advised attempt at a "healthy-looking" tan. If the worst happens and you do get a zit, a little dab of concealer will disguise it. Best to have tried on a few different shades of a higher-end concealer, so you'll have one that matches your skin tone at show time. To use it, work the smallest possible amount over the spot using a light dabbing motion.

Get your hair cut a week or so before the wedding, avoiding anything new or too drastic: now is not the time to experiment with a number 2. If you go to a traditional barber, ask for an old-fashioned wet shave, a luxurious experience that's come back into fashion (but don't mention Sweeney Todd). Other grooming jobs might include trimming nose (or ear) hairs, perhaps separating a monobrow, and making sure your nails are clean.

Finally, on the day itself make sure you floss (if you don't already) and drink plenty of water, as all that stress and alcohol can cause bad breath.

Parents, pageboys and flower girls

For whatever reason, tradition dictates that the mother of the bride should pick out her dress (or suit, or whatever) first, then show it off to the mother of the groom so she can buy a coordinating outfit. Or you can just let each mother pick out clothing that she likes and that goes with your wedding colours and level of formality.

While your mother would resemble an ageing bridesmaid were she outfitted in a matching costume, the dads look spiffy in the same stuff as the men of the wedding party. Even the most anti-suit father is likely to be willing to dress up a bit for his kid's wedding.

Pageboys are often dressed in the same outfit as the rest of the men in the wedding party, only in miniature. Since grown-up girl's fashions are often inappropriate for children, the principle does not hold for bridesmaids and flower girls. However, a flower girl's outfit may be made from the same fabric as the wedding party women's gowns, or may be a match in colour. Alternatively, children in the wedding party may simply be dressed up in adorable kids' clothes. They don't generally stand at the front of the church during the ceremony (this courts disaster), so it doesn't matter as much to have them perfectly coordinate.

9 Food and Drink

Like every other aspect of your wedding, there's no reason you have to stick to the traditional option if it doesn't suit you. A silver service lunch of smoked salmon followed by chicken with baby vegetables may be expected by your uncles, aunts and grandparents, but if your tastes run more towards burgers and fries, tofu crêpes or pâté de foie gras, then you can make your menu as creative as your budget allows – though don't forget your guests entirely, unless you don't mind your wedding being memorable for the wrong reasons. Food and drink will comprise a significant part of your wedding budget, so you want to spend wisely, though it's perfectly possible to leave your guests full and happy without breaking the bank. This chapter lays out a smorgasbord of options.

The food

Memorable menus

You want this to be a special meal, ideally one with **meaning** beyond simply filling your belly. Think about food that has some significance for the two of you: perhaps that fantastic starter you shared on your first date would work as an hors d'oeuvre? Foods from your **ethnic heritage** are a good way to personalize the reception and can be especially nice if you're bringing together two families with different food traditions.

Of course, pleasing yourselves doesn't mean being insensitive to the needs of others. If half your young cousins are **allergic** to nuts, a peanut-butter wedding cake would be a cruel joke. A lactose-intolerant mother-in-law will not thank you if the main course is loaded with cheese. **Vegetarian** dishes should be part of the mix, rather than an afterthought. You also need to make sure that you cater for any children or older people whose palates might not be as sophisticated as yours.

Memorable menus are often cost-effective too, for instance picking your menu based on what's **in season**. Foods cost less when they don't have to be flown halfway across the globe. A summer wedding can go all out with fresh fruits and vegetables. In winter, think about rich comfort foods based around store cupboard staples.

Consider any **local foods** you could use in your menu: it'll be cheaper and guests will enjoy the chance to sample regional specialities. French food is not the only ethnic approach to a wedding dinner, either – think about using a caterer from a local immigrant community.

Stations where food is cooked or served on demand make for a lively, memorable meal. For example, a **pasta station** where guests choose from a selection of sauces and watch while their pasta is tossed, or a **crêpe table** with cooks flipping and filling sweet or savoury crêpes on demand. Granted these may not come cheap and will depend on the type of venue you've chosen, as well as the catering team.

Table service or buffet?

There are two ways to distribute the food at your wedding: either you go to the meal, or the meal comes to you.

Sit-down meals

A sit-down meal with **table service** is traditional and there's no denying that it makes for an **elegant, well-paced event**, though it doesn't have to be a stuffy one. You can have waiters in tuxedos or in skinny jeans, depending on your style, theme and location. Leisurely served courses ensure that there's plenty of time to wander round and chat to your guests, plus people enjoy being waited on. On the downside, it's usually the most expensive option. Also, guests are less likely to

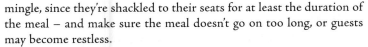

mingle, since they're shackled to their seats for at least the duration of the meal – and make sure the meal doesn't go on too long, or guests may become restless.

In planning a seated meal, be sure to talk through the **serving procedure** with your caterer. Decide how long to pause between courses, and ensure that an off-site caterer has visited the venue and worked out **traffic patterns** to avoid collisions of waiters with full trays. Check that those with alternative meals (kosher, vegetarian, etc) aren't going to be penalized by extra slow service. You'll also want to make sure the schedule allows for hot or cold items to stay at the **correct temperature** – leaning heavily on items meant to be eaten at room temperature, from cheese and fruit to sushi, can be helpful.

Buffets

Buffet stations can be as **formal** or as **quirky** as you like – depending on all the little touches you choose, from the tablecloth to the plates to the sort of food you serve, your wedding reception can feel like an Elizabethan banquet or Cinco de Mayo.

Buffet stations offer the possibility of setting out a number of **different eating options**, letting guests graze at will. One table may be loaded with fruits and cheeses and another salads, while across the room there's a spread of seafood, a carving station and a pasta chef. Talk through the preferences of your guests with your caterer to help them get a sense of how much of each type of food to provide.

With planning, a buffet can be less expensive than a sit-down dinner, though it's perfectly possible to drop a bundle on a buffet. After all, serving sizes are not controlled when guests help themselves, people will pick up second and third plates, and you need attentive staff to clear the empties and keep the space from looking like a scavenged mess.

Guests aren't pinned to their table during a buffet, so there will be more **mingling** and the party is likely to have a livelier feel. However, it may make for a shorter event without the downtime between courses, although you can compensate for this by having multiple buffet courses rather than setting everything out at the start.

Timing

The **time of day** you choose for your wedding determines in large part what kind of party you're throwing, from a decorous tea to a raucous party. It influences what **kind of food** you're likely to serve (though you can certainly put out steak in the morning or omelettes at night) and the **level of formality**, since black ties and evening dresses don't tend to come out until, well, evening. Prices are also generally lower the earlier in the day the reception ends. At a minimum, people tend to drink less while the sun is high, and alcohol is a big-ticket item.

All else being equal, a seated dinner is the priciest choice, followed closely by a buffet dinner. Seated lunch or brunch is next, then buffet. Breakfast foods are inexpensive across the board, or if you want a more formal affair that doesn't break the bank, afternoon tea is a lovely option.

Brunch

Brunch is the perfect meal if you're raring to catch a honeymoon flight or the idea of partying all night with your family does not appeal. In addition, you can go all-out on **breakfast foods** and still not spend a fortune, which makes it an appealing option for the frugal. Even mascarpone-stuffed French toast topped with berries and real maple syrup isn't anywhere near as expensive as steak.

On the downside, the horde of guests who have gone to the trouble of flying in may be disgruntled if they're hustled out of the door after an hour or two of coffee and pastries. A **seated brunch** will last longer than a buffet, allowing you to stretch out a simple meal into more of an event.

Afternoon tea

The ritual of afternoon **tea**, with its gorgeous little cakes and crustless cucumber sandwiches, provides an opportunity for a **formal party** that goes beautifully with your splendid attire but doesn't last all night. Flesh out the menu with a selection of fine teas and coffees and a champagne toast. A big wedding cake is optional, especially if you pile up the tea cakes on an elaborate stand.

While tea tends to be a fairly short event, no one's left wondering what to do with the rest of the day. By the time tea is over, it's nearly time for dinner, so guests can go their own way, and you're free to go yours, whether to enjoy a romantic tête-à-tête or collapse in exhaustion.

Tea has the added benefit of being fairly easy on the pocketbook, since it involves neither a big meal nor much alcohol – but it's lovely enough that guests will never realize how little it all cost. This is a great occasion to spend extra on flowers for a really lush feel to the party.

Cocktails

A cocktail party can be as swanky or as casual as you like. It's also a cheap evening option, since you don't necessarily have to fork out for a full bar, perhaps offering beer and wine and a single signature cocktail, or even just beer and wine.

A cocktail party necessitates snacks to soak up the booze, so plan on **hors d'oeuvres** as well. These can be passed around or set out at stations, or both. Make sure you have enough to last throughout the event – better to have a wheel of cheese left over than hungry guests picking forlornly at the final cracker crumbs.

Lunch or dinner

Lunch tends to be somewhat more elaborate and costlier than brunch, although of course that depends upon the level of formality. You've also got the conundrum of keeping the party going long enough that guests feel they've had time to enjoy themselves and you feel properly fêted.

Dinner and **dancing** makes for a fabulous party. Yes, it costs more, but that's because it's the most popular option, and it tends to last the longest, making both you and your guests feel like you've really done this wedding thing properly. For many couples, regardless of price, dinner is the only option.

In the UK it's common to have a formal sit-down dinner **starting early**, around 4 or 5pm. Often guests won't have had lunch because of dressing and getting to the ceremony and no one seems to mind eating at an odd time. You'll probably want to have a small buffet on hand during dancing later on, for guests who work up a fresh appetite.

> ### Tip
>
> Make sure your invitations state clearly what kind of food guests can expect and when. Anyone who comes expecting a meal will be disappointed with hors d'oeuvres, however delicious and substantial.

If you're set on dinner and dancing but cost is a problem, then think about the **day** of your party. A Sunday night dinner, even a Friday night, will cost less than Saturday. A Monday night dinner will be the most affordable of all, if you and your guests have flexible schedules.

Seating plans

If you go with a seated dinner, you could, of course, leave the seating to chance, but what about that old friend who doesn't know anyone? Or your deaf grandmother who needs to sit near the speech-makers so she can hear? It also makes things tough for the caterers: with a seating plan they at least have a fighting chance of knowing where the vegetarians are sitting. This brings you to the minefield of **building a seating plan**. Your guests are going to spend a long time trapped in their seats and if you want to ensure a good time for all, you'll need to put plenty of thought into it.

First of all, decide where you will sit. Even if you spend much of the meal table-hopping, you need a home base to return to – and where you can snatch a few bites between visits. Some couples set a table for two at the centre of the room; tradition has a long **top table** for the entire wedding party, facing the rest of the room, though there's no reason you can't have a round table. You could also have a smaller top table of you and your parents, allowing attendants to sit with their partners on other tables.

Many of the decisions are made for you: your wedding reception is a welcome chance for **families** who many not have seen each other in a while to come together, for **old friends** to meet up again. But it's also an opportunity for you to bring together people who might not know each other but will enjoy one another's company. One difficulty comes with **antagonistic forces**, whether it's ex-partners who loathe each other, feuding cousins or simply those who are polar opposites.

Once you've safely placed potential combatants in their respective corners, you're faced with everyone else. Age ranges, politics and interests all come into play if you want a hall full of cheerful chatter. **Splitting up** couples is very unpopular, but it can be good to split up groups of friends to avoid people retreating into cliques.

> **Tip**
>
> Consult both **mothers** about who gets on with who in the respective families, as they might know something you don't. It's also worth showing them the plan once you're happy with it, as they might spot a problem that you haven't.

Drawing up the plan

Physical props are useful for this project. Draw a **large map** of the room on A3 (double-letter-sized) paper, with tables in their proper places, and then use mini Post-its to shuffle your guests around like the pawns they are. Be sure to check the table sizes at the venue. Perhaps they can offer a couple of bigger or smaller tables to help make your scheme work. If you're happier working onscreen, there are some great resources on the Internet: check out tinyurl.com/perfect-tools or tinyurl.com/seat-chart, which require you to sign up to use them but offer other wedding planning tools too.

Caterers

If you've already found your venue, you'll know if it comes with on-site food production, in which case you've got your caterers already. Anywhere that doesn't have on-site caterers may still have a list of required or recommended off-site companies it works with, which provides you with a **short list.**

On the other hand, if food is a high priority for you, you can **begin with the caterer** and let the venue come second. Starting from scratch in a search for a caterer can seem daunting, but the process is just like finding venues: ask around. Ask newly married couples, ask foodies you

Dietary requirements

Some of your guests may have specific dietary requirements: low salt, no nuts, vegetarian, vegan, kosher, and more – there's a long list of possibilities a conscientious host must take into consideration. A choice of entrées or a buffet will take care of most of these, but some – such as guests with life-threatening nut allergies – will pose more of a challenge, one you'll need to discuss with potential caterers before signing the contract.

If you've requested preferences with your invitation reply card, then you know what you're facing; if not, then you'll need to do a careful read of the guest list. A phone call won't be taken amiss – your guests will be flattered that you went to the trouble of verifying their particular requirements. This prepares you to go into caterer interviews armed with specific questions about what can be supplied and how much it will cost.

know and enjoy eating with – even ask a favourite restaurant whether the chef does weddings. Any wedding professionals you line up can offer suggestions as well – a florist or photographer who gets your sense of style may have the perfect recommendation.

Check that your caterer and venue are going to **work together**. It's no good falling in love with a caterer and then trying to install him or her at a venue that already has a chef, or giving a caterer a venue that doesn't provide the right facilities. Whichever comes first, location or food, keep in touch with each party as you continue the wedding planning process, and pay attention to their needs and restrictions.

What's included?

Some venues provide all of the necessary objects to make a party go: tables, plates, linens, forks, glasses, even potted plants or tea lights. With others, you get a room – a blank slate for your wedding. Ditto with caterers: they may provide all the stuff that goes with serving your meal, or they may not. It's absolutely essential to find out whether the price a caterer quotes per head is foodstuff alone or that and everything else – or some variation in between.

Additional costs can appear seemingly out of nowhere. They may be the result of an innocent misunderstanding between you and the caterer, but if not then get out at the first sign. If the former, it's time to further open those channels of communication. Any reputable caterer will be willing to answer your questions about what's included and put it in writing for you. If they balk at this, then it's time to go, no matter how good the food tastes.

Especially if you're throwing an **outdoor wedding**, you may need to rent the tables, plates and such. If your caterer does not supply this stuff, ask them for recommendations for rental agencies, and get specifics on how many of each necessary item you ought to rent. The caterer will know from experience exactly how many salad plates you need for a hundred-person buffet.

Tastings

Once you've assembled a short list of caterers, it's time for the best part: the tastings. Most caterers will offer either to prepare a **meal just for**

you two or invite you to a **group tasting** with other affianced couples. Either is great – going alone ensures you get the staff's complete attention, while dining with others lets you chatter about the wedding planning process (and yes, your friends are tired of hearing about it) and also get useful tips about other venues and vendors in the area. Here are a few things to check:

❤ Verify that the food's **presentation** on the plate is exactly as it would be at the wedding, or ask if it can be modified to suit your preference.

❤ Be sure to taste **food and wine together**, since they will have a dramatic influence on the play of flavours. If your booze is coming from a different source, ask if you can bring a few bottles with you to the tasting. However, it's probably best not to get too sozzled. You want to be able to take good notes to help remember the experience. Note that you may have to pay for the wine even if the food is free.

❤ If you're after **complicated hors d'oeuvres** you may not find them forthcoming, especially if it's a two-person tasting. Ask if they're making these particular nibbles for an upcoming event, and if so to put aside a few of them for you to pick up and try.

❤ Even if the food is delicious and looks appealing on the plate, it may not be **right for your wedding**. Consider whether it fits in with the mood you're trying to evoke.

❤ Find out when they need **final numbers** by. Do you expect to have all your RSVPs in by that date?

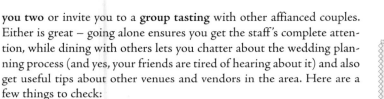

Tip

Don't forget to feed the photographer, DJ and band. They'll perform better fed than hungry.

The catering contract

Once you've chosen a caterer, make sure that both parties sign a contract that spells out the details of your event. In addition to the general points needed in all vendor contracts (see p.229), you'll need to stipulate the following:

❤ The date and time of the event, including the exact location down to the individual room.

❤ The type of service (passed hors d'oeuvres, staffed carving station) and the staff-to-guest ratio.

❤ The entire menu, including presentation notes and any special or expensive ingredients.

❤ What drinks are being served.

❤ Any sales tax, gratuities, overtime charges or bar fees.

❤ The name of the catering representative who will be present on the day, and a way to contact that person on the morning of the wedding if necessary.

❤ Proof of license and liability insurance.

Dealing with caterers on the day

Most caterers will make their first appearance either very early on the day, or the day before, to set the tables and unload their stuff. If you are dealing with various companies (supplying PAs, marquees, etc), talk to each about the **best order** to get things in place, trying to ensure they don't all appear simultaneously.

Though it depends on the size of the catering firm you are using, more than likely the administrator or manager that you have been dealing with up to now will not be present at the wedding. And because on the day the bride won't appear on-site until the very last second, it is up to the **groom** (or perhaps the best man) to make himself known to the staff before guests start arriving, specifically to find out who is in charge and go through the finer details of the day with them.

Basically, you need to make sure that all pre-arranged **plans and timings** have been communicated down the ranks and that everything is set up as you had intended. With any luck, the staff you're using will have catered at your venue before, and will more than likely have a better idea than you of how the whole day will unfold.

Aside from the catering manager and the chef(s), the caterers will have supplied you with a gaggle of **serving staff**. They are likely to be young, and it's worth remembering that theirs is a fairly thankless task, so if you want to get the best from them, be sure to say hello at the start, and make sure you have some cash on you to tip them at the end of the day (assuming their work warrants it), or at the very least, give them a mention and a clap during the speeches.

Questions to ask the caterer

❤ Has the caterer worked at your chosen venue before? If not, will he make a **site visit**?

❤ If you don't have a venue already, can the caterer **suggest anywhere**?

❤ Can you look at **sample menus**? Are there **photographs** of previous events?

❤ What are the caterer's **specialities**?

❤ How **flexible** is the caterer in planning a menu?

❤ How does the caterer **price** the menu?

❤ What comes **included** in the price? If needed, does the caterer provide tables, chairs, linens, plates, flatware/cutlery, glassware?

❤ Does the caterer provide **staff**? At what cost? How many per guest? Who sets up and cleans up, and is there an additional fee? What is the fee for overtime?

❤ **Who will oversee the events** on your wedding day? Can you make all of the arrangements with that person?

❤ Can the caterer provide a **wedding cake**? Is it a problem if you want to bring in a cake from elsewhere? Is there a cake-cutting fee? Do they provide a cake knife?

- ❤ Are there any **additional fees**? How will your bill be structured? Are gratuities included in the price?
- ❤ Does the caterer also manage the bar?
- ❤ Can you supply **your own drinks**?
- ❤ What is the **total estimated cost** for your wedding, including food, drinks, rentals, and staff? Get this in writing.
- ❤ Could you have a **list of references** to call?
- ❤ What is the **cancellation policy**?

The cake

An enormous white tiered cake may be the most potent symbol of a wedding – even more instantly recognizable than the white dress or diamond ring. Of course, your cake need not be enormous nor tiered, nor white – nor even cake. Most couples like to have some variation on this ancient fertility symbol (cake is made from wheat, which is grain, meaning seeds), not least because it's delicious.

The **act of cutting** itself is also loaded with meanings. One old superstition has it that the bride must cut the first piece or risk being childless. The cake is traditionally cut with the bride's right hand on the knife handle and the groom's hand over hers, symbolic of their shared life together, and the couple feeds one another the first bites, which demonstrates their commitment to providing for each other. Then all the guests get their pieces in order to share in the good fortune of the lucky couple, though they may choose to take them away if they prefer.

Sourcing cakes

Cakes aren't difficult to find, whatever your location. At the less expensive end, the bakeries in many large **supermarkets** are capable of turning out tasty wedding cakes at a great price. The local **bakery** with yummy everyday cakes probably does wedding cakes as well – just ask. Or the **pastry chef** at the reception location or on the catering staff is probably trained in cakes, too. You may even have a friend or relative who's a superb cake-maker. Bakers should be willing to supply you with a range of flavours to sample, and sample you should.

Choosing flavours and colours

> *Our cake was mocha. My aunts bought it for us from a Filipino bakery we've gone to since I was young. It was the same place we used to get our childhood birthday cakes.*
> **NENETTE**

The white-on-white cake – or fruit cake, in the UK – is always lovely, but wedding cakes can be **any flavour**, from chocolate to carrot to champagne. If you have trouble choosing just one, pick a different recipe with different fillings for each layer. The heaviest cakes (fruit) should be the bottom layers, topped with other flavours (chocolate with mocha cream, lemon with raspberry filling) and the very lightest sponge at the top. The colour of the cake is also up for grabs. Some couples like to coordinate the cake with the bridesmaids' dresses or the china pattern or the lace on the bride's gown.

Icing is a whole subject in itself. Consider not just look and taste, but how long the cake will have to sit out in what kind of temperatures when picking your icing. **Butter cream** is delicious but won't stand up to a long reception in warm weather. **Fondant** is perfectly smooth and provides a perfect canvas for further decoration, but doesn't taste like much, whereas **royal icing** is hard as nails and difficult to cut. **Marzipan** can stand in for fondant, but some people loathe it. **Chocolate ganache** is lustrous and rich, if you're ready to truly break with the white.

A brief history of wedding cake traditions

The **cutting of the cake** is seen as the first joint labour of a newly married couple, symbolizing their practical devotion to one another and commitment to feed and care for their extended family. A microcosm of a life together, there is an undertone of power struggle in the act: will they then feed each other delicately, or try to assert dominance by mashing it across each other's faces? This latter US tradition has not yet reached the UK.

As with many absurd traditions, there's a meaning buried within its pagan origins. **Ancient Romans** are responsible for the physicality involved in what might otherwise be a pretty routine cut-and-serve procedure. Long ago, a tunic-clad groom would break a loaf of bread over the head of his new bride, releasing her fertil-ity as guests scampered about picking up lucky crumbs. Over time the bread was replaced with sweet buns and even pies, stacked upon one another as prelude to the tiered constructions first popularized in the **English royal court**. The newlyweds would attempt to kiss above the towering stack without upsetting its balance.

Sometime later, but before the first column-supported constructions of Victorian England, someone decided to sweeten the outside of the wedding cake with **white sugar**. Matching the virginal dress of a chaste Western bride, the white was in this case a practical consider-ation, since colouring added to the cost, but quickly became a sign of status, with the finest whites only achievable through highly refined and expensive sugar.

When it comes to layers, be sure to check the ceiling height of your reception venue.

Cake decorations

As for decoration, these days wedding cakes can get as wild as your imagination. The edible arts have taken off in a big way, and one result is wedding cakes of every conceivable shape and colour, from stacks of

> *We wanted to give our guests some choice, so we ordered two tiers of vanilla cake with lemon curd filling and two tiers of chocolate cake with raspberry jam filling. The cake was iced with vanilla butter-cream and cream-coloured rolled fondant, and then decorated with satin ribbon and silk flowers.*
> **OLIVIA**

be-ribboned gift boxes to a meadow of cascading flowers. Be prepared to stump up extra if you want a truly weird or gravity-defying design.

Fresh flowers are an inexpensive and beautiful option for decorating the cake (make sure they're pesticide-free – see Chapter 12 for more on floral decorations), while the traditional bride and groom **topper** now comes in every possible pose, costume, ethnicity and gender. You can even get original look-alike toppers sculpted, for a hefty fee. Or use this as a way to stamp your individuality on the cake (see the alternatives box, below).

Cake logistics

Check with your reception venue before ordering a cake from elsewhere – they may not permit outside food, or they may charge a cake-cutting fee. Find out the details of where and when the cake will be set up and for how long. Does the venue supply a decorative **cake knife** for the cutting, or do you need to bring your own?

A common way to discreetly cut corners, especially for a large wedding, is to order a small display cake and then enough big rectangular sheet-pan cakes of the same flavour to feed everyone. After the initial cut by the bride and groom, the cake is generally returned to the kitchen for cutting and serving, so no one need be the wiser.

Wedding cake alternatives

If traditional cakes don't float your boat, try something a bit different:

- ♥ Towers of **profiteroles** – the traditional "wedding cake" in France.
- ♥ Tiers of **cupcakes**, a mountain of **muffins** or a **doughnut** pyramid.
- ♥ A **themed cake** that matches your interests, be they scuba diving or watching old movies.
- ♥ A **"cheese" cake**: a whole Cheddar at the bottom, with a Stilton on top, decorated with flowers and served with crackers and pickles.
- ♥ A sugar or chocolate **sculpture** – a pricey but impressive centrepiece.

There are loads of amazing alternative cake ideas to be found online, so get Googling, or start here: **tinyurl.com/nerd-toppers**.

The drink

Of course, food is not the only stuff consumed at most weddings. So festive an occasion lends itself to the imbibing of alcoholic beverages, and an exuberant wedding guest will tend to sop up the stuff like a sponge. Managing the event so that there's enough to go around – but not too much – takes some planning.

Your chosen venue may insist you use their bar and their booze, or you may be free to go the DIY route and provide your own drinks. Whichever is the case, **what you serve** and **how you serve it** will greatly impact both the kind of party you have and its cost. You'll have to decide whether to have a cocktail hour between the ceremony and the reception, what drinks will be served during the meal, and how much booze to make available during the rest of the reception.

How much booze and who pays?

First of all you'll need to work out what kind of drinks offering you have in mind. The most lavish option is without doubt an **open bar**, where either for a cocktail hour or throughout the entire reception, guests can go to the bar and order anything they want, on you.

At the other end of the spectrum is the **cash bar**, where the guests pay for their own drinks. This may be an acceptable way of doing things or it may raise hackles, depending on the circles you move in. If you can't afford to pay for alcohol, then you might be better off going for a brunch rather than a dinner, where booze isn't necessarily expect-

Tip

To lower costs, you may close the bar during dinner, especially if waiters are pouring wine to accompany the food, though make sure that any non-wine-drinkers have got drinks.

ed. Or perhaps offer a champagne toast with cake and a brief reception, followed by an **after party** at a nearby bar, where it will feel natural for those present to pay their own way.

By far the most popular option, though, is the **limited bar**, where you give your guests as much to drink as they want – but only of the things you choose. This limitation makes it more economical, not to mention more manageable, than an open bar.

Happy medium: a limited bar

There's nothing wrong with a **wine and beer bar**. Offer at a minimum a red, a white and a couple of beers appropriate to the season and the food menu, plus of course non-alcoholic drinks (see box below). Put sample bottles on display so that guests can see what their options are. To this basic menu you can add one of the following to glam things up a bit:

♥ **A single liquor/spirit**. Choose vodka, gin or rum and make up a menu of suggested cocktails. With only one spirit on offer, the enterprise is more controlled and therefore more affordable. Guests may enjoy trying a new and memorable drink at your wedding.

♥ **A signature cocktail**. Pick one cocktail that goes with the theme or season of the wedding, or ask the bartender to help you come up with a cocktail that matches your wedding colours, like a cosmopolitan to go with the pink roses and the pink frosted wedding cake. For more ideas, check out The Knot's excellent guide to choosing a signature cocktail by colour, season, or name at tinyurl.com/knot-cocktail.

Tip

In winter, guests will welcome a hot toddy or a warming mug of mulled wine. For summer, consider the classic gin and tonic, the festive Mai Tai, or the minty Mojito. Or mix up a batch of sangria – enough to last the night.

Non-alcoholic drinks

You could offer non-drinkers and kids the basic choice of orange juice, Coke or water, but it's nicer to give them something more **special** when the other guests are getting fancy cocktails and champagne. Don't underestimate how many people will be driving home afterwards, either. As well as the staples listed above, **home-made lemonade** or fruit-flavoured **iced tea** are good options, along with a non-alcoholic version of any cocktail you're offering. You could also hand out something fizzy, like sparkling elderflower, for the toast.

On-site drinks

If you're using the venue's bar service, then there may be several different **pricing structures**. The two main options are:

❤ **Per head** You simply pay a **fixed price per person** of legal drinking age. In this case, however, it benefits the venue to hand out fewer drinks so make sure you get details of the service in writing to guarantee there are enough staff and that it's not going to inconvenience guests.

❤ **By the bottle** You get charged for the number of open bottles at the end of the party, in which case you might ask if you can pick up any partially consumed bottles of spirits the next day. Some venues price by the **half-bottle** or even tenth of the bottle, so you don't have to pay for an entire bottle of Scotch with only one drink gone. Any **wine** will be priced by the full bottle, as leftover wine isn't much good to anyone.

Ask if you can **combine** these to meet the needs of your event. For example, you may be able to hold a cocktail hour with hors d'oeuvres and drinks at a per-head rate, and then go to by-the-bottle or partial bottle during dinner and after.

DIY drinks

Being responsible for the drinks can save you some money, but providing a full bar with every drink under the sun, every possible mixer and garnish is a daunting prospect. Choosing a **limited bar** is really the only sensible option if you're going DIY.

Of course, the first and most important question is whether the venue is **licensed** to serve alcohol at all. It's also necessary to find out exactly what the laws are on hiring bartenders and serving alcohol, since these vary dramatically from place to place. You'll want to find someone to mix and serve drinks if you're going to provide cocktails. But if it's simply beer, wine and soft drinks, then it's not unreasonable to have a help-yourself bar.

In addition, find out if any **corkage fees** apply. This is a sum per bottle that the caterer or venue may charge to open and serve the wine that you supply.

> **Tip**
>
> Serving **house wine** is perfectly okay, so long as you've sampled it yourself and made sure it meets your standards. If it doesn't, ask how much the price would increase to bump it up a notch. Same goes for offering "house" spirits (liquors) – just taste them beforehand and verify that they're at least one step up from battery acid.

> **Tip**
>
> Rather than forking out for both bottled sparkling and still water, ask your caterers to provide jugs of iced **tap water** in place of still – you'll be doing the planet a favour too.

> *Our caterer suggested charging £1 a drink for our evening bar – it stops people wasting drinks because they're free, but means that everyone can have a good time for a fiver!*
> **MATT**

Where to buy drinks

Shop around for good prices on drinks. Some US states sell booze at markedly lower prices than others – although you should also check out local laws on carrying alcohol across state lines. Buying **online** is another option, again with the caveat that US state laws vary. Some stores or vendors will also let you return unopened bottles for a refund, which lets you order more than enough without spending too much.

If you're in the UK, a time-honoured tradition is for someone to **drive over to France** for the day and load up a car or van with less heavily taxed wine and beer. The amount you can bring in from an EU country is unlimited so long as you transport the alcohol yourself, it's for your own use or a gift, and duties and taxes have been paid in the original country. You may be called on to prove you're not going to sell the bottles on.

DIY bar shopping list

Bar equipment

- Bottle openers
- Corkscrews
- Garnishes, knife and cutting board
- Ice buckets
- Ice scoops
- Ice tubs (to chill wine in)

Glassware (2–3 per person)

- All-purpose glasses
- Highball glasses (if needed)
- Wine and beer glasses
- Champagne flutes (if needed)

Liquid supplies

These will vary enormously depending on the drinking habits of your guests. However, there are a few guide-lines to help you estimate.

- For a litre bottle of **spirits**, estimate 20–22 drinks in the US, about 30 British measures of 35ml, around 40 of the smaller 25ml measure.
- A bottle of **wine** pours about 5 drinks.
- A litre of **mixer or soft drink** pours 5–7 glasses, depending on glass size and ice.
- A **bottle of champagne** pours 6 generous flutes.
- A **case of champagne** pours about 75 glasses.
- During a **one-hour cocktail reception**, estimate 2 drinks per person.
- During **dinner**, count on 2–2.5 glasses of wine per person.
- For a **four-hour dinner party**, 3–4 drinks per person.
- For a **longer cocktail party**, estimate one drink per person per hour.
- **Vodka** is the most requested spirit, followed by **whisky**, **gin** and **rum** in that order.

Cool as ice

You never want to run out of ice. Look at your storage options and, if there's nowhere to put it, arrange to have it delivered at the last possible moment.

❤ Plan on 1lb or 500g of ice per person to serve **in drinks**. This is a generous estimation, but ice is both cheap and necessary.

❤ For **chilling bottles**, make it 2.5lb or 1kg per person, more if you're holding the party outdoors during warm weather. After all, ice melts.

❤ A bottle of wine takes **two hours** to chill in the refrigerator and over an hour in ice alone. If you're in a hurry, submerge bottles in heavily salted ice water: they'll chill in under half an hour. However, the labels may also peel off, so this is an emergency solution.

Serving drinks

Consider how you're going to get drinks to everyone as well as what they'll be drinking. With more than 100 guests, you'll need two separate bars to avoid long queues of thirsty guests. Surprisingly, waiters with trays of drinks may be cheaper than bar service. You have to pay the waiters, but people drink less when they're handed drinks, plus they tend to drink what they're given – such as house wine rather than premium mixed drinks.

Even if you're not doing waiter service for most of the reception, consider having waiters with trays of drinks stationed at the entrance of the room as guests stream in from the ceremony. This ensures that everyone gets that all-important first drink promptly so they can begin to mingle and enjoy themselves, rather than waiting in line.

Champagne

Strictly speaking, Champagne (with a capital C) is the sparkling wine produced in France's Champagne region. All others are sparkling wines, which can be just as good and a lot less expensive. Consider Prosecco or Asti instead, or any delicious plain old sparkling wine from anywhere.

The terminology that goes with sparkling wines seem designed to confuse. Briefly, **Extra Brut** means totally dry (less than 0.06% sugar), **Brut** is very dry (less than 1.5% sugar), **Extra Dry** is medium dry (sweeter than Brut), **Sec** is slightly sweet, **Demi-sec** is considered sweet, and **Doux** is really sweet (and should only be served with dessert.)

You can have sparkling wine available at the bar, passed by waiters, or available only for a toast. It's undeniable that the sparkles are festive and will set a celebratory tone. If you're meeting guests with trays of drinks as they enter the reception area, flutes of sparking wine are a wonderful way to go – they look as festive as they taste.

If you want to stretch the bubbly further, champagne or sparkling wine **cocktails** do the trick. In the UK, guests enjoy **Buck's Fizz** (orange juice and champagne) at any hour, while in the US this same combination, known as a **Mimosa**, is strictly for brunch. Another terrific champagne cocktail is the **Black Velvet**: half Guinness, half champagne. Add a dollop of any tasty liqueur to the wine to buck up a plain glass of bubbly: Crème de Cassis makes a **Kir Royale**, or try Amaretto, mango liqueur, or even cherry brandy. But try any ambitious concoction out on a few guinea pigs first, before deciding to serve it to your guests.

10 Speeches

You invited all those who love you best to your wedding, and they've watched the ceremony – some of them probably even got a little choked up. Speeches provide a chance for guests to talk back and tell you how they're feeling, how full of love and how proud. They also provide an intimate moment for groups that have never met before – the families of the bride and groom, as well as far-flung friends – to gain a glimpse into your lives and what you mean to others. With a little planning, this can be an extremely moving part of the day – and a chance for the bride (if not the groom) to sit back, relax and listen to the nice things people have to say about you.

Who says what and when

Master of Ceremonies

The **MC** provides an invaluable service at many weddings: telling everyone what happens next. He or she keeps things moving along and prevents the dead air that can arrive when no one knows what they're supposed to do. This role often falls to the bandleader or DJ, mainly because they've already got the microphone. If you like and trust this individual (and if you have a bandleader or DJ) then by all means make use of them. The bartender has also been known to fill this role, as a public figure who is present in the capacity of employee rather than guest. Sometimes the

The origin of the toast

Oddly enough, toast (as in bread) and the practice of toasting are actually related. The ancient Greeks had developed a nasty habit of slipping poison into a rival's glass, so it became the practical habit, as well as a polite gesture, for the host to decant wine into a common jug and then serve everyone from it – himself first. The Romans followed in these Greek traditions as in so many others, with one addition: a bit of burned bread in each glass. The wines of yesteryear tended to be highly acidic, and they believed the bread improved the flavour (the charcoal probably did reduce the acidity, in fact). The Latin "tostus", meaning roasted or parched, came to refer to the drink as well as to the bread.

venue may supply a **toastmaster**: feel free to use this person if you like him or her, or to politely decline and make your own arrangements.

However, it can be a better idea to actively **choose from among your guests** an MC who you believe will be up to the job and will have your best interests truly at heart. It's also a great way to give yet another person an honoured role in your wedding – and ensure that you aren't stuck with the bartender's bawdy humour. Choose someone who isn't a mite nervous in front of crowds, who has an easy grace and charm and – this is really important – a loud voice and a commanding presence.

Talk through the **order of events** with the MC so that he knows exactly what happens when (see p.145 for ways to order the day). In particular, the MC is responsible for announcing the start of the speeches – and then for graciously cutting off overlong speeches, as well as handing off the mic from person to person.

Of course you don't need to have an MC at all, though someone (perhaps the long-suffering best man) will need to make sure that speeches begin and end when you want them to and announce the cake-cutting and the first dance.

The big three speeches – and more

As with so many other aspects of a wedding, a strict protocol exists for the order of speeches. Based on the assumption that the **father of the bride** has paid for the wedding and reception, he makes the first speech:

Tip

Absolutely anyone, including members of the wedding party, can act as Master of Ceremonies. Just pick the best person for the job, regardless of tradition.

the host welcoming his guests, speaking with affectionate pride about his daughter, and toasting the couple. The **groom** then rises and, speaking on behalf of himself and his bride, thanks all the parents for their support and all the guests for coming. He compliments his lovely wife and thanks first the men of the wedding party, then the women of the wedding party, and finally toasts the bridesmaids. Third comes the **best man**, whose brutal job it is to be funny, entertaining, and touching all at once. He also reads out any cards, emails, faxes or texts from absent friends.

It's certainly possible to change things around, though, so long as the guests are welcomed and someone close to the couple toasts them with a witty and loving speech. The father of the bride is no longer necessarily the actual host of the evening, in which case he may still play that role, but certainly doesn't have to. Also, the **bride** may wish to make a speech as well as the groom. And the **maid of honour** often wants to get in on the speeches – or may even be asked to take the best man's place if he's not much of a public speaker.

In the US, it's perfectly acceptable to keep the speeches going until everyone's energy and attention span runs out, with **friends and relatives** of the couple taking the mic to say a few words. If there's anyone you couldn't squeeze into the wedding party, you can also specifically ask them to make a speech: perhaps someone who may know you well

> " Since a Champagne toast is traditional in both America and France (our native countries), we definitely wanted one. Part of the groom's family hails from the Champagne region and they brought a few bottles that were specially produced for our wedding, making the toast even more special.
> **OLIVIA** "

Toasting etiquette

In the US, everyone rises at the start of the speech, except the recipients. However, unless everyone's standing already, the entire room probably won't jump to its collective feet, nor should you feel slighted when they don't. UK speeches tend to last longer, so the tradition there is to remain seated until the end of the speech, when everyone rises for the toast.

♥ When **offering a toast**, stand.

♥ To **complete a toast**, raise your glass and say the recipient's name(s) ("To Sean and June!" or "To my beautiful wife Lora!") and take a sip. Others will follow your lead.

♥ It's supposed to be bad luck to toast with an **empty glass**.

♥ Some even hold that it's bad luck to toast with **water** – make sure you provide an alternative for non-drinkers (see p.130).

" *We both hate champagne: we did have a toast, but it was with the drink of your choice.*
KATRINA **"**

Champagne is optional: toast with whatever drink you prefer, from pints to piña coladas.

or who has watched the two of you grow closer over time, or just a friend or family member who's particularly silver-tongued.

Ask any possible speech-givers for their consent a few weeks in advance of the day to give them **time to plan** what they're going to say. Some guidance on the length of the speech isn't amiss either.

When to do it

For a **cocktails-style reception**, the speeches can happen as soon as everyone's present and has got their hands on a drink. At a reception with a **sit-down meal**, then in the UK the traditional point is at the end of the meal with a champagne toast; the natural moment in the US is when everyone's been seated and served drinks. An excellent solution to avoid toasting burnout is to schedule the speeches between courses. You can also have the speeches and toasts immediately before or after the **cake-cutting**. See Chapter 9 for further suggestions of drinks for toasting.

Making speeches

The groom

On this day of all days, you have to give a speech, too. However, unlike the best man, whose speech is supposed to edify and entertain, the groom has a relatively easy task, with a few set points to hit. First of all, he has to **thank the father of the bride**, or whoever made the first speech. He does this on behalf of the couple – "my wife and I" – and this often gets a cheer, as it's his first opportunity to say this in public. He also thanks the rest of the **parents** for their love and support and his new in-laws for welcoming him into the family. The **guests** get thanked for showing up. The groom **compliments his new wife** and says how gorgeous she looks, how proud and grateful he is, etc. This is a moment where he can let loose a bit with some gooey yet manly sentiment – after all, it's his wedding day.

The groom then finishes up by thanking the wedding party, and if there are gifts for them this is the moment when these are given out. At last, he proposes a toast to the beautiful **bridesmaids**, and then he gets to sit down again. That wasn't so hard.

"Toasting a bride I didn't like"

"When my best friend told me he was getting married, I wasn't thrilled. It was obvious that his fiancée didn't like me, and ever since they'd started dating I'd seen him less and less. She was needy and overbearing, but the worst thing was that she was boring, and was dragging my friend down to her mundane level. All that aside, I knew she wasn't malicious and that in her heart she was a good person, and though I think he could have chosen better, I see that they love each other.

It took until about a month before the wedding for this guy, my friend for some thirty years, to ask me to stand up with him and make a toast at his wedding. I love him as a brother, and was proud to tell everyone how great I thought he was; unfortunately, I was going to have to talk about his wife, and I had no idea how to go about it.

I sat down to write out some notes after thinking about it for days. Hours went by and I picked at a sentence here and there. Finally it started to make sense. I didn't have to tell people what I thought about this woman, I had to tell them about how she made my friend feel, about how he believed his life was better for having her in it. That he thought she was a beautiful woman, who took care of him and loved him. I simply had to write my speech from the groom's perspective.

It went over extremely well, and ever since then his wife has considered me her friend."

JEREMY

The best man

The best man's speech is the most anticipated of all the speeches, a nerve-wracking job for nearly anyone. Unless he is a rugged individualist who can't stand doing as others do, his speech will likely follow the established template, which has him **introduce himself** and his relationship to the groom; describe how the couple met; offer an **anecdote** about how they're special; express **hopes for the future**; and then **propose a toast** to the happy couple. Tips specifically for the best man are covered in the box below.

The best best man's speech: some tips

♥ First and foremost, don't be afraid to let out your **love for the groom**. Tears are not necessary, but if you can muster some you will bring the house down.

♥ For a strictly serious speech, pick a **childhood story** that exemplifies the quality of man the groom had no choice but to become.

♥ If you feel that you're expected to be funny, do this by **gently roasting the groom**. His intelligence, his taste in clothes, his hygiene and ability to care for himself, whatever you sense is within bounds. This also sets up a natural transition into complimenting the bride. If it weren't for her, your pal the groom, that incompetent boob, would probably be dead.

♥ While the groom is fair game, **under no circumstances should you insult the bride**. It's poor form and is likely to make everyone in the room feel uncomfortable. Instead, concentrate on her beauty and intelligence, on how she makes the groom a better person. From there you might revisit a roasted groom, and this time point to his qualities, and how those qualities, mixed with the bride's, have made the amazing couple that everyone is there to celebrate.

♥ End on a high note by letting everyone know how **happy you are** for the couple, remind the crowd of how **happy they all are** as well, and don't forget to say **cheers and propose your toast to them** before taking a drink.

Speech-making: the dos...

Great speeches can be a real highlight of the wedding, but if the speakers aren't that good they run the risk of **sending everyone to sleep**. This should be a forgiving audience, all the same – everyone's here to have a good time.

❤ Watch the **length**. If your guests are standing, then keep speeches to under five minutes. In the UK, if they're seated and have drinks to hand, then ten to fifteen minutes can be fine for a great speaker. In the US snappy speeches are the rule.

❤ Bring **notes** to refer to (but not read from). If you're not sure **where to look**, focus on a point at the back of the room, or turn to the folks you're toasting and speak directly to them. Practise ahead of time, with a mirror or, better, an audience.

❤ **Compliments** always go over well, as does **humour**. However, if you're not sure if a joke is suitable, it's probably best left out. Your audience will forgive inept sincerity and heartfelt stumbles, but not tactless jokes. See box on p.143 for online joke sources.

❤ **Quotations** from famous people work nicely, and the Internet is littered with them, as are books written specially for those people who have to give speeches and don't know what to say. Feel free to use the words of others, but try to weave them in with your own to avoid sounding false or like you've got the whole thing from rent-a-speech.

> For inspiration, the poet Robert Haas assembled a lovely book *Into The Garden: A Wedding Anthology: Poetry and Prose on Love and Marriage*. Or check out The Knot's tips at tinyurl.com/knot-toast.

The way of the microphone

❤ Do a **sound test** early in the day to work out any kinks.

❤ Hold the mic about **six inches away** from your mouth.

❤ Talk **past the mic**, not directly into it.

❤ **Don't yell**. That's why you've got a microphone.

❤ Don't stand in front of a speaker, or you'll get gut-wrenching **feedback**.

❤ Any "b" or "p" sounds will **pop**, so if you're a true obsessive, plan a speech without these sounds – or simply try to say them gently.

... and the don'ts

❤ Unless you're absolutely certain that everyone present will enjoy a good dick joke, **keep it clean**. Save your naughty material for the bachelor/stag or the bachelorette/hen party.

❤ Don't **humiliate** anyone, present or absent, and avoid all mention of **exes**. Bride and groom shouldn't be shown in a **poor light** – even if the story is really funny. Any of these will bring a note of discord into what should be a joyous occasion.

❤ Don't dwell on religion, politics or any other **touchy subjects**.

❤ Don't apologize for being a **rotten speaker** and never say you didn't want to give a speech but had to.

❤ Don't refer to **inside jokes** that more than half the audience won't get.

❤ Above all, **stay sober**. A single drink will steady your nerves; you don't want to end up slurring your speech. This not only embarrasses you, but the couple as well. You can always get wasted after you give your speech.

Public speaking tips

Addressing a crowd of mostly strangers can seem a terrifying prospect, and so many of us have difficulty with it that an abundant business has arisen, feeding off our fear. Books, courses (both classroom and online) and videos promise to gently guide us through the stages of public speaking development. Beyond that, everyone you know will offer their own tidbit of advice, "imagine everyone naked" being both the most common and just plain worst of them all.

❤ The best possible advice anyone can give you is **get some practice**. Force yourself to address a group of colleagues or friends, even if just in a social setting, perhaps after a couple of drinks.

❤ Even if you plan on working from memory, **write down your speech**. When you do, structure it on the page as if it were a poem, putting line spaces and indents in places where you'd want to slow down to let a point sink in, or where you want to remember to take a breath.

❤ When standing in front of the assembly, **don't hold the paper** on which you've written your speech. Your nerves will show in the shaking paper, which will only make you more self-conscious. Set it down on a nearby table or chair, and refer to it when necessary.

Online gags

While it isn't all about the laughs, a few **good jokes** can really make or break a wedding speech. But very few people are capable of standing up in front of a packed room and making everybody laugh. And even those comedians who do it for a living have the advantage that at least a proportion of the audience will have come specifically to hear their gags and pretty much know what to expect.

Wedding speeches are very different: you will more than likely have an audience of mixed ages (including children) and what might be appropriate for your closest friends may very well cause great auntie Doris, assuming she understands it, to fall off her chair in shock rather than hysterics. And whatever you do, don't refer to exes!

The Internet is a fantastic source of jokes for speeches, and it shouldn't take you long to track down those sites that suit your sense of humour (which is important, as the speech needs to sound like it's coming from you … even if it isn't). For starters, try:

- ❤ thebestmanspeech.com
- ❤ tinyurl.com/weddingspeechdigest
- ❤ tinyurl.com/guysports
- ❤ tinyurl.com/bridegroom-speech
- ❤ tinyurl.com/hitched-jokes

PS: If you come across any sites that want a few dollars off you before showing you the funnies, move on – they almost certainly won't show you anything you won't find for free elsewhere. Oh, and DON'T REFER TO EXES!

- ❤ Make sure to **speak plainly**. A conversational tone will make both you and the audience feel more at ease. Use the sort of language you'd use with a kindly old lady you've just met on a bus.

- ❤ Undoubtedly, something you thought might come across as a joke will **fall flat**, and something else you say will bring the house down. Everyone will assume you meant it exactly that way, so just **go with the flow**.

- ❤ Most importantly, **be yourself**. If you believe in what you're saying, and you speak from the heart, you will make a genuine connection with your audience.

11 Party!

A wedding is a sacred occasion – but it's also a big party, perhaps the biggest you'll ever throw. You want your guests to cry at the ceremony and then get down at the reception. This takes planning, from the schedule of events to the ideal music volume for dinner and dancing to entertaining any little kids so the big kids can have some grown-up fun.

Before the party starts

Ordering the day

It's worth writing out a **schedule** of your big day with times roughed in – not that you'll actually hold to these precise timings, but it helps you organize the day, plus you can use it to coordinate the many players so that, for example, the caterers know when to wheel out the cake. Bearing in mind that things always take longer than expected, it's a good idea to schedule some **dead time** as a buffer to get you back on track if you get too far behind (just make sure guests won't be left with nothing to do if you are on schedule). Remember to account for transitions between different venues or rooms, too.

For the schedule – at least on your personal copy – begin at the beginning and end at the end, from the time you plan to set your alarm clock to realistic estimates for how long it takes to do the bridesmaids' curls to whether the speeches come before dinner or after. You can then hand out an **abbreviated version** to all of the main participants, providing both times and cues for events to help the ushers, photographer, bartender, Master of Ceremonies, DJ, waiting staff and anyone else involved to do what they're supposed to do in the correct sequence.

The receiving line

A receiving line just outside the reception area can be a great way to **greet guests** and make sure you get a moment of face time with each and every person, but it can also be a time sink. Spending 30 seconds greeting each of 100 guests will take nearly an hour. You may decide that hour could be better spent table-hopping, having longer and more meaningful conversations with groups of friends and family.

But it's a great opportunity to **introduce guests** who your parents or even your new spouse may not have yet met. If you do go with the receiving line, the key is to keep it simple: the two of you and both sets of parents. Though in the US the bride's parents traditionally head the line, this is another throwback to the days when dad was the real host of the event; if most of the guests are your friends or you paid for most of the event, you could head the line instead. In the UK, the bride's mother is usually paired with the groom's father and vice versa, so that at least one person in each pair has a vague idea of who the guest is and can introduce them to the other, rather than offending anyone by having to ask who they are. Make sure you arrange for a waiter with a tray to **deliver drinks** to the guests waiting to greet you, as well as the receiving line itself.

Music

The big decision: live or recorded?

The rise of digital has radically transformed the musical landscape, and not only for the recording companies' bottom lines. While many couples still choose to kick it old school with live music or a DJ, the possibility now exists to put together a few different **playlists**, then plug your digital music player into the stereo system and go. The fact that this option is practically free makes it awfully attractive to the bride and groom who are looking to throw a classy do on the cheap.

> " At my cousin's wedding, we had to queue for the receiving line in drizzle, which was getting progressively heavier, while they stood nice and dry in the doorway to 'receive' us. Boy, did that queue move slowly! It was a bit of a disaster – wish they'd thought to have some brollies at the ready.
> *ANDREW* "

That said, there are definite benefits to working with **live musicians.** They bring energy to an event. It's the difference between listening to a recording of your favourite song in your living room versus being at a show. It's more expensive, though, and the cost rises with the number of musicians. But you can **combine various forms** of music delivery to fit your style and your wallet.

For example, to wow your guests when they first arrive at the reception, hire a pianist to tickle the ivories and sing classic romantic tunes – and then you can switch to recorded music via your iPod during dinner and for the party after. Conversely, put on recorded music during cocktails and dinner, when it's mostly in the background, then have a DJ or band come on to ramp up the dance party. Or have just a few instruments from a larger band play during dinner, when you want a quieter vibe anyway.

The kind of music and the musicians you choose should go along with the **overall tone** of the wedding. If you want a raucous party, don't hire a classical quintet. On the other hand, a jazz combo can really make that swingin' vintage feel you were going for. Or consider a ceilidh or barn dance (see p.149) – always great fun as it involves everyone.

Working with the venue

The size and logistics of your chosen venue will make some of your musical choices for you: a small space can't fit a twelve-piece band, while a single acoustic guitar will get lost in an echoing hall. When you sort out the room layout with the venue manager (see Chapter 6), there are several things to discuss.

💜 Where will the **musicians** or **DJ** be able to set up? Where are the **speakers** and can they be moved if you want? (For more on the PA system, see the box on p.150.) You don't want some tables out in Siberia while others are deafened because they're slammed up against a huge speaker.

💜 If you plan on dancing, make sure you've set aside space for a **dance floor** in the table layout, and that there's appropriate flooring, whether indoor or out.

💜 Talk through, as well, **what time** the musicians can set up and how long they will have to break down when the party ends. Plan on **feeding** the band – musicians get hungry, too, and a good meal may make all the difference in coaxing a lively performance out of a jaded wedding band.

> *We're both musicians, so recorded music wasn't an option! We had a wonderful evening of live music in the build-up to the wedding, with all of our musician friends jamming with us. It cost quite a bit to rent sound equipment and some of the instruments, but it added such a personal dimension to the event, it was totally worth it. We had a couple of keyboard players (Western and Indian), guitar, bass, drumset, congas, tablas and all sorts of little percussion instruments played by anyone who wanted to join in. The music ranged from classic rock and pop to jazz and Indian film, sufi and bhangra. There was much singing along and dancing and everyone had a ball.*
> **PUNITA**

Finding a band

As always, **referrals** from newlyweds or other engaged couples are a great source of names, as are other wedding professionals. They've been there. They know.

Local music colleges are a great way to find talented young (read "cheap") musicians, especially if you want some standard classical or jazz played, although there will be other types of musicians in the mix there as well.

Those who **book bands professionally** are great sources of information, if you can get a concert promoter or a nightclub booker to chat with you about that great opening act they saw recently. And then there are booking agents, who bring together musicians and gigs for a living.

Take any names you pick up straight to the Internet, where many bands or musicians will have **audio files** available for you to hear. This is a great way to avoid going to the trouble of auditioning a group whose sound simply doesn't appeal to you.

Auditioning and booking a band

Any band that's looking for gigs will have a **demo** they can give you, which should provide a more substantial sample of their sound than the couple of songs you already listened to online (unless, of course, their entire demo is online). However, be sure to find out how long ago and under what circumstances the songs were recorded. A band's sound can change a great deal over time: perhaps they're working with a new style or have a couple of different musicians today. Plus, a studio recording will always sound different from a live show.

Ideally, you would get to hear the bands you're serious about **play live**, in similar circumstances to those of your wedding. But it's not a good idea to go crashing other people's weddings (or anniversaries or bat mitzvahs) to listen to the band: you wouldn't appreciate having a bunch of strange couples hanging around your reception. Should a group happen to have a gig coming up at a club or other public venue, definitely check them out. Otherwise, see if perhaps they'd be willing to let you listen in to a few songs at a practice session so that you can get the feel of their playing in person. If you're shelling out thousands

Tip

Space out band auditions over several days or weeks, if possible. After you listen to five jazz combos in a row, they all start to sound the same.

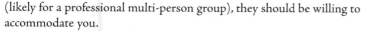

(likely for a professional multi-person group), they should be willing to accommodate you.

Once you've decided you like the music and style, then you'll need to work out the details.

- ♥ If there are **particular songs** that you definitely want to hear at your wedding, whether religious or simply some favourites, check the band is willing and able to play them.

- ♥ Also check up on **what clothes** they normally wear to a gig. If you like, you could ask them if they would be willing to show up in formal attire.

- ♥ Put all the details **in writing**: the time they'll arrive and depart, breaks, meals, clothes, songs you particularly want played (and ones you absolutely can't stand), how much overtime costs.

- ♥ For big instruments, especially the **piano**, check if they bring along keyboards or if you have to arrange to rent a piano for them (or if the venue has one you can use/rent).

- ♥ Also, find out how much of the **sound system** they supply, and how it meshes with what's available at the venue. For more on PA systems, see p.150.

- ♥ Musicians can be **temperamental**, but then again so can chefs and hair stylists. Don't hire a band you don't get along with or who don't take your requests seriously. They may roll their eyes at "Rainbow Connection" – but will they settle down and play it if that's what you want for the first dance?

Doh-si-doh your partner!

A popular choice in the UK, at least for the dancing part of the evening, is a **barn dance** or **ceilidh band**. The choice of music is taken entirely out of your hands, which can be a relief. Plus, you get someone calling the steps, which encourages the less confident dancers, and the event is far more sociable than dancing individually at a club.

Even the oldest can take part in the more sedate dances, and often partners are switched all through the dance, so guests get to meet and mingle far more than they otherwise would. It's also a good choice if you yourselves are reluctant dancers and dreading that first dance. You can lead off the first dance and your moment in the spotlight will be over in no time.

As with any other band, be sure to **see them in action** before committing: the caller really makes or breaks a band. Make sure their instructions are clear, unpatronizing, and delivered in a fun and friendly way.

Working with a DJ

The wedding DJ occupies the **middle ground** between a live band and plugging in your iPod. You still get a professional human being who can judge the crowd's needs in real time – when it's the moment to give a flourish as the bride and groom enter, when to mix in a slow song and when to play the stonking track that gets the crowd out on the dance floor.

The downside of a DJ is that you are, fundamentally, at his mercy. He can play the "Chicken Dance", and you can't stop him without causing a scene. DJs are notorious for ignoring the DO and DO NOT PLAY lists that every couple faithfully compiles. He also acts as an MC for the evening and might talk in cheesy radio style over the end of songs or make inappropriate comments that will make you and your guests cringe. That's why you need to check references very carefully or, if possible, go and see a DJ in action. As usual, the best way to find a DJ who will respect your wishes is through a recently married couple.

Once you have a person you feel you can trust, talk through the sort of music you like and the mood you're looking to create at different points during the reception. Look through his music collection

Filling the room with noise: PA systems

In many instances, PAs (public address systems) are already present at the venue or, if you are using a professional DJ, band or entertainer, they may well bring along everything they need to fill the room with noise. Don't assume anything, however: double check beforehand exactly what everyone needs and what's available on site.

When bands discuss their requirements, they will more than likely start blathering on about "DIs", "lines", "channels" (and whether they are allowed near the bar). All you really need to know is how many **microphones** they need and how many "**lines**" they need – the latter referring to instruments like keyboards that plug straight into the PA. When gathering this information, don't forget to factor in your own speeches (if it is a large room) and perhaps any amplification you might want during the ceremony.

If you do end up hiring your own PA, ideally you will want them to deliver and **set up** the equipment (speakers in particular can be very heavy) and then dismantle it afterwards. However, if you are using a small venue for the whole day, you may well only want to set things up in the evening, in which case you are going to have to do it yourselves… or rather, delegate the task to some techie ushers.

Equipment hire shouldn't be too expensive, but it's still worth getting several quotes to play off against each other. Also, look out for hidden extras such as **insurance**, as you might already be covered for damage to hire equipment by either your venue's policy or a separate weddings insurance policy (see p.16) if you have one.

and point out songs you particularly enjoy. Like every other wedding professional you work with, he should ask questions and seem to get your aesthetic and the kind of event you're after. Lists of songs you love and hate aside, a DJ who understands the overall tone of the party will be able to perform more fluidly than one who's simply working off a list. If strict adherence to a list is really what you want, then just go with the digital music player.

Your wedding soundtrack

Providing your own music by means of an iPod or other digital music player is the ideal option if you're pinching pennies – plus it's also great for control freaks. After all, there are **no nasty surprises** when you programme the music yourself. You'll need several playlists: for the ceremony (see p.65), cocktail hour, dinner, cake-cutting, dance party, and later dance party when the oldies have gone home. Think of it as the soundtrack to your wedding. Not every part of a soundtrack stands out, but it's all important.

You will need to designate one responsible and musically apt individual (the hip groomsman comes to mind) to **take charge of the music**, performing playlist changes, and sensing when a song isn't working and should be skipped. It can be a drag to be a guest yet have to stay focused enough on the music to perform this crucial service right through to the end of the night, so be sure to ask someone who's up to the task. Or find out if there's a staff person who can take care of at least the basic changes of playlist, based on your schedule (cake-cutting versus first dance).

> *Friends of ours set up a dedicated email address to which their wedding guests could send song requests to be passed on to the DJ. I emailed 'our' song through (something soppy and pretty uncool which will remain nameless), but we never heard it so I guess it got blackballed by either the couple or the guy at the decks!*
> **LENALISA**

Pump up the volume

What sounds perfect to your club-attuned ears may be excruciatingly loud to your great aunt Tessie. Yes, it's your party, but you want your guests to have a good time as well. When you establish the volume of the music, consider the crowd as well as the mood. During dinner, for example, people will want to talk without shouting; as the party wears on and some of the older generation head home to bed, you may choose to play more contemporary music, and louder.

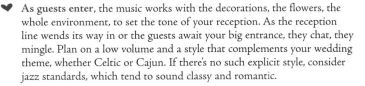

♥ **As guests enter**, the music works with the decorations, the flowers, the whole environment, to set the tone of your reception. As the reception line wends its way in or the guests await your big entrance, they chat, they mingle. Plan on a low volume and a style that complements your wedding theme, whether Celtic or Cajun. If there's no such explicit style, consider jazz standards, which tend to sound classy and romantic.

♥ Whatever songs you play **during dinner**, make sure they can melt seamlessly into the backdrop. Guests want to eat and to talk and to be able to hear one another – and you want to hear what they have to say when you table-hop to converse with them.

♥ Special **cake-cutting music** can provide an auditory cue that it's time to pay attention. This is another chance to play a meaningful and romantic song – either one that's already yours, or one that you make special by association. Lots of couples succumb to the temptation to pun and go with, for example, "Sugar, Sugar" (The Archies), "How Sweet It Is (To Be Loved By You)" (by Marvin Gaye or James Taylor, depending on your preference) or "Pour Some Sugar On Me" (Def Leppard).

♥ Though there's nothing quite like the crackle of vinyl and the panic-stricken look on your guests' faces as the needle skates across a scratched copy of "I Will Survive" just before the chorus, it's both easier and cheaper to **do your own digital DJing**. Make sure you bring enough variation in your party playlists, in case your default list isn't to everybody's taste. Both iPods and iTunes come with the so-called "Genius" feature, which assembles playlists for you automatically based on one particular selection, though you might find it a bit risky to chance on the day. If you're feeling very confident, you can also let trusted friends know about the setup, so that they can bring their own iPods along too. For specific technical help and advice, check out *The Rough Guide to iPods & iTunes*.

Wired for sound

If you have hired a PA system, then all you need to make the connection between your iPod, digital music player or laptop should be a cable with a stereo mini-jack (which looks the same as a regular headphone jack) at one end and two phono jacks (generally one is red and one white) at the other. It's worth checking with the hire company beforehand just in case their system doesn't have regular phone inputs.

Dancing

Where to dance?

Some venues come with an inlaid **dance floor**, in which case that's that. Set up the band/DJ/stereo nearby and you're good to go. If, however, you're working with a venue where everything's brought in, such as an outdoor venue, you first must decide whether to rent a dance floor (the answer is a resounding "yes" if you plan on dancing), and then where to put it. One end or the other is probably the best move; in any case, you need to ensure that no tables will be stuck with a view of the back of the band's heads all night. If you're going with solely recorded music you might be able to get away with putting the dance floor bang in the centre of the room, so long as all cords are safely covered or out of the way so as not to trip table-hoppers (like yourselves). Leave some space for those who aren't dancing to navigate around the floor even if the party gets really wild.

The first dance

Many couples dance a first dance together as yet another symbol of their pledged partnership. This doesn't have to be the very first time anybody dances at the reception, but it's the first time the newly married couple dance together and can range from a few simple steps to an elaborately choreographed performance. Choose **a song that's special to you**, or at the very least has romantic lyrics you can get behind. Crucially, it must be something you can dance to, since that's what you'll be doing, in front of absolutely everyone.

It works well to have the MC announce the first dance so that itinerant guests can assemble for the show. Some couples are filled with horror at the mere thought of dancing in public, in which case of course you can skip it. Or you could ask all the recently married couples, parents, bridesmaids or whomever you like to join you after a few bars.

If you are planning to take to the floor on your own, though, try dancing together to potential tunes in your living room. It might be

> *The sound system broke before our first dance so the groomsmen were called upon to sing 'Have I Told You Lately' while one tried to fix it! It was probably for the best, as I'd thought we were having the Rod Stewart version (my preference) and Chris had arranged for it to be Van Morrison (his preference).*
> *MEGAN*

Our first dance...

The old Dorothy Fields jazz standard "Exactly Like You": the Mark Murphy version, which is a little slower than most – OLIVIA

"Always and Forever" by Heatwave – SEAN

"These Arms of Mine" by Otis Redding – SAMANTHA

"The Universal" by Blur – ANDY

Don Byron playing Raymond Scot's "Charley's Prelude" in honour of my grandfather who was a heck of a ballroom dancer – GREG

"Most Beautiful Girl in the Room" by Flight of the Conchords – ALEX

"You and I" by Michael Bublé – KATRINA

"Weekends Away" by Math and Physics Club – DAVE

"You Are the Sunshine of My Life" by Stevie Wonder – it played a few times in the restaurant during our first date – NENETTE

"My Baby Just Cares for Me" by Nina Simone – KARLIN

"Michelle" by The Beatles: it started out as a dance between my dad and me, then Bart cut in and we finished the dance together – MICHELLE

Practice makes perfect – though a wooden shuffle is fine if that's all you can manage.

that your slow dancing has never developed beyond a slightly awkward shuffle, so you'll probably want to choose a shortish song, or ask others to join you on the floor after a minute or so. If, on the other hand, you're determined to do it properly, consider taking dance lessons in whatever style suits your music. Reasonably confident dancers who want to pick up some new steps may settle for an afternoon or weekend class; if you're not so light on your feet, sign up for a longer course and be prepared to practise in your own time, as well. But just be sure you've got enough moves to last out the tune – three minutes can seem a surprisingly long time when you're alone on the floor.

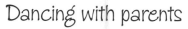

Dancing with parents

In the US, often the next tradition, right after you've paraded your smooth moves across the floor with your sweetie, is the **parent dance**: the bride dances with her dad, the groom with his mum. Music for this dance tends towards the saccharine, how-quickly-the-years-have-passed genre. Even more than for the first dance, you must double check the lyrics in the music for a parent dance. You really don't want any suggestion of sexuality to undermine the moment (see box below).

Some regions, in the US mostly, follow this with an entire **formal dance sequence**: after bride–father and groom–mother, then it's bride–father-in-law and groom–mother-in-law, followed by bride–best man and groom–maid of honour. At this point the rest of the wedding party also joins in the dancing, and then after that the party is on. If any of this takes your fancy, then go for it, but feel free to pick the parts that have meaning for you or to ignore it completely.

The no-play list

There's nothing more uncomfortable than watching a newly married couple dance their first dance to a song about heartbreak, except perhaps watching a father and daughter dance to a song about yearning. Unfortunately, certain popular first-dance songs you thought were charming and lovely may, in the context of your wedding, have awkward undertones. If in doubt, look up the lyrics online, and if you're not sure what we mean, the following examples should offer some guidance.

"Every Breath You Take" by The Police
Believe it or not, this is a popular first dance song. Sung from the perspective of a creepy obsessed stalker, this track suggests a restraining order isn't far down the line.

"I Loved Her First" by Heartland
One of the more popular selections for the daddy–daughter dance, this supposedly loving ode comes across as a thinly veiled warning to the new son-in-law. Do not mess with daddy's little girl.

"I Will Always Love You" by Whitney Houston
Usually associated with undying love and devotion, Whitney's enduring ballad (Dolly Parton's original now long forgotten) is actually about a love that can never be.

"You're Beautiful" by James Blunt
Unbearable falsetto aside, this is a classic example of getting lost in the chorus: Blunt's pop poison is about never, ever, being with the person you might possibly love, after having only really caught a glimpse of her.

"Let's Stay Together" by Al Green
Everyone loves Reverend Al, but this song might be a little more pleading than it is reaffirming. A borderline choice you could probably get away with.

"Butterfly Kisses" by Bob Carlisle
About a father's struggle to accept that his innocent little girl has, at this exact moment, transformed into a woman. Luckily, Jesus, groom to all women, is there to keep her safe now that dad's out of the picture.

155

Keeping people dancing

A few key elements will help to get guests dancing and keep them on their feet. The first and most important is of course **the music**. Talk with your band or DJ, or consider your music collection carefully when assembling playlists in order to choose songs that make the toes tap irresistibly. Take the **age range** of your guest list into account as well – if you want your grandparents to shake it, play music they like, perhaps big-band tunes. As the evening progresses and the older generation fades out, you might move more towards contemporary dance music.

Especially early on in the party, have a plan in place to gently **encourage guests onto their feet**. Have the wedding party on alert to ask unpartnered individuals to dance – getting a shy cousin out of his seat is half the battle. Many people will lose some inhibitions – and feel more comfortable getting their groove on – after a drink or two: worth bearing in mind if a rocking dance party is important to you.

Alternative entertainment

Fireworks, magic and more

Everyone loves fireworks, and though not the most original of wedding entertainments, they can be one of the most spectacular. Still, there are few things less impressive than a half-baked salvo of fountains that fizzle in the centre of a lawn, whilst a lone rocket zips into the sky and marks its demise with the kind of "pop" you'd expect from a Christmas cracker. This is one area where DIY isn't such a good idea. If you have an uncle or pal who claims to have the magic touch, it's probably best to say no to them, too. What's more, said guest may be slightly drunk by the time it gets dark and should not be let anywhere near a box of fireworks.

By choosing a reputable **professional company** to organize and choreograph your display, you should end up with a well-timed and composed spectacle that peaks in the right places and ends with a proper bang. Many companies offer standard packages that can be tailored to suit your tastes, perhaps to match your colour theme, and might offer extras, such as having your initials spelled out in the sky.

Chinese lanterns

A far more sophisticated, cheap and memorable alternative to fireworks are Chinese lanterns. The basic idea is that a large paper bag is held aloft while a small "fuel cell" attached below it is lit. As it burns, the paper bag fills with air and, when released, drifts off into the sky.

The really great thing about these lanterns is that all the adults can get involved and help with lighting them (a few strategically placed garden candles make this process much easier), and the more lanterns you have, the more impressive is the final result. The sight of dozens of the things drifting off until they become too distant to see is truly magical.

Of course, we are talking about unleashing burning paper to the elements, so a little common sense is required: check that the venue is happy for you to go ahead, and if you are holding your wedding out in the countryside, it might also be worth asking the permission of local farmers, especially if they have hay drying in the fields. Also be aware that rain and strong winds will make it a no-goer. It might also be worth informing local police of your intentions, as lanterns have been known to jam emergency services switchboards with reports of UFO invasions! More seriously, coast guards have been on occasions called out after sightings of lanterns in coastal areas have been mistaken for distress flares. Putting aside these concerns, they really are an amazing and memorable way of celebrating, and as they grow in popularity, so the range on offer has expanded. As well as oversized lanterns and coloured lanterns, you can now also track down heart-shaped and even football-shaped varieties.

In the UK visit **skycandle.co.uk** to place orders, and in the US, point your browser at **wishlantern.com**.

Most importantly, opting for a professional display ensures that what you get is going to be safe.

Here's a few more ideas for making your wedding party go with a bang.

- Rent a **photo booth** for the day, and place it in a discreet location. Leave out some sticky tape and encourage your guests to attach the pics in a guestbook alongside their good wishes.

- **Magicians** specializing in card tricks and sleight-of-hand can mingle among your guests, moving from table to table without making themselves the centre of attention. In similar vein, a **caricature artist** can roam the floor and create abbreviated pieces for your more sedentary guests.

- Hire in a **roulette wheel** or craps table for a little dance-floor-adjacent gambling action – group games where everyone is betting on the same "roll of the dice". Card games like blackjack or poker require an individualistic strategy that takes away from the easy ebb and flow of a party setting.

- Outdoor receptions lend themselves to all manner of **sporting events**, from the refined, like croquet or badminton, to the gruntingly aggressive, like football or ultimate Frisbee. For beach weddings there's always volleyball, and for dance-floor fun break out the limbo stick.

♥ For better or worse, many of us have singers in the family. Designate an hour or so for **karaoke**, being sure to limit the set list to wedding-appropriate tunes.

Kids' stuff

If you've chosen to invite children to your wedding, you're going to have to **plan for them**. During the ceremony, parents are responsible for maintaining some level of control over their kids, but during the reception your young invitees aren't going to want to sit quietly, and they won't be interested in speeches, an open bar, or dancing to your DJ's 80s-heavy pop mix.

Rather than have to deal with a rebelling force of small creatures running wildly all about your party, consider some of the following tips, keeping in mind that structure is the key when keeping children entertained.

♥ **Seat them together** at the reception, at a table near the back. It's likely that there's a children's menu from your caterer, so put them all at the same table for ease of service. This also lets them play together instead of bothering their parents, and since they're sitting away from the official activities (speeches, etc) they can get up, run around and generally freak out without being too distracting. You might also consider hiring a sitter to watch the kids, leaving your friends and relatives free to enjoy the party.

♥ Create an **activities kit** and have it at the table ready to go. Include bubbles, crayons, stickers, a puzzle or colouring book, and consider using a white paper table covering so they can draw right on the table. Remember that gender and age are factors, and that ten-year-old boys will not be as fascinated with glitter princess stickers as four-year-old girls.

♥ Provide a **small toy** in the activities kit. Firstly, it will serve as your special little wedding favour to them, and secondly, children can't focus on any one activity for too long or they get bored. The keyword here is variety.

♥ Too old to sit with the children, too young to find adults entertaining, **teenagers** deserve special consideration. If you can, dedicate some space away from the main event where they can hang out. Provide some board games and playing cards, and if a TV is available add in a gaming system. Be sure to have one of the waiters swing by occasionally to refill snacks and take drink orders.

12 Flowers and Decorations

So you've found the perfect place to say "I do", got something smart to wear, and arranged to feed and water all those who'll come to witness it. With these fundamentals in place, you're free to indulge your creative impulses in flowers and other wedding fripperies. These are the icing on your proverbial cake: a chance to put in that little extra effort that's a way of showing how much this day means to you. But remember: this is the small stuff – so don't sweat it. Spend as much time as you like on swatches and samples, but only so long as you're enjoying yourselves. If it's all becoming too serious, it's time to take the night off and let the odd unmatching accessory slip through.

Grand designs

Your wedding will probably involve several different phases, possibly multiple venues, and many small but heavily scrutinized details. A **colour scheme** is one of the easiest ways to pull all these elements together into a coherent whole. With a **theme**, you can go one step further, uniting each element around a central idea. Of course, a colour scheme – let alone a theme – is far from compulsory. But it gives a professional air to proceedings, helps your photos look nice, and shows you've made a bit of an effort.

Colour schemes

Don't let anyone tell you you can't have pink and orange, if that's what you want. Any colours "go" if they're used confidently. That said, if you're not confident with colour, stick to the following advice and you won't go far wrong.

Your safest bet is a **single colour.** But be sure to use different shades of that colour, else the end result will look flat. As a general rule, use **lighter shades** for large areas such as tablecloths, and **darker shades** for smaller objects. And don't forget that not everything needs to be coloured – the effect would be overwhelming – so complement with neutral **white or cream** to avoid overkill. After all, you don't want guests' strongest memory of your wedding to be your colour scheme.

If you do use more than one colour, go for **either pastels or brights,** not a combination of the two. Two or three colours is plenty: more than that and things will look haphazard and confused.

When it comes to choosing a colour, you can of course simply go for **your favourite.** But it's worth considering what will work best with the season and the backdrop provided by your venues. In autumn and winter, for example, rich reds and purples will add warmth and work in low lighting. As for your venues, think about what colours are already present in carpets, curtains and so on. Is there a lot of dark wood against

Online colour scheme resources

- **Tiger Color** (tinyurl.com/tigercolor). A rundown of the basics of colour matching.
- **Color Wizard** (tinyurl.com/colorwizard). One of the more user-friendly online colour scheme tools, this will generate a set of colours to complement a base colour of your choosing.
- **Palette Generator** (tinyurl.com/palette-gen). If you need some inspiration, upload a favourite photo and this nifty web tool generates a harmonious colour scheme based on it.

which whites and paler shades would stand out, or white walls that
would offset bright reds and yellows?

Before you go identifying your exact favourite shade, you might
want to let your **attendants' dresses** take the lead. Bridesmaid-dress
shopping is a delicate enough operation already; head out armed with
a precise colour swatch and you're doomed from the start. By all means
have a colour in mind, but be prepared to ditch it if the dress-to-end-
all-arguments is only available in a quite different hue. Once you've
fixed on a specific shade, **take a colour swatch everywhere with you,**
and especially to any vendor meetings – don't try to judge matches
from memory.

Wedding themes

Trekkies, football fans and tacky Las Vegas drive-thrus may have given
wedding themes a bad name, but having a wedding theme needn't
mean having a full-on "theme wedding", complete with guests in fancy
dress and vows in Klingon. It can simply be a subtle reflection of your
passions and personal style, perhaps showing through in the cut of
your outfits, your choice of music, even the food you serve, while never
distracting from what the day's really about. You might be inspired by
a particular **historical period** – say the flappers and jazz of the 1930s
– or an **art style** such as art nouveau or gothic. You could go **rustic,**

Tip

Even if you decide not to have a theme, **naming tables** is a nice way of injecting your personalities into proceedings. Name them after places you've been on holiday together, favourite books, films or bands, and decorate accordingly.

with cottage-garden flowers, cider and barn dancing, or recreate the cuisine and visual style of a **country you've visited** or your honeymoon destination. You could confine your theme to a simple **recurring motif** – hearts, butterflies, a sports team badge – that appears on orders of service, place cards, and perhaps your cake frosting.

Flowers

The most prominent part of any colour scheme will probably be the flowers. Many couples are torn between dismay at spending so much on something that's perishable but not edible and Martha Stewart-inspired dreams of being engulfed in sweet-scented roses. The good news is that with wise flower choices it's possible to put on a good show without breaking the bank. But first, here's a run-through of your likely flower needs:

- **Bride's bouquet** This can be anything from a small informal posy to an elaborate trailing extravaganza. Consider what's going to best suit you and your dress. If you're small, an enormous bouquet will dwarf you. Equally, if your dress is quite plain a dramatic bouquet could provide interest. Do take comfort into account: you'll be carrying it around for a good while so avoid anything too heavy.

- **Bouquets for bride's attendants** These often echo the bride's bouquet on a smaller scale. You might want something a cut above the rest for your chief attendant.

- **For hair** Any flowers used in your hair will need to be wired, and only certain ones will stand it without wilting – check with your florist.

- **Corsages and buttonholes (boutonnieres)** These are small pieces pinned to the lapels of the wedding party: mothers and fathers, best man and ushers. You may also want to give them to grandparents, godparents and anyone else special.

Tip

If you're getting married in a church, ask any other couples getting married there the same day if you can share the ceremony flowers. You'll save money, and avoid multiple-florist pile-ups in the porch.

- **For the ceremony** Civil venues often have their own floral arrangements, in which case you can save your money for the reception venue. In a church you might decorate pew ends and have a couple of large pedestal displays up front.

- **Table centrepieces** Avoid large displays at eye level, as they'll block guests' views of one another – keep things low, or go for tall and thin. Alternatives to flowers are listed on p.168.

DIY rose petal confetti

Fancy leaving the ceremony in a swirl of scented petals? A decent quantity from a confetti supplier will set you back about as much as a marquee, so if you've got access to a rose bush from which you can harvest some blooms it's well worth making your own. Fresh petals will spoil in a matter of hours, so gently dry yours to preserve scent and colour. Lay the petals in a single layer on a baking tray. Stick them in the oven at 100°C (210°F), then whip them out just as they start to shrivel, so that they're dry but not crisp – it'll only take a few minutes, so keep on the case. Stored in an airtight container, they'll keep for a few months.

💜 **For the cake** Fresh flowers can be used to decorate the cake. Tiny plastic vases (resembling a biro lid) can be sunk into the icing to keep flowers watered.

💜 **Petals for flower girls/confetti** (see box above).

Which flowers?

Flowers vary enormously in price, so you'd be wise to find out likely costs before setting your heart on a particular bloom. If you want orchids or armfuls of roses you'll soon rack up an enormous bill, but there are plenty of more reasonably priced flowers, so a small budget needn't mean scanty arrangements. Here are a few other things to bear in mind when choosing your flowers.

💜 **Colour** You'll want your flowers to be an integral part of any colour scheme. For the bouquets and hair flowers, think also about complexion, hair colour and dress colour. Although white's the traditional colour for the bride's bouquet, white on white may look washed out, particularly in the photographs.

💜 **Durability** Especially for the bouquets, which will be out of water all day, durability is important. A good florist will be able to suggest long-lasting alternatives for most things.

💜 **What's local and in season?** Local, seasonal flowers are both environmentally friendlier than their air-freighted fellows, and likely to be cheaper too. Check out tinyurl.com/flowersinspring for a slideshow of flowers in season in spring; click the links to see winter, autumn and summer flowers.

Fairtrade flowers

Growing flowers on an industrial scale involves the use of harmful pesticides and other chemicals. This is a particular problem with **roses** and other flowers grown in the developing world. Using fairtrade flowers means you can feel confident workers are adequately protected, and receive a fair wage too. There are a small but growing number of fairtrade-certified flowers on the market. You may struggle to find a florist who'll source them for their arrangements, but there are plenty of online wholesalers if you want to take the DIY route. See tinyurl.com/fairtradeflowers for more info.

❤ **Subtle messages?** The traditional "language" of flowers means you really can pin your heart on your sleeve: red roses for true love, violets for faithfulness, etc. (There's the odd negative connotation, too – yellow roses signify jealousy. But don't let that stop you using them if you think they look pretty!) See tinyurl.com/flower-language for a comprehensive list.

❤ **Formality** Cottage-garden flowers will contribute towards an informal atmosphere, while glossy hothouse blooms will ramp up the glamour of the day. The number of different flowers used also has an effect: arrangements of just one or two types tend to look more formal.

❤ **Scent and allergies** If you or your guests are going to sit close to arrangements, consider their scent. Lilies and hyacinths can be overpowering. Likewise, take account of any hay-fever sufferers. Some people choose silk or other artificial flowers if they have a real problem with pollen. Non-flower arrangements (see below) are also worth considering.

❤ **More radical options** Think beyond flowers. Especially if you're marrying in winter, when little's in season, consider arrangements of foliage, branches, berries – even fruit.

Who'll arrange them?

The flowers will need arranging no more than 24 hours in advance and setting up on the day itself, so if you're considering the **DIY option** be realistic about how much time you'll have to spare. Be realistic, too, about what you can achieve: bouquets and hair flowers especially

Four flower heroes

❤ **Hydrangea** With blooms up to eight inches across, hydrangeas are sturdy, reliable, and not afraid of a big space.

❤ **Daffodils** Marrying in early spring? Steer clear of Valentine's Day price hikes for roses, and fill your arms and venues with bucketloads of daffs.

❤ **Carnations** One of the cheapest flowers out there, carnations are the poor man's roses, and come in a huge range of colours.

❤ **Gerbera** With their big daisy heads in all colours of the rainbow, gerbera are great for adding dash to larger arrangements. They're also cheap as chips.

Four tips to score more bang for your buck

- ♥ If you've set your heart on a particular flower, save it for your **bouquet** and use similar-looking, cheaper alternatives for the other arrangements.

- ♥ Those fashionable bouquets of tightly packed roses were surely dreamed up by florists with an eye to a hefty price tag: get a similar effect more thriftily by substituting **carnations** or **ranunculus**.

- ♥ **Bulk out** expensive showpiece flowers with trusty supporting players (such as baby's breath), foliage and ribbons (in large bows or trailing).

- ♥ **Be flexible**. If impact is what matters, and you trust your florist, give them free rein to scour the flower markets for bargains and cook you up something with the finds.

need skilled assembly if they're to stand up to the rigours of the day. One option is to get a **florist** to do the tricky on-the-body pieces, and decorate the venues yourself. If you're getting married in a church, the regular **guild of flower arrangers** may offer to do your ceremony flowers for you: it'll save you money, though you'll lose some control – try to pop in on a few different Sundays to see their work before committing.

Hiring a florist

Service varies considerably: as ever, your best bet is a recommendation. Make sure the florist has **experience** of wedding flowers, and ask to see photos of their previous work. You'll probably need to reserve a florist about four months in advance, and to attend a planning meeting about eight weeks before the day. Take as much information as you can to this meeting: photos of dresses and venues, pictures of bouquets you particularly like. Give your florist a **firm budget** and ensure they understand it's not to be exceeded: ask for an itemized price list to ensure your money's being spent wisely.

Buying and arranging your own flowers

Ask around for **local wholesale flower markets** willing to sell to the general public – some will only deal with "trade" customers. Visit in advance to familiarize yourself with the setup and ask any questions.

These markets do their business in the early hours of the morning, so be prepared to get up at an unearthly hour. An alternative is to **buy online**. This has the advantage that you can order weeks in advance and from the comfort of your sofa. But if you're likely to fret about possible hitches – after all, there'll be little time to make alternative arrangements should your delivery not show up – this may not be the best option for you. Once you've got your flowers home, you'll need to **keep them cool** (in the garage is ideal), with their stems in buckets of water, until you're ready to use them.

If you are doing your own arrangements, your best bet is to **keep things simple**. If your flower-arranging expertise is nil, you can even stick to single showpiece blooms in tall, slim vases. Beyond that, it's all about preparation. On the day, you'll be under considerable time pressure, so make sure you've done your homework and have a clear plan of action. Be sure to enlist one or more extra pairs of hands, too.

- Videojug has an excellent series of **video tutorials** covering all your wedding flower needs, from making a buttonhole to arranging flowers in a vase (see videojug/tag/flowers).

- If you've little or no experience, or need to brush up your skills, a **flower arranging course** could be money well spent: you'll still have saved money overall, and you'll have learned a new skill to boot.

- **Practise** the arrangements in advance – if necessary, using cheaper flowers than you'll have on the day.

- Ensure you've got all the **sundries** you'll need: ribbon, pins, tape, wire, buckets of water and vases.

Flowers resources

Paula Pryke, *Wedding Flowers*. Traditional or experimental, Paula Pryke's arrangements are consistently classy, fresh and modern. At £20/$30, this hardback isn't cheap – and it may well inspire you to spend more on flowers rather than less – but inspired you certainly will be.

DIY-flowers.co.uk is a UK-based flower wholesaler catering to the amateur florist. Their prices aren't the cheapest around, but the advice and support (including a complimentary booklet of care instructions and arranging techniques) could be useful if you're feeling out of your depth.

Tossing your bouquet – the alternatives

With its message that all women are desperate to be married, tossing the bouquet is another of those traditions that makes many a modern couple squirm. What if your best mate lands one on your maiden aunt in the ensuing scrum? What if all your commitment-phobe friends dodge it and it lands on the floor? What if your long-coupled-up-but-still-not-engaged pal finds herself alone in the catching zone, her desperation plain for all to see? If you fear the worst, there are plenty of alternatives to take the pressure off:

♥ Dismantle your arrangement and distribute **a flower** to each of your female guests.

♥ Present your bouquet to the **longest-married couple** in the room.

♥ Go with the usual scrum, but insist the **men try for it too**.

♥ **Keep it for yourself!** You can even get it preserved for posterity (though there's a whiff of Miss Havisham in that).

Good hand–eye coordination is a must for wannabe bouquet-catchers.

Other decorations

A wedding with no flowers at all would be unusual. But there are other means of decoration that can brighten a space for a far smaller outlay. Use them to supplement your floral displays, or – perhaps if you're allergic or simply not a flower fan – go the whole hog and have flower-free festivities. **Scope out your venue** in advance, taking pictures if necessary: there may be ugly corners that need concealing, or dull walls that want cheering up. And rope in friends to form a **decorating team**: if setup needs to be done on the day itself, you may have to leave them to it. Here are a few suggestions:

- **Photos** of you as kids, and of your life together so far. Set up displays on the walls or in a quiet corner, or put a different set on each table.

- **Helium balloons** are great for adding height to table centrepieces without obscuring guests' view. Helium canisters are available for hire. Remember you need extra-strong balloons to hold helium. They don't last for ever, so blow them up as late as possible, or they'll start bobbing and sinking before dinner's over.

- **Bunting** is perfect if you've a marquee/tent or outdoor space to decorate and it's a cinch to make. Cut triangles of fabric (using pinking shears for a serrated edge), fold over one edge and sew a hem, then thread onto string.

- **Ribbon** is also useful for a marquee/tent: wrap the pillars with overlapping ribbons in maypole style. At any venue you can tie ribbon bows to chair backs and the front edge of your top table, and use ribbon in place of napkin rings.

- **Candles** work in all shapes and sizes. Narrow ones add height to table centrepieces while tealights are cheap and can be dotted all around. Bear in mind safety when planning arrangements: you don't want the tablecloths or worse going up in flames.

- **Fairy/holiday lights** are a safer alternative to candles and can be used to surround a door frame, peep out from among a large flower arrangement or trail along a windowsill. Be sure to check the location and availability of power sockets, and arrange extension leads if needed.

Tip

Nothing gives more bang for your buck than balloons. They're great for filling a large space with colour – just don't get too carried away or you'll look like you're hosting a kids' party.

13 Photos and Video

Sure, you can squirrel your dress away in a closet, get your bouquet preserved and freeze a layer of your cake, but none of these really brings back the full picture of that fleeting moment that was your wedding day. Photos and a video are your best bet for capturing the atmosphere and sense of excitement that marked your big day (not to mention how fabulous you both looked). And if you're lucky, they'll form treasured possessions to be displayed for years to come. That said, photos and video should be a record of a great day, not your primary purpose.

Photos

Good photographers get **booked up early** – almost as quickly as do the most popular venues – so don't expect to find one at the last minute. But don't rush to choose one either: your photos are about the only part of your wedding that'll last for ever, so you want them to do it justice. For the same reason, this is not an area to skimp on. With photography, **quality really does tell**: training, equipment and experience don't come cheap. By asking the right questions from the start, you can ensure you get the real deal and not an overpriced disappointment.

Which photographer?

Friends or family may volunteer to do your wedding photography, but unless they're in the business themselves, this is an offer you should almost certainly decline. There's a lot more to wedding photography than point and shoot: crowd control, dealing with inclement weather, time management, coaxing a dazzling smile out of a nervous or shattered bride… It's all best left to the professionals.

♥ Sidestep the classifieds and ask around for **recommendations** – many of the best wedding photographers don't advertise, word of mouth alone guaranteeing them a steady stream of work.

A shot of all your guests posing together works best on steps or a slope.

❤ Your best bet is a small studio or an **individual**, rather than a large operation. They're likely to be cheaper, and to take a more personal approach to your requirements. If you do go with a big studio, make sure to meet the person who'll be photographing your wedding, not sales staff, and insist their name is specified in the contract.

❤ Make sure your photographer is in the business full time, **specializes in weddings** and is passionate about them: you don't want some wannabe big shot doing this to make ends meet while they wait to get noticed by *Vogue*.

❤ Ask to **see their work** – complete albums, that is, not carefully selected "greatest hits". Try to see beyond stunning settings and catwalk-fodder brides: are the shots well composed and varied? You'll soon get an idea of a photographer's **personal style**: does it fit with the look you'd like for your day?

❤ Make sure you feel a **rapport** with your photographer: they're going to be hanging around you on your big day, and you need to be able to relax and have fun in their company if you're going to end up with the shots you want. If they put your hackles up or seem a real bore, keep looking.

How it works

The photographer will take many shots on the day; now that most are using **digital** it's likely to be many hundreds. They'll send you **proofs** of these, from which you select the pictures you'd like enlarged and put in your **album**. Proofs used to be small prints which you had to return once you'd made your selection, but photographers using digital are more likely to send you a **CD** or make the images available for viewing **online**; in either case, the images are likely to be low-resolution or watermarked. Online proofing systems win top marks for convenience, making it much easier for loved ones to buy prints, but when choosing your photographer, remember your priority should be the quality of their work, not their web-savviness. Your photographer probably won't sell you the **negatives** or **high-res images**, as they rely on selling extra prints for a large part of their income.

Work that camera!

"Picture your photographer naked. Or better, picture your new spouse naked, and let those happily married smiles take care of themselves." – JEAN

"Get rid of your audience if they're making you feel self-conscious: see if you and your photographer can find a quiet corner for those intimate couple pics." – TOM

"I've always had trouble relaxing in front of the camera, so I went for a spot of "immersion therapy": a friend and I spent an evening photographing me and going over the results until we'd found a smile I could live with and replicate on the day." – LIZ

"Forget "engaging your abs", standing at an angle and holding your elbows away from your body. You'll end up looking stiff and unnatural. Just stand up straight, relax and smile." –LAWRENCE

"Neither I nor Dave enjoy having our photos taken. We went for a basic package, and simply relaxed and talked between ourselves while the photographer did his work. We don't have an elaborate album, but we have a few good shots as a record of our day." – KATE

Tip

When choosing a photographer, check what their policy is on guests' photos. Some insist no other photos are taken of the event, or at least of groups they have posed. If this is going to upset your guests, find a photographer who's more laid-back.

Guests' photos

Gone are the days of putting disposable cameras on each reception table and ending up with a heap of blurry pictures of the ceiling. Now that most of your guests will probably have a better camera than that on their phone, it's an unnecessary expense. Instead, work on making it easy for your guests to give you copies of their best shots – see box on p.174 for tips on publishing photos online.

Here are a few suggestions for making use of the images when you get them:

❤ **Digital albums** (where the photos are printed directly onto the pages rather than being mounted on them) are the latest hot trend among wedding photographers. Create your own using the "photo book" service at Photobox (photobox.co.uk) or Kodak Gallery (kodakgallery.com).

❤ For a more old-school, tactile memento, get some prints done and stick them in a **scrapbook** along with the order of service, pressed flowers from your bouquet, your speech script, etc.

❤ Print personalized **thank you cards** at moo.com. Each card can have a different image, so pick one specially for each addressee, perhaps one of you and them together.

What it costs

Different photographers have different pricing structures. Some have wedding **"packages"** specifying a set number of hours' work and number of pics in your album. Others will charge an **hourly rate**, or will simply **charge per picture** and build the cost of their time into that price. Make sure you find out what they'll charge for **extra prints**, and ask to see an example of the **album** itself – they vary markedly in quality, and poor-quality albums can make your photos deteriorate. Beware of cheap deals that include only a few prints in your final album: canny photographers know that once you see the pics you'll want loads more, and will charge a premium for supplying them. Once you've reached an agreement, get all the details in writing, and check the **small print** for hidden extras – overtime, travel expenses, etc – as well as their deposit and refund policy.

What pics and when?

These days, there's a lot more to wedding photography than endless **posed shots** of the couple sandwiched between various combinations of relatives: **reportage-style** work, where the photographer roams around your party capturing informal moments, is increasingly popular, and can make for a much more interesting album. Most probably you'll be looking for some combination of the two: reportage takes the pressure off if you haven't the patience to pose, or feel camera-shy, but those posed shots will always be in demand for relatives' mantelpieces. Here's a rundown of some key moments you may want captured on camera:

♥ **Preparations at home** Your hairdresser at work, that first glance in the mirror, tearful last-minute advice: all this can be preserved for posterity. Of course, if the house is likely to be a war zone once five bridesmaids have fought over the curlers and croissants, you may prefer this particular part of the day to go unrecorded.

♥ **During the ceremony** Check with your officiant whether photography is permitted during the ceremony. They may not allow it, or may restrict it to certain parts of the proceedings, such as the signing of the register.

♥ **Formal posed shots** These are usually done between the ceremony and the reception. And it's best to get them out of the way at this point: hair and make-up will still be holding up, and you won't want to be dragged away from the party later on. Work out a shot list, consulting with your photographer about what will be feasible within the time slot available. One increasingly popular memento is a shot of **all your guests together**, which you can blow up and hang on your wall; this may need some planning, as you'll need a slope, steps or a high vantage point for the photographer to ensure everyone can been seen.

♥ **During the reception** This is where the reportage-style work comes into its own. But if you don't want to pay your photographer to stick around for the entire reception, you could rely on guests' photos for this part – there's likely to be the odd corker amongst them. If you choose this option, you can toss your bouquet and mime cutting the cake right after the formals so your professional can take care of these shots before leaving.

♥ **Decorations and location** After all that hard work, you'll want some record of those painstakingly crafted favours and flower arrangements, the venue and that extortionately expensive car: make sure someone gets it all on film.

Publishing photos online

Whether you want to display your wedding photos to everyone you know, or you're looking to make something more exclusive, it's easy and inexpensive to post images online. The easiest way to get the job done is by uploading them to Facebook, or perhaps a more photo-oriented community such as FotoThing or Flickr:

❤ **Facebook** facebook.com

❤ **Flickr** flickr.com

❤ **FotoThing** fotothing.com

If you have signed up for Microsoft's Windows Live services, utilize the Photo Gallery features to share the pictures; if you are a Mac user, you have several options open to you from the most recent version of the built-in iPhoto program. It allows you to pub-lish your photos directly to Facebook and Flickr (see above), or when signed up with Apple's MobileMe you can upload directly to your very own Web Galleries with the click of a button.

❤ **MobileMe** apple.com/mobileme

❤ **Windows Live** photos.live.com

You might also want to investigate Google's Picasa picture management application. Whatever you use to organize and store your photos at the moment, Picasa is worth looking at as an alternative, and its Web Albums feature gives those with a (free) Google account a wealth of online space for displaying a wedding album.

❤ **Picasa** picasa.google.com (PC & Mac)

There are also many services that, for a small fee, will provide you with a ready-made photo gallery online. For instance:

❤ **Fotki** fotki.com

❤ **Phanfare** phanfare.com

DIY photo printing and wedding albums

Given the surprisingly high print quality that can be achieved with a relatively inexpensive domestic printer, putting together a wedding album at home is a real option, can be a lot of fun, and might be a great way to save a few pennies if you are planning your big day on a tight budget.

Of course, if you are going to go down this road you need to get hold of the photos from the day as image files, normally JPEGs, though any image format will do. What does matter is that the files are of a **quality good enough to print** – as a rule of thumb, if the image file is bigger than 1Mb in size, it will print out just fine up to about A4/Letter size. Most professional photographers won't give you their high-resolution images but you could create an album using guests' photos to complement a professional's more formal shots.

As for touching up and tweaking your shots, any computer bought in the last couple of years will more than likely have some basic image manipulation software built-in. There is also a very good, free-to-use online picture editing tool called **Pixlr** (pixlr.com) that's worth investigating. If you do start playing with contrast, saturation, "warmth" etc, make sure you keep an original copy of each file, just in case it all goes horribly wrong.

Perhaps the only real drawback is that home-printed images kept out in a frame **tend to fade** much faster than those created in the traditional way at a lab. That said, as long as you have access to the original files, you can simply reprint the image every time it starts to look a little tired. You could also use one of the many "**print on demand**" photo services found online, which offer anything from individual prints to professionally bound albums with whatever finish you might desire. Among the best services out there are Photobox (photobox.com) and Kodak Gallery (kodakgallery.com).

Videos

A wedding video is by no means an essential piece of kit – before shelling out, it may be worth considering how many times you're likely to watch it. However, for a sense of really "being there", video wins hands down and so could be a real boon if someone special to you can't be with you on the day (talk to your officiant if this is the case – they may be more accommodating than usual about filming the ceremony). It'll also likely show you things you missed on the day, and can preserve those speeches for posterity (though the downsides of this are readily apparent!).

If you're not bothered about slick editing and special effects, you may be better off saving your cash and asking a **friend or relative** to hold the camera – you can edit the footage and add background music yourself on your computer (see box overleaf). As with photography, however, be prepared for the end result to be more YouTube than Discovery Channel.

As for choosing a **professional**, the same advice applies as for stills photographers: follow recommendations, ask to see their work, and go for someone whose style and personality you like.

> ### Tip
>
> Some videographers like to collar guests for an impromptu "piece to camera". If you think your guests might wilt under that kind of pressure, consider installing a video booth that they can visit at their leisure: their more considered messages can be incorporated into the final video.

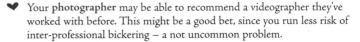

❤ Your **photographer** may be able to recommend a videographer they've worked with before. This might be a good bet, since you run less risk of inter-professional bickering – a not uncommon problem.

❤ When watching demo videos, remember the **sound** is at least as important as the pictures: are the vows drowned out by background noise?

❤ Confirm in writing what **editing**, **graphics** and **background music** are included in your package.

❤ Check what **format** your video will come in: can they supply a copy on VHS for your granny? They will probably encrypt DVDs to prevent you making copies, so find out what they'll charge for extras.

DIY video and editing

Gone are the days of second-rate DIY wedding videos with shaky camera work, endless shots of tablecloths and the occasional snippet of whichever movie happens to have been on the VHS that was being taped onto.

Most **camcorders** these days record either to a built-in hard disk or MiniDV tape. Both allow for TV-quality end results, and both allow you to edit your footage to a professional standard on any half-decent computer, using relatively intuitive software: on a PC go with Windows Live Movie Maker, and on a Mac iMovie. Both these applications come preinstalled on new machines and offer roughly the same tools.

Though a detailed walkthrough of the **editing process** is way beyond the scope of this book, the basic idea is to drag and drop chunks of your footage in a timeline, use "transitions" and "fades" to smooth over the cracks between clips, add music and commentary where necessary and splice in titles at the beginning and, if you wish, credits at the end (which always go down well with young bridesmaids, who love to know that their moment in the limelight has been recognized). Once you're done, use the "Export" or "Share" options to either burn your masterpiece to DVD or publish it straight to the Web. For more detailed help with all this, visit:

❤ **Windows Live Movie Maker** download.live.com/moviemaker

❤ **Apple iMovie** apple.com/ilife/tutorials

On the big day itself, make sure that whoever's playing cameraman has a good idea of what you are after (and doesn't harbour delusions of being the next Ridley Scott), preferably has a decent-quality directional microphone connected to the camcorder and, most importantly, uses a tripod.

14 Gifts

Your wedding will probably elicit more presents for you than any other life event. It can be positively overwhelming, but if you can set aside any feelings of awkwardness at such collective extravagance, presents are a lovely side effect of tying the knot. Whether gifts are from a registry or your loved ones' own inspiration, they'll furnish your home and your lives with daily reminders not only of the givers but of your wedding day. You'll have the chance to give gifts in return, especially to those trusty souls who've helped make your day a reality, but for many of your guests a big thank you – and a party to remember – are all they'll want in return.

Gift registries

It's not so long since **gift lists** were considered just a little vulgar. These days, while of course it's not obligatory, a gift list is pretty much par for the course, and most guests are glad of one – it saves them hassle, and means they know they're getting you something you really want. Be careful not to imply that no other gifts will be welcome, however: the gift list should be presented as an **option** for those who want it, not a diktat of what's acceptable.

The standard gift list is registered with a **department store**. Some will even supply you with **hand-held scanners** and set you loose to roam the floors. Most will make the list available to guests **in-store** and **online** or over the **phone**, and will let you view what's been purchased and possibly top up or amend your list online too. **Online gift**

> *The wedding was ages away so we didn't bother looking at the gift list until nearer the time. What a mistake that was. There were a few things left but I didn't want to buy any of them! In the end, we went off-list and bought them an antique photo frame. I don't know if they liked it or not. But a Kenwood mixer wasn't in our price range and the cheaper things – toilet brush, soap dish, tea towels – were just too cheap and boring.*
>
> *Lucy*

Prepare for battle...

You love shopping, right? Especially when someone else is paying. Go about it the right way and choosing your gifts really can be fun, not fraught.

- ❤ **Do your homework** beforehand. Draw up a shopping list, and discuss your overall philosophy for those big choices: do you want formal crockery for dreamed-of dinner parties, or a set that you can envisage actually using for your famous curry nights?

- ❤ **Pace yourself** and be prepared for the long haul. Remember how long it took you to choose that last set of bed linen? With all the choices you've got ahead of you, you could be in here for weeks. At least you can expect to need a second trip.

- ❤ **Rest and restore**. Bring provisions for a crafty pit stop in the sofa department, or take regular trips to the café. Everyone knows your decision-making abilities are that of a drunkard when blood sugar or water levels drop too low.

registries are the fast-growing challenge to the department stores' dominance of the gift-list market. Generally working with a large stable of retailers, they can offer greater choice than even the biggest department stores; some can even arrange for the purchase of anything available on the web. They are, however, that much harder to get hold of when things go wrong.

Drawing up that list of normally out-of-reach desirables may sound like a blast, but the gift list is possibly the most common source of wedding frustration and misery. Items are discontinued; your list is muddled with that of a similarly named couple; items purchased are not removed from the list, resulting in duplicates; deliveries are postponed or incomplete…

Your only protection is to go with a store you trust – one that has good **customer service** to resolve the inevitable glitches. Ask married friends for their experience of local department stores, and if considering an unfamiliar online store, do an Internet search to see if you can dig up any dirt.

What to put on your list

♥ Make sure to include a **range of prices**. As well as providing options for cash-strapped mates, a range of small, cheaper items will allow guests to "top up" to the amount they want to spend. And don't be afraid to include some more expensive items – friends may like to club together for them.

♥ List plenty **more items than you expect to receive**, so latecomers aren't faced with slim pickings. Depending on which store you go with, you may be able to highlight **priority items**.

♥ Even if they know only one of you, most guests will want to buy **something for you to share**. That said, brides should remember that many ostensibly shared traditional list items are not particularly groom-friendly – unless you're lucky enough to have a kitchen whizz for a fiancé – so it might be politic to include some items which he can get excited about.

Tip

Many department stores offer the option of adding **gift vouchers** in various denominations to your list; these are a good way of getting your hands on expensive furniture or white goods that people are unlikely to buy you outright.

Cash, charity and other alternatives

If you've been living together a while, you may feel you've already accumulated all the bath mats and knife sharpeners you'll ever need. Never fear: there are plenty of alternative gift-list options these days (see box below).

Four alternative gift lists

♥ **Amazon.com** Already got an Amazon wish list as long as your arm? Make Amazon your wedding-list home and stock up on books, music, games and gadgets for those newly wedded nights in. Its ever-expanding range means you can still throw in the odd towel-bale for good measure.

♥ **Honeymoon registries** Rather than simply requesting money towards your honeymoon, invite guests to buy you specific "experiences": a candlelit dinner on the beach, an elephant ride… There are websites out there who'll arrange this for you, although the mark-up on those "experiences" can be extreme. See p.198 for more on honeymoon options.

♥ **Oxfam Unwrapped** Sign up for Oxfam's gift list service and guests can treat you (or rather the world's poor) to schoolbooks, drinking water or his'n'hers goats.

♥ **Your favourite local shop** That fab indie boutique down the road may well be willing to arrange a gift-list service for you – it'll be a hefty chunk of custom for them, after all. You may want to combine this with a more widely accessible option, to accommodate out-of-towners.

Or you may want to invite guests to give **money**, perhaps to put towards larger **furniture** items, a **house deposit** or a **honeymoon**.

Bear in mind, though, that if some still bridle at a gift list, many more are unhappy about being asked for money. In particular, cash with no specified purpose is unpopular – people don't want to feel they've simply covered the cost of their dinner. And even the honeymoon option will be offputting for some, who'd like to buy you something that'll last a lifetime, not a couple of rounds of cocktails in an expensive resort bar. The golden rule here is **know your audience** and, if necessary, test the water with the odd casual question. Make sure that any request for money is optional: don't put an outright embargo on other gifts, unless you want to offend.

If the rampant materialism of wedding gifts just doesn't fit with your life philosophy, consider **nominating a charity** to be the beneficiary of those guests who just won't take no for an answer.

Receiving and unwrapping

If you've a wedding list, the majority of your gifts will probably be delivered by the store all together some time after you return from honeymoon. But it's likely that some guests will still bring gifts along on the day. It's a good idea to have a **table** for these near the receiving line, with a glammed-up shoebox or other receptacle to act as **mailbox** for any cards. Especially if you've asked for money, you don't want these to get mislaid. Assign a member of the wedding party responsibility for looking after the gifts and cards, taking them home at the end of the

 The strangest gift we received was a hand-made pottery bowl. Which would have been lovely had it not been moulded in the shape of the giver's bottom. It gets a lot of use in our house all the same – just not as the table centrepiece it was designed to be. Instead, it's become our dog's favourite water bowl.
JEN

Saying thank you

Your honeymoon tan may be fading, but don't consider the wedding over until you've done your **thank-you cards**. Personalize them if you can by saying what a special part of your life that new toast rack will be, and how much you enjoyed their spirited dancing on the day. But don't neglect them altogether, unless you want to begin your married life with a store of puzzled resentment among your friends and family.

day, and keeping a discreet **note of who gave what** if any presents are unwrapped then and there. Do the same when opening presents later too – it's all too easy to go from one to the next and quickly lose track.

Gifts for attendants and helpers

It's customary to give gifts to your **best man** and **bridesmaids**, as thanks for their support and hard work. You might also want to give something to your **parents**, and to anyone else who made a particular contribution to your wedding day: doing a reading, singing during the ceremony, arranging the flowers… Gifts can be presented at your stag/hen/bachelor/bachelorette night, at the rehearsal dinner, or during the speeches at the reception, whichever suits best. A **bunch of flowers** or a good **bottle of wine** will act as a fine token, but following are a few suggestions if you want to give a little more to the real troopers in your bridal team.

As ever, you'll probably find the **girls** in your life easier to buy for. If given before the day, **jewellery** or a bottle of their favourite **perfume** could

Flowers for the mothers

It's traditional for the groom to dish out "thank yous" to a few key players during the speeches, along with a smattering of token presents. You really don't want to go over the top or the whole proceedings can end up feeling like school Prize Giving Day. That said, this is the perfect opportunity to make a special gesture towards your **mother** and brand spanking new **mother-in-law**.

Flowers are a great choice (they show your feminine side, assuming you have one) and even better is something that is going to last longer than the trip home in the car. Potted plants work well, as do traditional "trugs", ornamental rustic baskets planted up with… erm… plants – mums love 'em! Though you could use the same florist as for the rest of the wedding, it is probably better to use a separate firm, to avoid either mum catching wind of your heart-melting offering.

add the final touch to your attendants' outfit, while being something they really can wear again. If you feel they deserve pampering after weathering all those bridal tantrums, a **spa voucher** might be a good choice.

Parents might like **photo frames** or albums, either filled with childhood pics of you both, so they can get to know their new son or daughter, or ready to hold the wedding photos when they arrive. Alternatively, how about **dinner vouchers, theatre tokens** or **concert tickets**? See the box below for a spin on the traditional option.

For your groomsmen, think utility first. You might consider classics like monogrammed **flasks** filled with twelve-year-old Scotch, or customized **cuff links** to complete the wedding-day look. Even more useful are locking-blade **pocket knives** or **multi-tools** with a simple, personalized engraving on the handle. Each use will bring back some memory of your wedding, and the special role your groomsmen played that day. Or if you're not so bothered about the keepsake aspect, **tickets** to a gig or sporting event are another good option.

Favours

Sure, not every guest goes home with a thank-you gift under their arm – not unless you really went to town with the whole army-of-volunteers approach to wedding planning. But the custom of **favours** means no one leaves a wedding empty-handed. Favours are small tokens presented to each guest – either at their place setting or as they leave – to thank them for coming. However, they're by no means a universal custom, so you shouldn't feel obliged to go along with it if money is tight or you feel it's an extra complication.

As you research your wedding you'll likely come across adverts from hundreds of favour suppliers, tempting you with overpriced chocolates or soaps and tiny boxes or pouches in which to present them. But before you get carried away, remember favours are only meant to be a **gesture**. They're one of those "small" unplanned-for items that can eat a substantial hole in your budget, with any regrets about overspending compounded when you see a good number of them abandoned on the tables by forgetful guests. The good news is there are plenty of more economical options. If you're sick of the whole wedding industrial complex by this stage and would like at least some part of your wedding to be homespun and personal, favours are a great opportunity for some **low-risk DIY** – far less ambitious or critical than the cake or bouquets.

You could go the whole hog and make your own chocolates or cookies, or bulk-buy the goodies and focus your attentions on home-made wrappings. For something really personal, why not spend a couple of evenings crafting something with your partner? Remember that favours don't have to be a physical object: you can use them as another opportunity to spread the love worldwide. Here's a few ideas to get you started:

- ❤ Home-made **lavender bags** or **pot pourri**.
- ❤ **Sparklers** or **indoor fireworks**.
- ❤ Oxfam Unwrapped **water purification tablets**, a few square metres of **Amazon rainforest** or a **tree** planted on behalf of each of your guests, with a card to tell them.
- ❤ **Flower seeds** or **tree seedlings** that guests can take away and plant.
- ❤ A special **lottery ticket** for prizes later in the day.
- ❤ A little box of home-made **mini-cookies**.
- ❤ Personalized **fortune cookies**.
- ❤ **Fans** for an outdoor summer wedding.
- ❤ **Penny sweets** for a retro feel.
- ❤ Lego **mini-figures** for the geeky wedding.

15 The Other Parties

Your wedding may be the mother of all parties, but it spawns a series of satellite celebrations along the way. With any luck, you won't be taking the strain of organizing most of these, but you may want to stick your oar in from time to time. Here's everything you need to know in order to direct proceedings from the sidelines.

The engagement party

When you tell them you're getting married, you may find your parents offer to throw you an engagement party as a formal way of spreading the news. If they don't, you can always throw your own. A formal engagement party is by no means obligatory, however. Friends and family will want to congratulate you in person, but you could just as well fill up your diaries with a series of **dinner dates** or **drinks outings**, so as to touch base with people on a more intimate basis.

If you do want to go the whole hog and have a "proper" engagement party, be sure to get moving pretty sharpish. It shouldn't be too close to the wedding itself, and if you're hosting it yourselves, you'll need to get this mini-project off your desks so you can get going with the wedding planning proper. For the same reason, **don't make it too big a deal**: it's not a dry run for the wedding – rather, you'll want to save your ener-

Tip

If lots of your guests won't know many other people, have each person wear a **name tag** showing their name and their relationship to you. Alternatively, create your own ice-breaking discussion pieces in the form of **photos** of your life together so far, positioned strategically around the room.

gies and best ideas for the real thing. You'll want to provide drinks and nibbles and perhaps some music (see Chapters 9 and 11 for help with this), but don't get dragged into specially printed invites and floral centrepieces unless you have a serious masochistic streak.

If you're just having a few **informal drinks** after work, there's no harm in inviting all and sundry, but if you're having a more formal party, don't invite anyone you suspect may not make it onto your **final guest list** for the wedding: an engagement party invitation will raise expectations that ought not to be dashed.

The bridal shower

One tradition that has yet to cross the Atlantic is the bridal shower. Sadly for UK brides, this is one exotic wedding ritual you most probably *won't* get the chance to emulate. Of course, even in the US you can't just throw your own: you have to wait for someone to throw one for you. But the chances are someone will come up trumps for you – and quite possibly more than one.

Showers are usually held a couple of months before the wedding; any closer to your big day and you'll have too much else on your mind. Unlike bachelorette parties (see opposite), showers are generally **family-friendly** affairs, to which you can safely invite any grannies or younger relatives. The gifts are, of course, the main entertainment, but it's common to play a couple of **games** and have some refreshments, perhaps cake. **Gifts** are opened there and then, so everyone can see what you got and how you react (rehearse expressions of delight if you think there's any danger they won't come spontaneously). Get someone to subtly keep a note of who gave what, to help with your thank-you notes.

There's no need to get overly involved in planning your shower: others will probably enjoy the chance to get in on the party-planning action, while you've already got enough on your plate. The only area you ought to keep particular tabs on is the **guest list**. Any guest invited to a shower will have to be invited to the wedding, so make sure your host's list of invitees doesn't include anyone who didn't make the cut. And if you're having multiple showers, make sure the guest lists don't overlap beyond the bridal party and close family members – or people will be obliged to buy you multiple gifts. Showers are usually **women-only**, but there's no reason why your fiancé or close male friends can't come along.

Last night of freedom!

While these parties go by different names – **stag and hen** parties in the UK, **bachelor and bachelorette** parties in the US – the basic principle is the same: one last night of freedom before you settle down to your new life of domestic bliss. These days it's unlikely to be much of a watershed – most probably you've not considered yourself "free" to get up to any funny business for quite some time now, and being married won't prevent you from going on the odd bender with your single pals. But it remains a chance, amid all the wedding-related activities, to celebrate some of the other important relationships in your life – to commit some quality time to **bonding with your closest friends**.

Who exactly constitutes your "closest friends" can be your first headache: if you're finding it hard to draw the line, one option is to invite a select group for the whole day, and invite others to join you just for the evening. While the bridal shower gives girls in the US the chance to involve all the special females in their life, without putting

Stag parties can be as elaborate as a weekend of skydiving or as simple as a slap-up dinner for the boys.

the brakes on any bachelorette outrageousness, UK brides might want to consider including a family-friendly activity before the real action kicks off.

These parties are traditionally organized by the **best man** or **maid of honour**, with the details kept secret from you until the day itself. But you may well need to give them guidance and support, in particular with drawing up the **guest list**. Even if you trust them wholeheartedly, there's no harm in dropping a few heavy hints about the kind of party you'd prefer, also talking through what's absolutely **not acceptable**, and what the **budget** should be.

On this point, stag and hen nights are increasingly turning into weekends, with dinner, drinks and dancing extending into pricey pampering sessions or extreme sports lessons, and the whole thing taking place in another city or even country. While flying abroad simply to spend your time on the inside of a bar is hard to excuse in our climate-conscious world, even local parties can raise cost issues. Weddings are expensive for guests as well as hosts – what with outfits, accommodation, gifts, etc – and a luxury hen/stag weekend could be a bridge too far for some. Rather than be faced with dwindling numbers or reluctant participants, be sure to consider your guests' bank balances when making your plans.

These parties were customarily held the night before the wedding – but this is one tradition now wisely ignored by most, hangovers and weddings not making good bedfellows. Arranging for your respective parties to take place the **same night** is a good plan since it prevents any stewing about what your other half is up to. As for ensuring you have nothing to worry about on that score, the golden rule is **communication**: make sure you let each other know what you consider reasonable behaviour, and pass this on to your best man or maid of honour. See p.207 for more on stag and hen fallout.

Stag party ideas

There is no escaping the fact that the bachelor or stag party has fallen into the same pot of commercialism as Easter or Mother's Day. Where once the event might have been marked by a few drinks in a favourite haunt followed by a curry, today the norm involves an entire weekend, along with fancy-dress costumes or perhaps T-shirts printed with the groom's face.

> *I wanted to be able to celebrate with my female friends – they're just as important to me as my male friends – so I had a hag do as well.*
> **Matt**

Going co-ed

Why should some of your dearest mates miss out on the fun simply because they're the "wrong" sex? There is, of course, nothing to prevent your having **male hens** or **female stags** – and we're not just talking gay best-friends. A joint hen-stag party may raise a few more eyebrows ("Can't you bear to be apart even for one night?!"), but if most of your friends are shared it can feel like the most natural thing in the world.

While the wedding day will likely require a degree of restraint and "best behaviour", this can be a chance for your united friendship group to send you off in style. An increasingly popular option is to split along gender lines during the day but **reunite** in the evening at a restaurant or club.

If you fall into the camp that says you should make this a weekend not to be forgotten and hang the expense, here are a few ideas for possible activities to incorporate.

♥ Mini Panzer tank **paintballing.**

♥ **Zorbing** (rolling down a hill in a large plastic ball).

♥ **Archery.**

♥ **Watersports** are always a winner (surfing, kayaking, sea fishing, etc).

♥ Indoor **skydiving.**

♥ **Quad biking** (or anything else you can find with a noisy motor).

♥ **Sumo wrestling** (in oversized rubber fat suits… you will never have laughed as much).

On the other hand, if you'd prefer something less physically active for your stag do, there are plenty of alternative options, and they don't have to break the bank either.

♥ A **pub crawl** back in your old college town (assuming you don't still live there).

♥ Going to a **music festival.**

♥ A wilderness **camping trip.**

♥ Top seats to see your **sports team** play (fans of other teams will have to support them, like it or not).

♥ Organizing a weekend trip around a **cultural festival.**

♥ A day at a **theme park.**

And for the girls…

While the "traditional" hen/bachelorette formula is well established – including such questionable accessories as veils, male strippers and forfeits – there's no reason to go along with that if it doesn't float your boat. It's hardly a tradition of long standing, after all – bachelorette and hen nights only really took off in a big way in the 1980s. Your best bet is probably going for a **supersized version** of the things you usually enjoy doing together, rather than following someone else's idea of a good time. With that in mind, these suggestions are merely intended to get your own ideas flowing. Most of them are achievable on a small budget, and none of them involve strange men getting their bits out…

- Have a **DIY pampering day**: an afternoon in a luxury spa may be beyond your budget, but you can recreate the experience at home. Ask each guest to come armed with props to offer her very own spa treatment, whether that be a manicure, hair braiding or a face massage. Make sure everyone gets to both pamper and be pampered.

- Hold a **movie night**. See *The Rough Guide to Chick Flicks* for the best girl-bonding movies of all time, or turn to p.237 for wedding-themed suggestions.

- Create your first heirloom by holding a **quilting bee**: at these traditional gatherings, each participant stitches a patchwork block for inclusion in a "friendship quilt" that's presented to the hostess. (See tinyurl.com/quilt-making for patchworking basics.)

- Hold a **safari supper**: have pre-dinner drinks at one girl's house, starter at another, main at another, and so on. Any guests who live too far away to host can provide an entertainment between courses.

- Have an old-fashioned **sleepover**. Get out your cutest pyjamas, stock up on midnight-feast goodies, magazines and music, and prepare to push on till dawn.

- Go **learn a new skill** together, whether that be salsa dancing, sailing, circus tricks or cookery.

- Book yourselves into a **self-catering cottage**, bolt the doors and have a man-free weekend of chilling out, cooking, drinking and exchanging stories and advice.

- Have a **poker night**: pop on your cocktail frocks, crack open the bubbly and turn your living room into an exclusive casino. Hire a cute croupier if your budget allows.

- Have a **picnic** in the park, followed by a game of softball or Frisbee.

The rehearsal dinner

As the name suggests, the rehearsal dinner is usually held directly after your **wedding rehearsal**, usually but not always the night before the wedding itself (see p.69). The guests are generally all those who've attended the rehearsal, plus their significant others and any other close family members. You might want to invite the odd other special person, and it's nice to include anyone who's travelled a particularly long way.

> *The hen do was one of the rare times that my friends and family from different parts of my life would all come together, so I tried to make sure there was something for everyone. We'd allocated a whole weekend, but not everyone had to join in with every activity. Some of us flew out to Dublin on Friday for a Robbie Williams concert, staying in a dorm room at a hostel to keep costs down. We spent most of Saturday lazily exploring Dublin. By the evening the others had arrived and we had a nice dinner, followed by a night of drinking and impromptu Irish dancing. The next morning we staggered out of bed and went to a day spa for some healthy, restorative treatments.*
> **MEGAN**

But don't go overboard – you'll be seeing everyone soon enough, and this is your chance to spend some quality time with those who are most important to you; on the day itself, you'll need to focus your efforts on speaking to everyone at least a little, so you won't be able to spend long with your nearest and dearest.

The rehearsal dinner is your cue to **relax** and start enjoying your wedding. It needn't be a formal affair – after all, there'll be plenty of formality the following day. You'll be pretty tired of party planning by this stage, so keep things **simple and casual**. Have pot luck, pizza or a barbecue, or head out to a restaurant so no one has to cook or wash up. Whatever you choose, don't turn it into an all-nighter: you'll need to turn in early, so you're well rested tomorrow. And, of course, **don't drink or eat too much**, and choose food that won't upset your stomachs.

16 Wedding Night and Honeymoon

Your wedding may be a celebration and a cementing of your relationship with one another – but with so many friends and family around to entertain, thank and generally talk to, it can often seem as if your new spouse is the one person you haven't connected with during the day. If, despite your best intentions, you find this is the case, never fear: that's what the wedding night and honeymoon are there for. They're a chance to hole up together for a fortnight, a week, or as long as you can manage and simply enjoy being husband and wife.

The wedding night

Where to stay

For some couples the wedding night and first night of the honeymoon are the same thing: they head straight off on honeymoon after the ceremony, perhaps spending the night in an airport hotel. But it can be less stressful to stay somewhere **near the reception venue** and head off at your leisure the next day, or even a few days later (giving you time to pack). That way, you can spend the morning after your wedding unwrapping presents, saying your goodbyes and generally reminiscing about the day before. If your reception has been in a hotel, try to **spend the night there** if you can. It saves on transport, and if some of your guests are also staying over you'll get to post-mortem the wedding with them over breakfast; by the time you get back from honeymoon it'll be old news. On the other hand, if you know you won't feel like being the centre of attention again the next morning, with everyone searching your hangover-crumpled faces for signs of wedding-night bliss, slip away to another nearby hotel or B&B.

What to pack

Even if you're heading straight off on honeymoon, make sure you've got a separate bag for your **overnight kit**: you'll have better things to do when you finally arrive in the room than rummage through suitcases. Aside from the basics of clothes and toiletries, don't forget the following:

- ♥ **First-aid kit** Stow a headache remedy, plasters (Band-aids) and any other medicines you're likely to want.

- ♥ **Car keys** If you've been thinking ahead, you'll have had your car moved to your wedding-night venue the day before; don't forget the keys!

- ♥ **Food and water** Many couples are so busy meeting and greeting that they hardly eat during their wedding – pack a few snacks in case you get the munchies, or ask the caterer to pack you a box of leftovers. Likewise, pack a big bottle of water to pre-empt hangovers.

Wedding-night brownie points for grooms

These days, many couples choose to spend their first night as man and wife relatively close to the venue, rather than having to rush straight off on their honeymoon and deal with airport check-ins and a long-haul flight. As well as being eminently sensible, it gives you a great opportunity to show just what a romantic soul you really are. Why not keep the location of your wedding night a secret from your partner, and book some fancy local hotel?

Whatever venue you choose to retire to after the party, it's a good idea to have prepared things in the morning, before the ceremony. How about some rose petals on the bed (but no thorny bits)? If there's a fridge, make sure there's some champagne on ice (even if you don't end up drinking it all, it's a cool gesture). Candles might be a good move, and some massage oil to get things started (though nothing too soporific, like lavender). You are both going to be fairly exhausted after the day's happenings, so you are going to need all the help you can get if you want to see any first-night action.

- ❤ **Comfy shoes.** It's easy to forget footwear when packing your clothes; don't put yourself in the position of having to squeeze party-battered feet back into the same itsy-bitsy heels that did the damage in the first place.

- ❤ **Presents for one another** Now's your best chance to exchange any gifts you have for one another.

Wedding-night sex

How common is it for you to have mindblowing sex after a long day on your feet, with liberal quantities of food, alcohol, dancing and small talk with distant relatives? If that's exactly the sort of thing to get you in the mood, then you're in luck. If not, don't expect your wedding night to buck the trend. That said, while it may not be your most elaborate and energetic performance, sex on your wedding night is likely to be one of your most emotionally charged, intimate times together. Throw what energies you have left in that direction: run a bath, pour one last drink, nibble some wedding cake or left-over canapés, talk over the day and focus on **romance and togetherness.**

If this will be the first time for either or both of you, the advice about expectations applies doubly, simply because the stakes are that much higher. **Talk to one another** in advance as much as you feel able about your expectations and hopes for this part of the day.

> ### Tip
> Flirt with each other (subtly!) during the reception, to get yourselves in the right frame of mind.

Getting in the mood: aphrodisiacs

As noted elsewhere in this chapter, if you want your wedding night to go with a bang, you're going to have to do something to counteract the fact that you and your new spouse are more than likely going to be zonked. One way is to dabble in the alchemical dark arts of the aphrodisiac. When it comes to sexy food, it isn't purely about the effect that ingestion can have. Some food is a turn-on because of the way it **looks** (asparagus, bananas), **smells** (truffles or liquorice, the latter particular effective for women) or **feels** (honey, chocolate, cream).

There is the **chemical influence** on the body to be considered as well. The aforementioned asparagus is said to heighten the sensitivity of sex hormone receptors; bananas are rich in potassium (essential for producing sex hormones); and it is no secret that the ingestion of zinc will keep men (and their sperm) at the top of their game – load up from pine nuts, sesame seeds, pumpkin seeds and yogurt. For more pointers, visit tinyurl.com/aphrodis. Still, however much you read about the potent powers of a particular dish (say oysters), if the thought of eating them turns your stomach, they aren't going to do much for your libido.

If you've still got the energy to carry her over the threshold…

If you partner does throw you a curve ball by falling asleep, fully clad, the moment they stumble across the threshold, don't take it personally. Likewise, don't let yourselves be upset if "performing" proves difficult through alcohol or nerves. Instead, how about saving yourselves for a spot of **post-wedding-morning sex** instead? Unless you seriously overdid it you'll wake up refreshed, with the stresses of the previous day a distant memory, and your honeymoon – and the rest of your lives together – to look forward to. And even if the morning brings only headaches and grumpiness, you've got your whole honeymoon ahead of you – no one's hangover lasts that long!

The honeymoon

Compared to the meticulous planning that goes into the wedding itself, organizing your honeymoon is a breeze. There's no agonizing over who to invite, what type of music you should play, or who's going to get lumbered with sitting next to the great uncle that nobody really knows. Indeed, it's the one part of the entire process where the only people you need to consider are yourselves. You might want to go for something quiet and simple after all the fuss of the wedding – or you might prefer to blow out on the trip of a lifetime. In either case, if you're going to do it right, you'll need to **start planning early**. Much the same rationale for sorting out the big day as far in advance as possible also applies to the holiday that comes after: generally speaking, the sooner you book your honeymoon, the cheaper things will be, and the more likely you are to get exactly what you want.

Planning your trip

Depending on the importance you place on your honeymoon, you might want to consider **where you want to go** and **what you want to do** (see p.199) at the same time as you decide on your wedding date – when you get married can determine your choice of destination. Having said that, there's nothing to stop you enjoying a couple of days' break immediately after the wedding (a "mini moon") and delaying your honeymoon proper until a later, more convenient date.

It's good to agree on a **budget** as early as possible. This might range from whatever's left once the wedding's been paid for to a size-able separate kitty. Remember, though, that this can be a good chance to do something that you may not have the money (or excuse) to do again. Some travel agents now operate honeymoon gift lists (see box overleaf), so you could raise extra funds that way.

You'll also need to decide who's going to **organize it**. As the bride-to-be is often responsible for more of the big wedding-day decisions, it can make sense for the groom to take on the job of planning the honeymoon. Keeping the honeymoon a secret from the bride may be a tradition, but remember that just because she once said she thought it

Tip

Be sure to book your flights in your maiden name. See p.222 for more on this.

> *Even if you normally take a suitcase twice the size of your partner's, I'd advise splitting your honeymoon packing between bags, just in case one goes astray. Unless, of course, you don't mind doing as I did and spending the first week of a once-in-a-lifetime Tanzanian safari wearing your new husband's underwear.*
>
> **SUSAN**

would be brilliant fun to go to bog-snorkelling in Ireland doesn't mean that she'd want to do it for her honeymoon.

Even if you'd normally buy your flights online and book your accommodation direct with the hotel, this is one holiday when, no matter who's doing the organizing, using a **travel agent** will likely be worth the additional expense. A good specialist tour operator will have someone you can speak to who has been where you want to go and stayed where you want to stay, and can advise you on everything from the feasibility of your itinerary to which local restaurants you'll need to book in advance. They'll also know what extras are available, and can arrange the relevant free room upgrades, complimentary champagne on arrival and all those other touches that can help make your honeymoon just that little bit more special. And should anything **go wrong** – flights can still get cancelled, luggage can still get lost, even though it's your honeymoon – you'll have the support of a company whose job it is to make things right.

Honeymoon gifts

A **honeymoon gift list**, a service offered by some travel agents, allows you to pay for your holiday with contributions from your wedding guests. It can be a good option for couples who have lived together for some time and already have the requisite crockery, or for those struggling to raise a big enough budget for their honeymoon, and can also make a refreshing change for guests (but see p.180).

With some gift lists, such as Trailfinders' (trailfinders.co.uk), guests make a donation to the overall cost of the honeymoon or flights. With others, like Honeymiles' (honeymiles.net), they can buy specific experiences from your itinerary. Some companies, including Turquoise (turquoiseholidays.co.uk), offer a bit of both.

If you're unsure who you want to book your honeymoon with or you want to do it independently (though see the note above), you could create a **honeymoon registry** instead. These services, such as honeymoney. co.uk and senduspacking.co.uk (in the UK) and honeymoonwishes.com (in the US), essentially act as online accounts, which hold your guests' "gifts" until you're ready to spend them. Some registries charge a set-up fee, and all levy commission (around 5–7 percent) on each contribution.

Choosing where to go

In the avalanche of questions you'll have to field once you've announced your engagement, "Where are you going to go on honeymoon?" is right up there on most people's want-to-know list, third only to "How did he pop the question?" and "When's the big day?" This, after all, might be the most amazing – and expensive – holiday you'll ever go on, so it goes without saying that you need to choose the right destination for you. Wherever you decide to go, and whatever you decide to do, it's important to consider the following factors:

❤ **When are you getting married?** A summer wedding in the UK and US means honeymooning in the southern hemisphere winter: Sydney could be grey, Cape Town rainy, and Patagonia under five foot of snow. At various times of the year, Southeast Asia, the Subcontinent and the Indian Ocean are affected by periodical monsoons, the Caribbean is hit by annual hurricanes, and many other countries have distinct wet seasons, where hotels shut up shop and travelling can sometimes prove difficult – all times of year that you'll want to avoid.

Home is where the heart is

When weighing up where to go on honeymoon, it's very easy to ignore what's on your doorstep: the merits of your **home country** can quickly get lost in excited talk of sugar-soft sands and gin-clear seas. There's nothing to say that you have to fly halfway around the world for the trip of a lifetime, though. The environment will thank you if you don't. Staying closer to home can be far more rewarding for you too – and not just for your bank balance.

You could use the time to explore your own backyard, going to places you've never quite got around to visiting and holing up in a hotel you'd normally never need stay at. You could venture slightly further afield by train and make the honeymoon the **journey** itself: maybe London to Venice on the Orient-Express, or the less luxurious but more epic Amtrak service from Boston to LA. Or you could try something completely new. You might have been to Cornwall before, but have you ever walked its spectacular South West Coast Path? And you might have "done" the Hamptons, but this time you could actually learn to sail there. Who said honeymooning at home had to be cheap?

> *Lynne and I honeymooned not far from home, on the Cornish coast. On the Tuesday, her parents turned up, expecting to hang out for the day. We ended up going on a boat trip round the bay, but my mother-in-law got seasick. While I leaned over the side of the boat to catch her false teeth in a bucket as she vomited into the ocean, I reflected that this wasn't the romantic break I'd envisaged – perhaps we should have gone further afield!*
> **DAVID**

❤ **What do you want to do?** Consider how you actually want to spend your time on honeymoon – there's no rule to say your honeymoon has to involve lying on a beach with a cocktail in your hand. One option is to go for a mega version of the kind of holiday you normally like to take, for instance walking the Inca Trail instead of your usual hiking weekends. Alternatively, think about doing something you wouldn't usually be able to afford, something that will stand out from all your other holidays together. Have you always dreamed of a safari in Botswana? Or do you want to do something completely different and go volunteering in Central America or backpacking around Asia? Whatever you do, you'll want to factor in some downtime, a few days on the beach at either the start or the end of the trip – safaris make a fantastic honeymoon but the early mornings can be tiring after a hectic wedding. Remember, too, that if you centre your honeymoon on an activity, such as diving or wildlife-watching, you'll also be restricted to certain times of the year and may have to change your destination – or wedding date – accordingly.

❤ **How much do you want to spend?** You'll have decided on your budget by now, but how do you want to use it? Do you want to spend more money on getting to a far-flung destination or will you stay closer to home and upgrade your accommodation? How many expensive extras – hot-air-balloon rides and the like – do you plan on doing? Remember to factor in, too, anything else that might not be included in the price, such as visas, alcoholic drinks and tips.

Greener long-haul honeymoons

Your honeymoon might be expensive but it needn't cost the earth. More and more couples are making their holiday an **environmentally friendly** one, and by taking a few moments to think about where you intend to stay, how you plan to get there and what you're going to do, there's no reason why you can't be one of them.

You'll reduce your carbon footprint considerably if you don't have to fly, but if you are honeymooning in a far-flung destination, you can "offset" any harmful emissions from your flight at sites such as carbonoffsets.org and carbonfund.org. Ask the company that you plan booking your trip with how they contribute to the local economy and if they've taken any steps to help protect the local environment – do they employ local people in their hotels? Is their accommodation solar-powered? Better still, book your tours with a local company or local guides and ensure that the money you spend is going straight back into the community.

Remember, though, that with the ever-increasing number of stylish eco-resorts, having a green honeymoon doesn't necessarily mean camping in a field with a bucket for a toilet. For an idea of how good an eco-resort can be – in more ways than one – check out Morgan's Rock in Nicaragua (morgansrock.com), Chumbe Island Coral Park in Tanzania (chumbeisland.com) or the Daintree Ecolodge in Australia (daintree-ecolodge.com.au).

17 The Big Day

As your wedding day approaches, here are some last-minute tips to ensure you're fully prepared to negotiate the final hurdles and make the most of those all-too-few celebratory hours that are the end result of all your hard work.

The final countdown

A few days before your wedding, **phone all your vendors** to confirm arrangements. Try to get this and any other final preparations done at least **36 hours** before kick-off, so that you can spend the final day winding down and savouring the moment. This really is important: if you're still running round like your pants are on fire just hours before you're due to say "I do", your mind and body will be in overdrive. Result: you'll feel like you're watching your day in fast-forward mode and, worse, a buzzing brain is less able to store memories, meaning whole patches of your big day will be a blank when you come to look back.

Avoid alcohol in the run-up to your wedding. It goes without saying that even the smallest hangover will take the edge off your just-married joy. **Keep your diet simple**, too: jittery nerves make for delicate stomachs.

Make time for some **exercise** the day before your wedding. Go for a run, a walk, a swim, and feel those last-minute worries sloughing off you. If exercise really isn't your thing, book a **massage**, or run yourself a long, hot **bath** – whatever it takes to take you out of yourself for an hour or so. It'll help with what ought to be top of both your to-do lists today: a good night's sleep.

Before you turn in, **lay out** all your clothes and accessories to check nothing is missing. If you're worried you won't be able to nod off, by all means take something to **help you sleep**. But don't use anything you've not tried before, just in case it doesn't agree with you.

Perhaps the thing most likely to help you sleep is **each other's presence**. It may be traditional to sleep apart the night before your wedding, but then the real traditionalists would have you sleep apart every night before your wedding, and make that kiss at the altar the first skin-on-skin contact you've ever had. Brides, by all means banish hubby-to-be Juliet-style at the crack of dawn, but if you're used to sleeping together – and, presumably, prefer it that way – why condemn yourself to a night in solitary just when you most need a calming presence?

The morning

Make sure you get going early enough in the morning that you've time to get ready at a calm pace. As a minimum, take the time you usually need to prepare for a really big night out and multiply it by two.

Be sure to eat a decent **breakfast** and drink plenty of **water** – no matter how close a fit your outfit is. For both of you, the bubbly will likely start flowing long before you next get to eat; being well fed and watered will stand you in good stead when it comes to coping with this.

Before you leap into the car, take a moment to make sure you've got everything. Grooms, that's the rings and your speech notes; brides, your bouquet, the emergency kit, your mum…

Tip

Brides: don't forget to wear a top with buttons this morning, so you can take it off easily after your hair and make-up have been done. Many a T-shirt has had to be removed with scissors from girls who forget this essential pre-wedding outfit rule!

Tip

Grooms: don't go and sit down at the front of the ceremony venue too early. Stay out in the fresh air as long as possible (though be sure you're in place five minutes before the bride arrives).

Your wedding-day emergency kit

It's only a party, right, not an assault on Everest? Take it on trust: at least some of the following will earn their keep.

Headache tablets ♥ Wipes to freshen up ♥ Vaseline for chafing necklines ♥ Spare stockings ♥ Breath mints ♥ Spare hairpins and hairspray ♥ Tissues ♥ Plasters (Band-aids) ♥ Deodorant ♥ Safety pins ♥ Pocket mirror and lipstick ♥ Powder ♥ Perfume ♥ Lipsalve ♥ Mascara ♥ Needle and thread ♥ Shot list for photographer ♥ Vendor phone numbers and mobile phone from which to call them ♥ Vendor tips and fees

Let your maid of honour help you with any last-minute adjustments before you head out the door.

And you're on...

First off, **relax**. Everyone's rooting for you. No one expects slick perfection from you in the vows or speeches. They just want you to be yourselves, and enjoy your moment. See p.212 for advice on handling those last-minute nerves.

One of the keys to a successful wedding day is **keeping on schedule**. If things start falling behind, problems will soon mount up: from overtime fees for photographers to a cold or overcooked wedding din-

Tip

Decide in advance who you plan to tip, and have the tips ready in sealed, labelled envelopes, so you don't have to worry about it at the time.

ner. Hopefully you've built some slack into your timetable to allow for unexpected hitches (see p.145 for more on this), but make sure to nominate someone cool-headed to keep things on track without chasing everyone about like a drill sergeant.

Something will go wrong. But weddings are such complex events – multiple phases, quite possibly multiple venues – that it's hard for even the most catastrophic cock-up to spoil the whole day. If a problem arises – the wedding car's got a flat, dinner's running late, the photographer's lens is broken – get someone on the case, then make good use of the delay: go talk to someone you've not spent enough time with yet. Have someone primed to deal discreetly with any **unacceptable behaviour** (from drunken uncles or emotional exes, perhaps). That way, you can safely ignore it, knowing it's under control.

It's ironic that on a day celebrating your relationship, you may not be alone together until the end of the night. Think about when you can **grab five minutes alone together**, and be prima-donna-ish about getting it if needed. A good time can be just after dinner, or immediately before your first dance.

Time to call it a night

It's traditional for guests not to leave before the bride and groom. So, if you're intending to dance the night away, let guests know they really needn't wait around for any grand farewell. That said, you'd be advised to leave before things get messy. Don't be tempted to hang on in there until the bitter end. Exit on a high – and leave others to do the tidying up.

18 Emotional Crises

It'd be a pity indeed if your engagement, marriage and first days of being wed weren't an emotional time for you both. But amid all the heightened romance and nuptial joy, there are more difficult emotions to handle too. Here's how to take them in your stride.

Being prepared

It may not be fashionable to say it, but if you're taking your vows seriously (and if you're not, then it's a lot of bother to go to for just a party), then no matter how long you've been living together, there's a **major life change** disguised underneath all those logistics: marriage signifies a shift in your relationship not only with one another, but with others too. Most notoriously, you're each inheriting a whole **new family**. But you may find your relationship with **friends** changing subtly too, as they adjust to the reality that your partner is now officially a permanent fixture, with first dibs on your loyalty and attention.

It's easy enough to let your **reasons for getting married** slip out of sight in the midst of a million small details and big decisions. But if you don't give yourself head space to explore your feelings, you may find they catch up with you later on, perhaps ambushing you when you return from honeymoon, or expressing themselves in irrational bridezilla-style outbursts. You'll get more out of the day, too, if you've mulled over those vows and really let their full meaning sink in. See p.54 for the lowdown on marriage prep, and how to cook up your own marriage prep course if none's on offer from your officiant.

Aside from these big-picture adjustments, other emotions are likely to rear their heads before, during and after your wedding. With so many decisions to be made – and so many potential stakeholders involved – the **potential for conflict** is huge. Likewise, your chances of getting through the experience entirely stress-free are slim.

Conflict with your partner

Conflict with one another about your wedding day is especially painful since you're planning a celebration of your relationship. You may find yourself worrying that if you can't even plan your wedding peacefully then you've no hope when faced with more serious challenges in the future. But remember:

- ❤ Every couple **argues**.

- ❤ Planning a wedding can be extraordinarily **stressful** – it's certainly up there with buying a house.

- ❤ You're **just starting out**. See wedding planning as training for coping with bigger challenges in the future – learn from the experience how each of you copes with crises, and thus how you can support one another through them.

Professor John Gottman, an expert in what makes for **long and happy marriages**, says one key determining factor is the way a couple deals with conflict. Below are a few tips on conflict handling; for more, visit gottman.com/marriage/self_help or get hold of his seminal book, *The Seven Principles for Making Marriage Work*.

- ❤ Raise problems "**gently and without blame**".

- ❤ When in an argument, "**edit yourself**" – that is, avoid voicing every critical thought that may be running through your head.

- ❤ **Be positive**: focus on your common ground, and the good things about your relationship, rather than making negative statements.

- ❤ Learn how to repair damage and **exit an argument**: change the topic; make a joke; make physical, comforting contact; back down…

- ❤ If things are becoming heated, agree to **take a break** and return to the topic when you're both calmer.

 We thoroughly enjoyed planning our wedding every step of the way. That's not to say we didn't have any disagreements, but we found ourselves trying to understand each other's differences more than ever and working as a team to resolve all those challenges and disagreements that preparing for a wedding can cause.
HARYUN

One frequent source of tension between engaged couples is the groom's perceived **lack of interest** in wedding planning. See p.7 for advice on how to head this one off at the pass, by making sure there are parts of the day that each of you can be excited about. But you may both simply have to accept that those clichés are true and man will never keep pace with woman when it comes to pre-wedding excitement. Most importantly, the bride should remember that **enthusiasm for wedding planning is not the same as enthusiasm for marriage.** Again, communication is key: grooms, there's no harm in verbalizing how the most exciting part of the day for you will be when you get to carry your brand new wifey off into the night.

Stag and hen fallout

Stag and hen nights (bachelor and bachelorette parties in US parlance) can seem explicitly designed to throw a spanner in the works just at the moment of greatest pressure – in those last few weeks before the big day. That's one thing to be said for the old-style night-before send-off: there's no time for recriminations about strip joints and random snogging before you're down the aisle and it's all water under the bridge. That said, a late night and lots of alcohol isn't the best way to wind down before your big day.

A better course of action is to pre-empt problems, by establishing between yourselves a set of **ground rules** of what's acceptable, and then communicating this to your best man and maid of honour. Ensure your partner is in no doubt about how hurt and disrespected you'd feel if they did end up getting a lap dance, for example – that way, they'll be more likely to stand their ground when drunken mates start trying to break their resolve.

Finally, remember people do screw up: the combination of alcohol, peer pressure, the weight of "tradition" and a dash of pre-wedding nerves is a lethal cocktail. It's not an excuse – but at least let your own hangover subside before making any sudden decisions to call things off. Your marriage can offer a clean slate to both of you, and a last-minute crisis could even help bring into focus just how important it is to both of you not to jeopardize what you have by making any silly mistakes in the future.

Conflict with others: am I turning into a monster?

Conflict with your family can be just as painful as arguments with your other half. Underlying everything may be a consciousness that you'll soon be leaving them, and in some sense choosing your new partner over them. Fights in which you're seen to take sides with your fiancé(e) may carry an extra sting for soon-to-be empty nesters.

Probably the most common source of conflict is the question of who's **making the decisions**. Parents – especially of the bride – may have been looking forward to this day for even longer than you have and may, perhaps unwittingly, start trying to impose their "vision" of the day on you. Perhaps they didn't have such a fab wedding as they hope you'll have – but this is no excuse for appropriating what is, after all, *your* big day.

The best advice is that if it's a question of **taste** (the design of your invites, the flowers in your bouquet, your favourite dish included in the dinner), then it's fair to follow your own hearts. But if it's a question of **money** (they're footing the bill, and don't feel they can stretch to those luxury Portaloos) or **people's feelings**, then it's time to ask yourself if you'd behave like this under normal circumstances. It's an emotional occasion for family, too, signifying an ending that may feel as momentous as your beginning. And the rest of your guests have (smaller) needs too: the need not to wear a bridesmaid's dress that makes them feel hideous, the need to have a meal that suits their dietary requirements, the need not to find themselves next to an ex just because that's how your first draft of the seating plan came out.

If it becomes clear that parents or others offering to help you out financially want lots of control over proceedings in exchange for their contribution, sit down and **talk things through** as soon as you become aware of this, and decide together how to proceed (and see Chapter 2 for more on paying for the wedding). Finally, **pick your battles**. If you don't really care about flowers then why not let someone who is passionate about them push you around on this one?

Sometimes it's not a question of control but simply one of **involvement**: someone is just too eager to help, and wants to tag along to every

> **"** Don't let things build up! I let myself get in a furious state with my mum, who was constantly 'taking the initiative' with local suppliers while I wasn't around to have a say. We had a huge blow-up over Christmas and she was distraught to discover how angry I was with her. I wish I had nipped things in the bud, so we could have avoided all that upset.
> **HELEN "**

wedding appointment. If you think this is likely to be the case, you may need to straighten things out at the outset: explain that it's important to you that your day be something you and your fiancé have organized yourselves, but that you hope you can come to them for advice when needed.

One of the most notorious causes of pre-wedding strife is **battles with bridesmaids**. Again, hidden factors may be exacerbating emotions: your friends may be jealous of your soon-to-be-married status, or, like your family, they may feel they're losing you as you head off to join the ranks of the smug marrieds. On p.107 there's practical advice on the vexed issue of bridesmaid dresses; beyond that, it's a question of communication – being vocal in your gratitude for their support and help, and letting them know how much they mean to you.

Falling out with your maid of honour is never a good idea.

> After living together for five years I was very sceptical about the changes that marriage could bring to our relationship. I thought of our wedding as a kind of reassurance to family members rather than a milestone for us as a couple. But I've been pleasantly surprised. For me, marriage is like a piece of art in progress that requires continuous commitment and hard work to avoid routine. On our wedding day, we merely started the journey.
> **HARYUN**

"The best thing about being a married man...?"

"Wow, what a question... where to start? I think the first thing to say is that marriage has really strengthened the bond between Jessica and me. It sounds corny, but there is something really cool about introducing her as 'my wife'. It just feels right. I think, as a man, wearing a wedding ring demands a certain amount of respect from peers and those that you meet for the first time. I find that I am taken a bit more seriously. It has also changed the way I can behave around women. I'm not sure what Jessica would say about this, but being married allows you to chat with the opposite sex far more freely, without them having to worry about whether they are being chatted up or not. It sounds like a small thing, but it really does make quite a difference.

Having gone through the whole process of a wedding has changed me too: it's made me more able to deal with the unexpected, and having organized such a major event and dealt with all those people on the day has done wonders for my confidence. And, of course, Jessica and I have this amazing day to look back at together. I really couldn't be happier... unless I had a better car, of course."

JOHN

Cold feet

While some issues are best brought immediately out in the open, cold feet should be **kept to yourself** until you are sure of your feelings. It's a painful blow for your other half to put behind them, should you decide it was just a case of the jitters; you may even find that your moment of indecision prompts them to have second thoughts too, and there's no guaranteeing theirs will evaporate when yours do. Talk things over with someone you can trust, but avoid confiding in too many people. If you decide it was just a temporary wobble, you may regret having wavered so publicly, and if you do decide to abort the wedding, your fiancé(e) deserves not to be the last to know.

If you're not careful, wedding planning can so dominate your life that the good bits of your relationship – the reason you decided to get married in the first place – can seem a distant memory. Ease the pressure by making space in your week for a time when **wedding talk is banned** and things can be as they were before the whole crazy project kicked off, whether that means rambling conversations that stretch into the small hours, or playing *Mario Kart* and sharing a few beers.

> I know I want to be married to my fiancé and am really excited. But it is such a huge commitment... I've told him how I feel and we laugh about it. He tells me not to worry as we can always get divorced!
> **LIBBY**

In case of death or illness

The death or serious illness of someone close to you may mean you feel unable to go through with the original plans for your wedding – after all, you'll be on display for the whole day, and expected to wear a permanent smile. You've various alternatives, from which it's simply a case of picking the one you feel most comfortable with:

♥ You could **postpone your wedding** for a few months or more, until you feel ready for it.

♥ You could opt to go ahead with the wedding, but on a **smaller scale**, perhaps simply a quiet ceremony with your very closest family, and no reception.

♥ Especially if you feel – or know – it's what the person would have wanted, you could continue as planned, but find ways within the day to **remember them**. You might include them in prayers during the ceremony, or ask everyone to take a moment to think of them during the speeches. Instead of throwing your bouquet, you might save it to take to a hospitalized or housebound person, or to place on the grave of someone recently deceased.

"We said a prayer for her..."

"My husband's Aunt Anna was in a car accident a week before our wedding and was in bad shape all week. She was his godmother, and her son Billy was his best man, so it certainly seemed wrong to be happy and excited about the wedding.

She died on the Friday, a day before the wedding.

It was very depressing but her husband, our Uncle Bill, immediately decided that everything would go as planned, including Billy and his sister Sandra being in the wedding.

Naturally, they were given some kind of medication to help them through it. People were crying for us and for Anna. My husband took one of his mother's pills, whatever they were, to settle him down. Everyone still had a good time but they all knew that the next day they would be going to a viewing for Anna. Uncle Bill said (as most would) that Anna would have wanted us to go on with the plans and be happy."

We said a prayer for her on Sunday en route to Miami in our little MG."

JOSEPHINE

> *The worst thing about being stressed out is that I've had loads of bad dreams. Including recurring ones about the wedding dress being wrong (one of these was pink with black lace on it – totally gross!). I told my dress fitter and she said it's incredibly common!*
> **SARAH**

Stress

Getting stressed about your wedding isn't a failure of character. Nor is it a sign of incurable egotism, simply a natural reaction to the fact you've got a lot on your plate right now: a crash course in events management, combined with an impending change to your most significant relationship. Accept the fact that you're not going to get through this without a bit of freaking out now and then. And console yourself with the thought that **stress is good for you**: stressed people live a little longer, on average – and they're also much less likely to forget to pick up the DJs before the hire shop closes.

The best cure for stress can be a quick **reality check**. If you're still hanging on to the dream of the "perfect" day (and who can blame you, given the blandishments of the wedding industrial complex?), now's the time to let that dream go. **Lower your expectations**, just a little. Once you accept the fact that it won't be perfect, you can stop agonizing over every tiny detail, and actually enjoy the ride. Work out your priorities, and don't be afraid to let some things go. Ironically, you'll probably have a more "perfect" day after all, as you relax and focus on what matters and let the rest slide by in a happy haze.

Taking some **time out** can help you regain perspective: have a couple of weeks off from wedding planning and remember there's nothing that can't wait until you're back on the case.

On the day

If a part of the day is terrifying you (walking down the aisle, posing for the cameras, reading your vows or making that speech), take a few moments in the days leading up to the wedding to practise some **visualization**. By vividly rehearsing that moment in your head – running through it in slow motion, imagining it going well, picturing not only what you'll say or do but what will be going on around you – while in a state of deep relaxation, you'll be primed to sail serenely through when the time comes.

On the day itself, while you wait for things to kick off, take a few **long, deep breaths** through your nose, focusing on lengthening your out breath. Not only will this calm your nerves, it'll slow your mind down so you're ready to fully take in what's going on rather than experiencing the day through a fog of adrenaline. If, as the day wears on, you find yourself feeling overwhelmed, slip away for five minutes on your own, or with your other half or a close friend, and just sit quietly until you're ready to re-enter the fray.

Negotiating the post-wedding slump

There's really no knowing how you'll feel when it's all over. Maybe you'll find yourself furiously jealous of those who've got it still to come. Perhaps you'll be horrified by how old and conventional you feel every time you refer to your "husband" or "wife". Perhaps you'll simply feel exhausted, and fed up with all those questions about babies.

Planning a wedding can consume a huge amount of your spare capacity, possibly for a year or more: you may find that once the dust settles you're ready for a new challenge in some other part of your life.

> " Almost as soon as I returned to work after our honeymoon, I realized I didn't want to be there any more. I'd not given my career much head space in the months leading up to my wedding, but now there it was, staring me in the face. And so, three months after our wedding, 'real life' had come rushing back with a vengeance: I had a new job and we were moving house.
> **AMELIA** "

19 Red Tape

While the bureaucratic side of getting married needn't distract you too long from more enjoyable tasks, it's important to jump through the necessary hoops in good time. Before your wedding, you'll need to sort out your marriage licence, and possibly a pre-nuptial agreement; in the aftermath, you should think about wills and ensuring everyone knows about your new name, if applicable. For the red tape involved in getting married abroad, see Chapter 7.

Getting your marriage licence

In England and Wales

In order to be married in a **Church of England** or **Church of Wales** ceremony you must live in the parish or have one of the other qualifying connections (see p.48) and **banns** must be read. Banns are a formal announcement of your intention to marry, and need to be read out in the church you will marry in, as well as your local church if different, on three Sundays in the three months preceding your wedding.

If one or both of you is not a British national or is not currently living in England or Wales, you can apply to be married by **common licence**; this method can also be used if there isn't sufficient time for

> See the Church of England's weddings site, **yourchurch-wedding.org**, for more information; it also includes lots of useful advice about the wedding ceremony.

Been married before?

This might seem obvious, but if you have been married before, then you have to be **divorced** before you can marry again. What's more, at one of the official meetings that you have with your registrar, or when you first register to be married, you'll have to present some **documentation** to prove that your divorce is complete. If you don't have copies of your divorce papers, you'll need to get in touch with your local records office or court office to get copies and present them in plenty of time before the date of the wedding.

banns to be read – but you'll need a good reason. If you have a long-standing attachment to a particular church but none of qualifying connections, you can apply for a special licence to be married there – but these are granted only in exceptional circumstances.

If you're having any **other religious ceremony** (Methodist, Catholic, Quaker, Jewish, Muslim, Hindu, Sikh…), you need to go through the **civil procedure** for obtaining a Certificate of Authority (see below). If your proposed wedding venue is not in the registration district in which you live, you'll need to prove it's your regular place of worship. The superintendent registrar will need to attend if the minister conducting your ceremony is not authorized to register marriages. If you're having a Muslim, Sikh or Hindu wedding, the mosque or temple may not be registered for the solemnization of marriages; if this is the case, you'll need to have a separate civil ceremony before your religious ceremony – and it will be this that legally marries you.

You can have a **civil wedding** or register a **civil partnership** at any register office or approved premises (see p.49) in England or Wales. However, you must begin by giving formal notice of your intention to marry at the register office of the district in which you live. Each of you must do this in person, and you must produce documents to prove your age, marital status, address and nationality. A notice including your details and your intended marriage venue is displayed at the register office for fifteen days, after which your "**Certificate of Authority**" to marry is issued; this authority is valid for twelve months. If you're not getting married at the register office where you gave notice, you'll need to collect the certificate and give it to your officiant on the day.

See **tinyurl.com/ CivilMarriage** for more information, including a search facility to find your local register office, and details on registering civil partnerships.

In Scotland and Northern Ireland

In Scotland and Northern Ireland, both of you must give notice of your intention to marry in the district in which the marriage is to take place. In Scotland, this must be done between three months and fifteen days before the wedding; in Northern Ireland you can do it between a year and fourteen days before the wedding. Religious marriages may take place anywhere; civil marriages must take place in a register office or approved venue (though in Scotland you can apply for temporary approval if, for example, you want to marry at home). After the registrar has checked you are free to marry, they'll issue the **Marriage Schedule**. If you're having a religious ceremony you'll need to collect this and give it to the officiant on the day; if you're having a civil ceremony, the registrar will bring it along.

> See **tinyurl.com/scotmarry** for more on getting married in Scotland and **tinyurl.com/ NImarry** for Northern Ireland.

More than just a piece of paper

Despite increased legal recognition of cohabiting couples, marriage still confers a number of **benefits** not available to unmarried couples. These vary from country to country and state to state, but typically include the following:

♥ Entitlement to make certain **medical decisions** on behalf of your spouse if they're unable.

♥ Entitlement to **time off work** to care for your spouse if they're sick.

♥ The option to add your spouse to any employer **health insurance** plan.

♥ The transfer of **pension rights** to your spouse in the event of your death.

♥ Exemption from **inheritance tax** on any property you inherit from one another.

♥ The option to file **tax returns** jointly (in the US).

♥ **Immunity** from testifying against one another in court.

In the UK, **civil partnerships** now offer many of the same rights to same-sex couples. For more information see tinyurl.com/USlegal (for the US) and tinyurl.com/marriedornot (for the UK).

See **tinyurl.com/USlicense** for links to information about obtaining a marriage licence in each US state.

For info on the legalities of getting married in other territories, check out:

Ireland
tinyurl.com/IrelandMarry

Canada
tinyurl.com/CanadaMarry

Australia
tinyurl.com/AustraliaMarry

New Zealand
tinyurl.com/NZmarry

South Africa
tinyurl.com/SAMarry

In the US

In the US, things are more straightforward. Whether you are having a religious or a civil ceremony, you must obtain a **marriage licence** from the state in which you will be marrying (not the state in which you live). While the exact procedure for obtaining it varies from state to state, the basic steps are the same.

To be absolutely sure of completing the paperwork on time, you'll generally need to start the process about a month before your wedding – but not very much earlier than that, as some licences are only valid for thirty days or so (find out in good time, of course, what's the case in the relevant state). In certain states you may be asked to take a **blood test** to check for STDs. No states currently require you to take a test for HIV/AIDS, but many require you to receive information about testing.

You'll need to apply for your licence together, and to take along your birth certificates, plus proof of age, citizenship and so on. There will probably be a short wait of between a day and a week before your licence is issued. Brides: you'll need to have decided on your married name by this point, as you'll have to sign the licence with your new name.

Obtaining this licence doesn't mean you're married – it just means you have permission to get married. For it to become valid, it needs to be signed by a religious or civil official, the two of you, and generally some witnesses. Once all the necessary signatures are in place the officiant will forward it to the relevant state office.

International couples

Many countries impose **legal requirements** on foreign nationals before allowing them to settle in their partner's home country. Foreign spouses of **UK citizens**, for example, must apply for a marriage visa before coming to the UK; if the couple have been married for less than four years, the foreign spouse can stay for an initial two-year period. Likewise, in the US, foreign nationals married to a **US citizen** require a spouse visa (I-130 or K-3), which can take up to six months to be granted – and, in the case of the K-3 visa, can only be applied for outside the USA. Make sure you've completed the necessary paperwork well ahead of time.

Cultural issues

The majority of international couples live in one of their native countries, which can immediately alter the dynamics of the relationship – the exotic **cultural nuances** that formed part of the attraction in the first place can seem alien and frustrating once you're immersed in them on a daily basis. One spouse has the concept of marriage – big enough on its own – to get used to; the other the added pressure of acclimatizing to a foreign way of life, sometimes away from family and friends, and often in a different language to their own. Even if you've lived together previously, becoming officially part of your spouse's family can mean significant changes to your way of life. Adopting the following attitudes should help the transition:

 Be patient Change doesn't come easily, especially when you're trying to assimilate into a completely different culture. It takes time – and understanding from your partner – to adapt to a new set of social mores.

Be positive It's unlikely that everything will be different, so focus on the similarities, no matter how trivial, and use them as a positive link.

Compromise One culture may be dominant in the outside world, but that doesn't mean your home life has to be so one-sided. Take an interest in each other's traditions and try to achieve a balance between them.

"Two cultures coming together as equals..."

"My wife Haryun is Korean, so we married in her home town in Korea. Having a traditional Korean wedding with a few Western elements (like exchanging rings) was really meaningful for us – signifying two cultures coming together as equals rather than one subsuming the other.

It was a little overwhelming at first for my parents to learn their roles. As joint hosts they had a big part to play: greeting guests in traditional dress, participating in formal introductions between the two families (outnumbered many times over by all my wife's relatives), and offering their own blessings to the bride and groom. But after some initial trepidation they had a great time, and they were delighted (if somewhat surprised) to learn they would have six grandchildren, when at the end of the ceremony we managed to catch that number of the dates and walnuts they threw at us in the hem of my wife's wedding dress."　　　　　　　　　　　　　　　　　　　　　　*GRAHAM*

US website **myfamilylaw. com/library/prenuptial- agreement** offers lots of advice on creating a legally valid pre-nup.

Pre-nups

When you're making a lifelong commitment to one another, and fully intending to honour it, any reminder that not all marriages last for ever is unwelcome. But for some – particularly couples with a large disparity of wealth – a pre-nuptial agreement can offer peace of mind.

A pre-nup is an opportunity for you to agree how you wish your assets to be divided up in the event of a divorce. It is not the place for laying down rules about who cleans the toilets, whose family you'll spend holidays with or whether you're allowed to keep in touch with your ex. A pre-nup must be **in writing**, and signed by both of you. It must be essentially **fair**, and must involve **full disclosure** of your financial assets and circumstances.

In the US, pre-nups are legally binding. However, if a judge considers a pre-nup to be **grossly unfair** or suspects that it was signed **under duress** (this might include one partner springing it on the other at the last moment), they can set it aside. In addition, laws about pre-nups vary from state to state (some don't allow alimony waivers, for example), so you may find parts of your agreement are invalid in the state where you divorce.

In the UK, pre-nups currently have **no legal standing**. A divorce court judge may take a pre-nup into consideration, but they are under no obligation to abide by it when dividing up assets, and will ignore it if they deem it in any way unreasonable, particularly if children are involved. Largely for this reason, pre-nups are currently much less common in the UK than they are in the US, though their adoption is on the increase, perhaps in response to high-profile messy divorce cases such as that of Paul McCartney and Heather Mills.

Changing your name

It's still overwhelmingly common for brides to take their husband's name on marriage. But, post-feminism, there are few women who haven't given at least a passing thought to the alternatives. There's no simple answer that will please everyone, so you just need to **do what feels right for you** and stick to your guns.

Aside from issues of gender equality, you might want to keep your name in order to maintain a **professional reputation** you've built up at work under that name, or simply because you've become attached to it over the years and feel losing it would undermine your sense of identity. But there are also some not-inconsiderable arguments for taking your new husband's name. First off, there's no denying doing so will make for an **easier life**: although you'd think they'd be used to the idea by now, many people (and organizations) are confused by a married couple with non-matching names, perhaps not even quite sure you're "really married". And there's also the question of what name any **children** will take. Finally, it's simply a nice feeling to share a name with the man you love.

It's not a simple either/or decision, of course. You could **double-barrel** your names, create a **merged name** or even pick a totally **new name** to share after your marriage. If preserving your professional reputation is the key issue for you, you could continue to use your maiden name at work, but take your husband's name the rest of the time – though you may find this muddling in practice, never quite sure

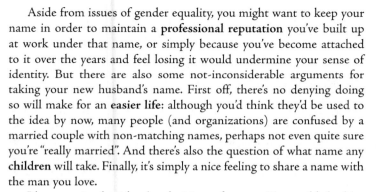

> *The simple fact is Chris is now my next of kin – we're a unit, a family – and it just seemed natural for us to share a name. Something had to give – and me taking his name raised fewer eyebrows than the reverse would have done.*
> **MAGGIE**

What's in a name?

As men, we naturally assume that whatever we do is best, and to be near us is to bask in our glory. What bride, then, wouldn't want to take her husband's name and share that much more in his greatness? This, ladies, is the mindset you should prepare yourself to meet when first discussing keeping your maiden name with your fiancé. Not that we are egomaniacs dripping with machismo, but there is some precious part of us that still wants to be the young boy whose surname the pretty little girl substituted for her own, over and over, in loopy handwriting, on the back pages of her school notebook. It's romantic and traditional – and even humbling.

But please realize, we do appreciate the sacrifice a woman must make in shearing off her old name, just as we appreciate the many reasons a new bride would want to retain it. Why, for instance, should a woman cast aside her name and join her husband's family, not the other way around? While the wedding ceremony is no longer considered the passing of a possession from father to new husband, remnants of said exchange remain, including the changing of a bride's surname from one man's family to the next. It doesn't seem quite fair. More practically, we understand that our women need to maintain their presence in the professional sphere, where projected identity can be as important as the work you produce.

The real and serious issue over naming concerns any future children. As part of a desire to extend our family line, we men will want children to the bear the family name. What happens, then, when there isn't a single name shared by mother and father? And… discuss.

> **"** *I didn't change my name. Doing so would have felt like a transfer of allegiance from my parents to my new in-laws, and that just didn't feel right. I'm not sure what we'll do if we have children, but for now it's just the two of us and having separate names is simply a reflection of the fact we're still autonomous individuals, not each other's 'other half'.*
> **UNA "**

what name you've booked an appointment in or used to fill out a form. If you're forming a **civil partnership**, all these options are available, with the added benefit that no conventional choice has yet emerged to push you in a particular direction.

Letting people know

If you do decide to change your name, you'll need to pass this information on to everyone you have dealings with. Government departments and banks will generally need to see your original **marriage certificate** (in the UK you'll have been given it on the day; in the US, you'll have to wait for it to come through), while most companies will be satisfied with a certified copy.

Although this might seem like a bureaucratic nightmare it's really very easy, so don't be waylaid by companies offering to do it for you – that's money for old rope. In the US, you should start by getting a new **Social Security** card: phone 1-800/772-1213 or visit tinyurl. com/ofabo. Then pop down to the DMV to get yourself a new **driver's license**. Once you've got these two, and notified your employer, the rest should fall into place. In the UK, there's no particular order necessary, so just get stuck in.

Passports, name changes and honeymoons

Beware of rocking up to the airport check-in desk, only to find your flight reservations are in one name, and your passport in another. In the US, you should make all your honeymoon reservations in your maiden name, as you won't have a passport or driver's license in your new name yet. In the UK, you can apply for a new passport in your married name up to three months before the wedding, allowing you to travel under your new name.

However, the new passport will be post-dated to the date of your wedding, and you'll have to send in your old one when you apply, so don't do this if you'll need your passport in the intervening period. And if you're travelling to a country where a visa is required, trying to acquire it in your new married name may be near impossible. All told, you may find it easier to travel in your old name one last time.

Type out a standard letter, print off a dozen or so copies, send them off with proof of your new name and the job's done. Here's a rundown of the key people you'll need to tell. The odd extra will probably come out of the woodwork over the next few months, but that's not a big deal.

- ♥ Your employer
- ♥ Social Security
- ♥ Revenue & Customs/IRS
- ♥ Electoral roll/Voter registration records
- ♥ Banks, credit card companies
- ♥ Insurance companies
- ♥ DVLA/DMV
- ♥ Your doctor and dentist
- ♥ Utilities companies
- ♥ Pension plan
- ♥ 401(k) account
- ♥ Passport office
- ♥ Telephone listings

Tip

Assuming you haven't been practising your new signature since your second or third date, now's the time to settle on one: once you've started signing things in your new name you'll be stuck with it, so make sure you like it!

Wills

Although it'll probably be the last thing on your mind as you make your final preparations for your big day, you should think about making a will when you get married, most particularly because getting married will **invalidate any wills** you have made previously.

If you die without a will, your estate will be divided up under fixed rules of law. In the UK this is straightforward if you have no children: your spouse will automatically inherit everything. In the US, however, many states will give a half or more to your parents or siblings. A will is particularly important if you have children, either jointly or from previous relationships: not only will it ensure your assets are shared amongst them and your spouse in the way you wish, but it can also specify who you want to act as their legal guardians, should both of you die at the same time.

The UK Citizens Advice Bureau outlines the basics of getting yourself set up with a will (tinyurl/willsUK).

A will relates to one person only, so you will each need to make a separate one. Solicitors or lawyers often offer a discount, though, if you draw up matching or "mirror wills". You don't need a lawyer in order to write a will – but it's advisable to use one so as to be sure that your will is legally valid and will have the effect you want. If you are taking the DIY route, there are **kits** available to help you get it right. Check out Lawpack in the UK (tinyurl.com/DIYwillUK) or Megadox in the US (tinyurl.com/DIYwillUS).

20 Suppliers

It takes an army to create a wedding, and dealing with flaky or uppity vendors can be one of the most stressful parts of the planning process. Yet the alternative – trying to do everything yourself or accepting help from loved ones – can be equally problematic. This chapter will help you choose the right person for each job, and keep them on the straight and narrow.

Finding reputable suppliers

There's no shortage of wedding suppliers. Open any wedding magazine and you'll find a slew of glossy adverts; visit any weddings website and you'll be similarly bombarded. Bear in mind, though, that many of the best suppliers don't need to advertise, since word of mouth does the job for them. By the same token, smaller suppliers may not be able to afford expensive ad space: tracking them down may take a little more effort, but they'll often be cheaper than the big boys, as well as offering a more personal service and more original ideas. Here are a few avenues to explore in your hunt for the perfect vendor:

♥ Wedding fairs These can be great time-savers, with hundreds of vendors under one roof. A word of caution: avoid giving anyone your contact details – ask for theirs instead. And definitely don't commit to anything or hand over any deposits then and there. See these fairs as an opportunity to amass lots of ideas and information, take it home, supplement it with information from other sources, and only then think about which is the right vendor for you.

Tip

Try contacting your local music, catering, photography or floristry school: tutors may be willing to recommend students or recent graduates who'll work for a much cheaper rate than established professionals. Be aware, though, of the risk involved in employing people with limited experience, and see as much proof as you can that they're up to the challenge.

♥ **Personal recommendation** Ask recently married family and friends for recommendations. Remember, though, that just because your friends were happy with a supplier doesn't necessarily mean it's right for you. And don't let it make you complacent: a single success story is no guarantee that you'll get the same unless you ensure it through a solid contract (see p.229).

♥ **Recommendation from other suppliers** A photographer may be able to recommend a skilled videographer, while your venue coordinator may be able to recommend reliable caterers.

♥ **The Yellow Pages** This has the benefit of including most if not all of the local suppliers. Taking a look in here ensures you won't miss the perfect vendor just because they don't advertise heavily or have a prominent web presence. Usually, you'll quickly be able to narrow the list down to a small number worth following up.

♥ **Internet search** For non-location-specific vendors, such as stationers, the Internet is an important resource, and it's also handy for looking at pictures of venues before visiting. Beware of online weddings directories, however, as they're neither impartial nor complete, giving prominence to suppliers who've made it worth their while.

Are they right for you?

When considering a vendor:

♥ Check out their **credentials**: are they a member of the relevant professional organization? Do they have the relevant qualifications?

♥ Ask to see **previous work** – real samples if possible, or photographs of their work in use at real weddings. Beware of glossy portfolios that give no indication of what's really possible on the day.

♥ Ask for testimonials or, better, **references** whom you can contact yourself.

Beyond these basic facts, pay attention to their **attitude** and behaviour during your initial contact: do they listen to your ideas and needs, or are they only interested in getting you to accept their standard package? Are they friendly, helpful and respectful, or patronizing and dismissive? How quickly do they **return your calls**? If vendors don't respond to your initial messages in a timely manner alarm bells should ring: cut your losses now, rather than risk their being equally elusive in

One of the first questions to ask is whether they're friendly and helpful.

the final few days. The bottom line is **listen to your instincts**: if you don't trust them to come through for you with a great product and with a minimum of fuss, then take your money elsewhere.

Negotiating price

If you fall in love with a particular venue or flower arrangement, don't reveal this to your vendor, but get comparable quotes from other suppliers to help you gauge whether the price they're quoting you is fair.

Tip

Many vendors require a non-refundable **deposit** on signature of contract, but avoid paying in full in advance: this gives your supplier very little incentive to ensure you're happy with the finished product.

Let them know they've got **competition** for your business, even if in your heart they're the clear front-runner. Don't allow emotion to cloud your judgement – remain businesslike in your negotiations and save any soppiness for the day itself, when you can reap the rewards of your cool-headed hard work.

❤ Don't be afraid not to accept the first price you're quoted. Many vendors expect to haggle (see box) and will be willing to offer **discounts** to get the job. Ask yourself if there's any reason why a discount would be applicable in your case: is it a quiet time of the year, or day of the week?

❤ Ask for a detailed **breakdown** of costs and consider each part: have they included some outrageously expensive flowers or ingredients that could be replaced with cheaper alternatives? Have they added on a huge fee for something you don't need or want? Ask them to adjust their plans and amend their total price accordingly.

❤ When comparing prices, **check what's included**. Tax and tips will add significantly to the final tally, as will extras such as delivery and set-up charges. Make sure you're comparing like with like, and that the final price won't creep up beyond what you've budgeted.

Tips on haggling

When it comes to negotiating prices with vendors, it pays to keep the following in mind.

❤ **Be polite.** The person you're dealing with needs a certain amount of money to make a deal worthwhile. You're attempting to get their price as close to their break-even point as you can. You won't achieve this by being a jerk.

❤ **Know the value of what you're asking for.** Get quotes from other vendors and do research online. Similar products shouldn't vary widely in cost just because they come through different sources. Let the vendor explain why their services/products cost more, and determine whether you feel the extra cost provides extra value.

❤ **Consider the time of year and the economy.** Vendors need your business more at slow times of the year. You'll be able to negotiate better prices for days when others aren't hounding them for their services.

❤ **Be flexible with payments.** You may be able to get a discount by offering to pay more up front or some or all of the amount in cash.

❤ **Be prepared to walk away.** If you've gone through the other steps but they still won't budge on the price, then get up to leave. You'll be surprised how quickly a vendor/hotelier/supplier will come around after they've seen you crack open your wallet, only to see you getting up to walk out.

Confirming details and protecting yourself

When you've agreed to go with a particular supplier, get all the details **in writing**. A signed contract is your most important safeguard against problems. It not only protects you against wilful dishonesty and backsliding, it also ensures that there are **no misunderstandings** between you and your vendor about what has been agreed. If you don't understand something in the contract, don't sign it until you've sought qualified advice.

Your contract should specify everything that's important to you: the exact flowers to be used in your bouquet, the exact person who'll be taking your photos, the make and model of car that'll pick you up…

It should also state:

❤ The **time** at which the vendor will arrive or deliver their goods, and how long they will stay.

❤ Whether you get **final approval** of any designs.

❤ Details of any **extras** that may be charged, such as travelling expenses, breakages and overtime, plus tips and taxes. It should also clearly state that nothing else can be charged for except by mutual agreement.

❤ The **payment** schedule and the **cancellation policy**.

❤ What the supplier will do to help if for any reason they are **unable to fulfil their part of the bargain**.

In addition to your contract, keep every receipt and letter, and make a note of any phone calls or meetings. If anyone does try to screw you over, or threatens to do so, the more comprehensive a **paper trail** you can produce the better chance you have of getting redress. You may

Pre-empting delays

The problem you're most likely to face with wedding vendors is their **failing to hit deadlines**. For goods and services to be supplied in advance of the wedding day, such as stationery or bridal gowns, fix a delivery date well in advance of when you really need it, to allow for delays. As for those who need to show up on the day, phone each a few days before the wedding to ensure everything is in order and remind them what time they are due to arrive.

also want to consider taking out **insurance** against vendor default (see p.16). While this is no substitute for proper contracts (indeed, your insurer will want to see paperwork in the event of any claim), it does provide extra protection. And if a vendor goes out of business, it's probably the only way you'll be able to retrieve any deposits paid. Another important safeguard is paying deposits on a **credit card**: credit cards and services such as PayPal often offer some amount of fraud protection; check with your company for details.

If a supplier lets you down

Although it's a miserable prospect, the truth is that with so many different suppliers involved there's a fair chance that someone will let you down. No matter how carefully worded your contract, your caterers may go bust, your photographer or even venue may double-book, your hairdresser may fall ill, or a vendor may simply fail to deliver goods or services to the quality you were led to expect.

If this happens, your first priority should be **damage limitation** rather than recriminations. In most cases, negotiating compensation or a refund can wait until later. More importantly, you don't want your wedding day to be overshadowed by unpleasantness, even if that does mean letting someone off more lightly than you normally would.

The best-laid plans

There's a very obvious reason to **arrange help** with this wedding you're planning – it's a big event, with a lot of elements, and there is no possible way for you to do everything by yourself. Still, there will be a lot of little things in the final stretch that you can't push off on someone else, and those things will pick away at your time right up to the point when you walk down the aisle.

While you can allocate for most things on your to-do list, be sure to give yourself plenty of **space in your schedule** for the inevitable last-minute disasters (best to call these things disasters within the last 96 hours, it'll get your helpers that much more motivated to problem-solve). If something goes wrong, you'll have time to take care of it, and if all goes according to plan, then you've just given yourself a chance to relax and appreciate all the effort you've already made.

No-shows

Professionals such as caterers, photographers and car rental firms should have contingencies in place in case of broken equipment or sickness. And so it is rare for a vendor simply to fail to show up, especially if you've phoned them to confirm arrangements just a few days ago. But do be aware of who's due when, and if someone doesn't arrive at the appointed time don't delay in phoning them up and checking they're on their way.

If you get hold of them and they say they're unable to complete the job as contracted, tell them they must arrange a **replacement** at their own expense. If they've gone entirely AWOL, or they refuse to cooperate, it's time to start making **alternative arrangements** of your own. This might mean asking your uncle to take on the role of photographer, or sending an usher off to buy some ready-made bouquets and bunches of flowers. Or it might mean phoning round other suppliers to see if anyone can step in at short notice. You'll probably have to settle for something less than ideal, but don't despair: the benefit of weddings being such complex events is that a let-down in one area really needn't mar your whole day.

Substandard goods or service

More likely than a complete no-show is the supplier who simply fails to meet your reasonable expectations as to the quality of their product or service.

If there's time for them to remedy the problem, give them an opportunity to do so (for example, reprinting botched invitations), telling them exactly why you are unhappy with their first attempt. But if they can't or won't put things right, focus on finding another supplier, before beginning the process of obtaining a refund (see overleaf).

If there's no chance to put the situation right (for example, dinner's served cold), do try not to let anger spoil your day. Tell the vendor you're not happy and that you'll be in touch later to discuss appropriate recompense. Delegate someone to gather evidence (photographs, for example), to be used to show why you'll not be paying the balance of what you owe them, or want a refund.

> **Tip**
>
> If you have wedding insurance, contact your insurer as soon as you can after the problem has emerged to find out what action you should take in order to be covered.

> The **Citizens Advice Bureau** outlines your rights when buying goods (tinyurl.com/CABgood) and services (tinyurl.com/CABservices) in the UK, while US site **consumeraction.gov** provides lots of advice about how to file a complaint, plus general tips on buying with confidence.

Seeking compensation

Remember not to sweat the small stuff. Sometimes, especially if the sums involved are small, it might be better to just let things go, rather than tarnish your wedding memories with a lengthy coda in the small claims court. However, if a significant amount of money is involved, as it easily can be with weddings, you will want to make a concerted effort to recoup your loss. When it comes to claiming a refund or refusing to pay for unacceptable goods or services, try to settle your complaint directly with the vendor before involving other parties.

❤ **Write to them** formally, outlining why you are unhappy with their service and what you feel they should do in restitution.

❤ If they refuse to accept your complaint, **write to them again**, threatening to refer the matter to the Better Business Bureau (US; bbb.org) or Trading Standards (UK; tradingstandards.gov.uk), or to take the matter to the small claims court.

❤ In many cases, the threat of **legal action** will get you the result you're after; but if necessary, follow through with it. There's plenty of support available (see box on p. 231).

Help from family and friends

Chances are, soon after word gets out that you're getting married you'll receive offers of help from loved ones keen to put their talents to good use in the service of your big day. A wedding which is the combined result of a series of such friendly gestures can be extra special – but think carefully before accepting offers.

First of all, assure yourselves that the person is **up to the challenge**: has your kitchen-goddess pal ever catered for so large a number; does your prospective DJ's music collection extend to family-friendly tracks? A gifted landscape photographer may have no idea how to work a wedding crowd. If you're not sure, do a bit of tactful sleuthing.

Even if you've no worries about their professional ability, there is the question of your **working relationship**. In short, you'll have to be nice to them! You may simply not feel able to boss friends or family around in the way you might a paid supplier, and may feel obliged to go along with their creative ideas, however far they might be from your own vision. And if you do that, you may find yourself resenting them for ever after.

If you do need to decline offers of help, soften the blow by explaining that you want them to relax and enjoy your day rather than be "on duty". You might want to suggest they help in a more limited way that still makes use of their particular talent.

Non-wedding suppliers

It's true, you often **pay more** for wedding supplies than you would for comparable goods and services in other circumstances. Some suppliers will play on your emotions to press upon you their most expensive offering, while others will have separate wedding packages or a separate weddings tariff which they insist you take. The popular advice is to pretend you're hosting a birthday or anniversary party instead. But mind your step if you do try this approach: things can get messy if the supplier discovers your ruse.

But while dedicated weddings suppliers may kick up a stink if they're deprived of their bridal premium, by thinking laterally and matching your requirements to people who've never even considered a bridal market for their products you'll very often be able to make big savings.

This is true even of some of the **big stuff**, such as bridesmaid dresses, for example. Dresses from regular stores are very often much cheaper than the gowns on offer at bridal shops. They're far more likely to be suitable for wearing again, too. Likewise, venues that don't advertise themselves specifically for weddings – or don't regularly hire themselves out for events at all – can be surprisingly good value. They may not provide all the added extras you'd expect from a regular wedding venue, but by the same token they may well not have thought of charging a fortune for corkage or cake-cutting.

But where this strategy comes into its own is with the **bits and pieces** – the miscellaneous items you find yourselves scurrying around for in the last few weeks before your big day. Wedding stores charge outrageous sums for various trimmings and you really can make substantial savings by buying the same products from non-wedding shops: balloons from a regular party store, envelopes from a sta-

> ### Tip
> Resist the urge to have everything brand new: you'll save a tidy sum if you're willing to have the odd thing that's nearly new or even antique. Remember a dress or pair of shoes is hardly second-hand after only a day's wear. Try **freecycle.co.uk** in the UK or **freecycle.org** in the US and you may even pick up things for free.

> *£1.50 to hire a linen napkin! 50p each for fancy paper ones! We ended up buying cloth napkins from IKEA for less than it would have cost to hire them, and they're still coming in useful five years later for barbecues and parties.*
> *ALISON*

tioner's, sweets from a supermarket. Check out **wholesalers**, too, both in town and online: for a wedding, you'll often being buying enough of things to qualify – for example, the minimum order for ribbon is easily reached with a hundred chair backs to deck out. eBay is a good source of job lots.

21 Resources

While the preceding chapters have included sources of further information on specific topics, listed below are some more general sources of inspiration and advice, as well as resources catering to particular overarching wedding philosophies, whether that be DIY, ethical or alternative. There are also resources specifically for same-sex couples.

What's covered

The listings include some **books**, but the majority of recommendations are for **websites**, simply because the Internet is such a great weddings resource. You'll come across a lot of sites that want to extract cash out of you, but there are plenty of others offering good-quality, detailed advice for free: the very best are listed below.

As for weddings **magazines**, they're great for getting you in the mood, helping you figure out what kind of dress or flower arrangements you might like, and for picking up the odd nice idea, but think twice before taking out a subscription: truth is, things don't change that fast in the weddings world, no matter how fashion-conscious you are, so after your second or third mag they'll all begin to look much the same.

General information and advice

Confetti.co.uk

Confetti want to do your wedding for you – from the gift list and favours to, well, the confetti. But if you don't mind that they're always trying to flog you something, there's a lot of great content on this site. As well as advice pages (in which South Asian-style weddings are unusually well catered for), there's an "inspiration" section with lots of pics of bouquets, cakes and decorations. There's also, of course, a well-stocked suppliers directory and a busy forum.

TheKnot.com

One of the biggest US weddings sites, The Knot has plenty of magaziney articles on all the usual topics. There's loads of in-your-face ads, but the site is pretty to look at and easy to navigate. Members get handy tools to help with budgeting, scheduling and managing guest lists, as well as their own wedding webpage. There's a good forum, plus a huge and compulsive dresses section with photos of literally thousands of gowns.

Weddings for men

Iamstaggered.com

A wedding site for "blokes" – grooms, best men and fathers of the bride. After wading through pastels and prettiness ever since you dropped to one knee, you may appreciate its spare, monochrome design. There's stag-do ideas, brownie-point-winning tips and competitions, plus some seriously blokey editorials on everything from best women to pizza cakes. Might just help you find your feet in the female-dominated world of weddings.

Alternative weddings

Indiebride.com

Aimed at the "independent-minded bride", this site features intelligent essays and interviews, down-to-earth advice on the etiquette dilemmas posed by alternative weddings, plus a friendly forum.

Offbeat Bride
Ariel Meadow Stallings (Avalon, 2006)

Stallings' regularly updated blog (offbeatbride.com) includes profiles of offbeat weddings, sassy, sensitive advice, and shout-outs for gorgeous alternative bridal goodies. Her book talks you through crafting your own offbeat wedding, drawing liberally and intimately on her own experience.

Ethical/green weddings

Ethicalweddings.com

Whether you're concerned about fair trade, organics, your carbon footprint or the sheer wastefulness of the standard wedding model, this UK site offers thoughtful suggestions – if not yet all the answers. The "real ethical weddings" section is great for garnering ideas from like-minded couples who've gone before. There's also a small ethical suppliers directory, and feature articles on topics ranging from wooden wedding bands (no, really – they're beautiful) to bagging yourself a charity-shop frock.

How To Get Married in Green
Suzan St Maur (How To Books, 2008)

St Maur's interested in "green" in the broadest sense, so this book covers other "ethical" issues too. In fact, the net's cast pretty wide, and the research feels correspondingly thin in places, but it will certainly get you thinking – about everything from e-invites and recycled confetti to energy-efficient appliances for your wedding list and writing your own green poetry.

DIY/budget weddings

Videojug.com/tag/weddings

Like YouTube, Videojug has thousands of online video tutorials offering step-by-step advice on subjects as diverse as bleeding a radiator and undoing a bra with one hand. Check out "Fold a t-shirt in two seconds" to be truly amazed. It's great for wedding-related topics, with clips on make-up, favours, memorizing your speech using mind-mapping techniques and much more.

Five wedding-themed films to get you in the mood

Plunder them for decorating ideas, or simply sit back and enjoy these topical flicks.

Four Weddings and a Funeral The classic wedding movie, it's a brilliantly accurate portrait of how a certain segment of British society weds.

Monsoon Wedding Gorgeously shot, each frame dripping with flowers, this charts the chaotic and emotionally intense run-up to a traditional family wedding in Delhi.

Mamma Mia ABBA, Meryl Streep, and romance on a Greek island: what's not to love? It's great for rustic/homespun decorating ideas too.

Wedding Crashers One for the guys. There are plenty of dresses and table centrepieces here too, but they're mere backdrop to Owen Wilson and Vince Vaughn on top comedy form.

Corpse Bride Tim Burton magics this fairy tale into something truly haunting – she may be dead, but she's the love of his life and, like all good wedding movies, it has a happy ending!

Do-it-yourself-weddings.com

DIY wedding catering, stationery, favours, jewellery and more. Not only are the instructions clear and well-illustrated, but some of the ideas are genuinely original and creative: check out their asparagus and artichoke table centrepieces.

eBay

While you'll find everything here from second-hand wedding dresses to wedding rings, eBay comes into its own in the last few weeks before your wedding, when you can pick up those last few sundries for next to nothing.

Bridal Bargains
Denise Fields and Alan Fields (Windsor Peak Press, 2008)

A budget-conscious guide to choosing and hiring wedding suppliers, including detailed technical information about everything from stationery to videography, plus recommendations and warnings of who to avoid. This comprehensive book is written for the US market, but much of its information will be of use to readers everywhere.

Gay weddings and civil partnerships

A Very Pink Wedding: A Gay Guide to Planning Your Perfect Day
Nicola Hill (Collins, 2007)

Gay weddings needn't be that different from straight weddings – unless you choose to make them so (and you don't need a book to tell you how to do that). And so, excellent though it is, this book won't add that much to what you've read in this Rough Guide. The real bonuses are a useful set of Q&As on the UK's Civil Partnership Act, pointers on finding gay-friendly venues, blessing celebrants and honeymoon destinations, and inspiring testimonies from gay couples who've tied the knot. Also check out the author's website, gay-friendly-wedding-venues.com.

Stonewall.org.uk/at_home/civil_partnership

The civil partnerships section of LGB charity Stonewall's website tells you everything you need to know about the legal side of civil partnerships.

Index

Alastair Sawday's

Special Places

Venues in Britain

Weddings, parties & meetings

Find the perfect venue for a wedding, celebration, conference or meeting – whatever the occasion, size or budget. Tie the knot in a country manor or on an organic farm, celebrate a 21st birthday in a Scottish castle or host a gathering in world famous Edwardian gardens.

Publishing June 2010

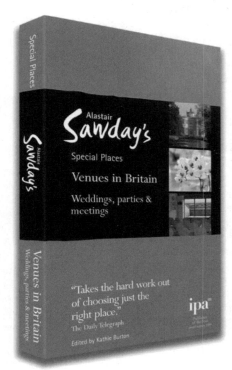